The Middle East, Oil, and the U.S. National Security Policy

The Middle East, Oil, and the U.S. National Security Policy

Intractable Conflicts, Impossible Solutions

Donald M. Snow

ROWMAN & LITTLEFIELD
Lanham • Boulder • New York • London

Published by Rowman & Littlefield
A wholly owned subsidiary of The Rowman & Littlefield Publishing Group, Inc.
4501 Forbes Boulevard, Suite 200, Lanham, Maryland 20706
www.rowman.com

Unit A, Whitacre Mews, 26-34 Stannary Street, London SE11 4AB

British Library Cataloguing in Publication Information Available

Library of Congress Cataloging-in-Publication Data
Snow, Donald M., 1943– author.
Title: The Middle East, oil, and the U.S. national security policy : intractable conflicts, impossible solutions / Donald M. Snow.
Description: Lanham : Rowman & Littlefield [2016] | Includes bibliographical references and index.
Identifiers: LCCN 2015042625 (print) | LCCN 2015046204 (ebook) | ISBN 9781442261969 (cloth : alk. paper) | ISBN 9781442261976 (pbk. : alk. paper) | ISBN 9781442261983 (Electronic)
Subjects: LCSH: National security—United States. Energy policy—United States. Security, International. United States—Foreign relations—Middle East. United States—Military policy.
Classification: LCC DS63.2.U5 S596 2015 (print) | LCC DS63 (ebook) | DDC 355/.0335730956
LC record available at https://lccn.loc.gov/2015042625

Printed in the United States of America

Contents

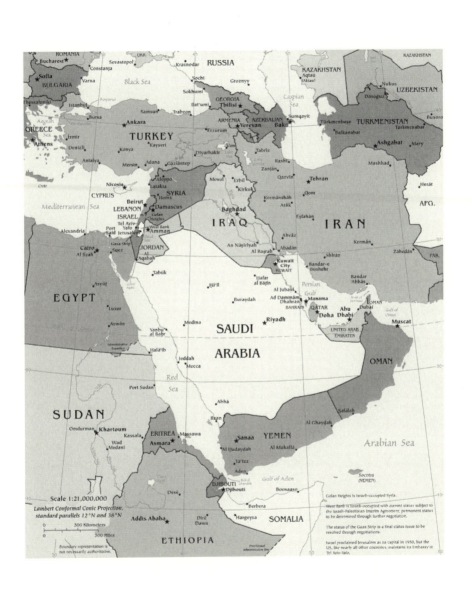

What This Book Is About

As the 2016 election approached, the United States found itself in what seems to be one of its perpetual crises over national security policy. The heart of these crises always revolves around questions of the circumstances in which the United States should use force (when force is justified to fulfill national interests) and how to use that force (what uses will reasonably assure realizing goals at an acceptable cost in blood and treasure). These considerations reflect three basic categories of concern: the importance of using force in certain kinds of situations, the attainability of desired ends using different means, and whether the use of force is worth the costs.

Americans have almost always disagreed on the answers to these questions, depending on the circumstances. In unusually stressful situations like World War II of the Cold War, there is an essential national consensus on each concern and thus very little disagreement on policy, but those periods are relatively infrequent. More often, there is substantial disagreement on all three criteria; the country is in that condition today.

There are two basic positions that different people tend to take on these questions. One side, that is labeled the position of the "hard men" or even more uncharitably the "chicken hawks" in the pages that follow, argues for an expansive, aggressive American military posture to support a "muscular" policy intended to enforce American policies through the application of American power, which includes, most prominently, military force. The other side argues for a much more restrained national security policy wherein the application of American power, and especially military force, in the world is limited to securing only the most important, vital interests, where that force can reasonably be expected to achieve those national ends, and where the costs of doing so are acceptable. This more liberal position maintains that there are very few places and circumstances in the world that currently meet those criteria and that the United States should therefore exercise considerable restraint in its national security policy. This book is largely an explanation and defense of this proposition.

The current locus of national security concern for the United States is the Middle East. It has been the central concern, one might even say fixation, of the policy debate since the Al-Qaeda terrorist attacks on New York and Washington on September 11, 2001. Given the trauma of that awful event, this obsession was by no means surprising or inappropriate. The Middle East had spawned a new horror that in many ways supplanted the Soviet nuclear threats at the heart of American fears in the world.

That obsession is still with us a decade and a half later. The events of 9/11 are farther away, but their evocative power remains firmly in place in the fear that the attack could somehow be repeated. Guarding against that contingency is a central focus in the debate about national security direction for the present and future.

What to do about the threat to the United States emanating from the Middle East has been the central national security theme of the 2016 presidential election campaign. Candidates, largely but not completely on the political right, have fallen over themselves trying to establish themselves as the "toughest" and "most muscular" potential leaders on how to cope with the world. Their arguments have been focused on the threat posed by the Islamic State (IS). The argument is familiar: IS has threatened terrorist attacks on American soil, and they must be prevented from doing so. That means the fight must be taken to this enemy where it is: if we do not engage and defeat them on their home grounds (currently parts of Iraq and Syria), we will have to fight them here. South Carolina Senator Lindsay Graham, who claims his six years of active duty as an Air Force lawyer makes him the most national security–qualified candidate, avers, "I want to be president to defeat the enemies that are trying to kill us." Without saying it in so many words, he means IS and other Islamic terrorists. He does not explain in any reasonable detail how this goal will be accomplished, except to say it is a military problem. Maybe so, maybe not.

If all this sounds depressingly familiar, it should. The United States has repeatedly stuck its heavily armed nose into conflicts in the Middle East in the past quarter-century that turned out to be primarily internal wars, and has failed to produce the desired outcome through prolonged, expensive application of its power. Why? The answer is simple enough: outside military intervention in people's internal affairs is inappropriate—it does not work. The United States should know this, having misapplied its might in places like Vietnam, Iraq, and Afghanistan. If the chicken hawks—James Fallows's delicious phrase—have their way, we will do it again against IS. It is almost certain we will not succeed—again.

This book thus explores what is wrong with American national security policy, why recent changes have made it possible to think of alternatives, and how it might be changed to produce better results. It is argumentative rather than being academically neutral and apparently objective. Its major point is that current policy is dysfunctional and needs to be changed. It is not only an analysis, but also an argument. I make no apologies for its stances, which is the result of looking at and thinking about these problems for a long time. Military activism by outsiders has repeatedly been attempted in the Middle East throughout history, and it usually fails for one or both of two reasons explored in these pages: the situations are not important enough to the United States to justify intervention—for example, why do Americans care if Sunnis or Shiites rule Iraq?—and American military forces are not appropriate for the tasks at hand. The Middle East is a mess, and so is American policy toward the region.

A discussion about the direction of national security policy is long overdue. The implicit assumptions of current policy are essentially extrapolations and modifications of American Cold War policy. That policy was crafted to deal with problems that no longer exist, and the contemporary environment is sufficiently different that the policy and assumptions for dealing with Cold War reality are no longer obviously relevant for organizing and thinking about today. Communism is not the same thing as terrorism, and a posture well attuned to one does not necessarily work as well against the other. No one openly admits that taking on IS in Iraq and Syria is an extension of Cold War thinking, but it really is.

Attacking this problem by examining policy toward the Middle East is also appropriate. For one thing, that part of the world has been the seedbed of the terrorist phenomenon that has been the central concern of national security policy since 9/11. The Middle East has also been the part of the world where most American national security–justified military actions have taken place over the past quarter-century. The Middle East, in other words, is where the action is.

Moreover, elements of the national security environment are changing enough to make such a reexamination both timely and possible. Two of these are featured here. One is the question of military power and the extent to which the all-volunteer military has been stretched to its near limits by repeated Middle Eastern deployments. The other is the changing energy equation, notably the emergence of alternate sources of petroleum energy and the consequent reduction of the American economy's dependence on Persian Gulf fossil fuels. Each of these factors contributes to an atmosphere in which changes in policy can occur.

My purpose is not to convince the reader that the stance I take is correct and should be adopted—although I certainly would not mind if I manage to convince some people that what I have to say makes sense and represents considerations relative to the ongoing political debate. I strongly feel that that concerns I have raised here have merit and should be part of that set of discussions, and it is in that spirit that they are provided for the reader's consideration.

The book's contents and organization may at first blush seem anomalous, but it is not. Rather, it consists of five related propositions that individually and collectively lead to the conclusion that a new national security policy toward the Middle East is both possible and desirable. The steps in this argument are as follows:

1. The United States remains, 25 years after the end of the Cold War, effectively stuck in a conceptual framework on national security on a framework—the Cold War paradigm—that is an artifact of that period and does not apply well to current threats in the environment, especially in the Middle East. Many veteran analysts (the "hard men") reflect this orientation.

2. The Cold War paradigm has led to extensive military activism in areas like the Middle East, and this level of deployment is not compatible with an all-volunteer force (AVF), which produces a very good but not very large force. Overuse in the past decade suggests the AVF needs a reduced operational tempo (op tempo, in military terms) or more troops. The AVF cannot produce a larger force, and conscription is not a politically viable option. A reduced level of deployment thus makes sense.

3. Less use of force in the Middle East, where most force deployment has occurred in the new millennium, is now possible because of changes in the American energy situation. Dependence on Middle East oil, the historic base of American vital interests in the area, has decreased due to innovations like shale exploitation. It is now possible to contemplate a different national security policy without endangering vital interests.

4. The nature of individual and general Middle East problems is complex, almost entirely not caused by the United States, and beyond our ability to solve. Only residents of the region can solve their differences (if anybody can). American military activism is irrelevant at best, and harmful at worst both to regional actors and the United States when inserted into these internal problems.

5. The United States needs a new, less aggressive policy in the region, which conditions now permit. It may be that a highly visible American military "footprint" is one reason regional terrorists target this country. A framework based on the triple criteria of the importance of issues (e.g., vital interests), attainability (do American efforts have a reasonable prospect of success), and cost (can the United States bear the cost of different alternatives) may yield a more acceptable policy and strategy.

The logic of the book's argument and the title proceed from this structure of the argument. The conflicts that mark the region are indeed intractable, based deeply on long-held hatreds and animosities that simply go beyond the ability of Americans (or most other outsiders) to understand, much less to do anything about. As a result, solutions have proven impossible: the antagonists themselves have proven this for literally thousands of years, and outsiders have proven no more successful. Why American policy makers believe they can do what no one else has proven capable of doing is a matter of considerable puzzlement. A major theme in these pages is that maybe we should follow the first order of politicians and shovels: when you are digging yourself into a hole, the first thing to do is to quit digging.

The book's formal organization also reflects the arguments. The first is to look at the inheritance from the past (Part I). The first chapter looks at the conceptual framework (paradigm) inherited from the Cold War, an intellectual device that remains the implicit standard today but does not really "fit" current and foreseeable circumstances. The second is the military manpower legacy of the AVF adopted toward the end of the Vietnam War. That concept has been politically very popular and has fulfilled most American needs. There are, however, inherent quantitative limits on the size of such forces, and these limits have been tested by repeated, constant Middle Eastern deployments since September 11, 2001. The American military could use a break from this pattern.

The second step in the process (Part II) is the changing pattern of energy, to which two chapters are devoted. Chapter 3 looks at the historic pattern of U.S. "addiction" to oil from the Persian Gulf, the consequent dictates that being an oil "junkie" has had on American policy priorities in the region, how the Iranian Revolution of 1979 thrust the United States into a permanent oil-induced military presence in the region, and how changes in consumption patterns are lessening that dependency. Chapter 4 focuses on the current source of shrinking dependency, the discovery and exploitation of shale gas and oil reserves. While this development promises to change greatly America's relative standing in the global oil market, there are also environmental and ecological cautions that should condition the most expansive advocacy and hope for this new source. It has, however, helped change the calculus of U.S. policy.

The heart of the analysis is the three chapters of Part III that focus specifically on Middle Eastern problems and issues. Chapter 5 focuses on the "vexatious" nature of the region as a central focus on American security policy, looking at the complex nature of the region and its problems and the specific contemporary threat posed by the IS. It argues that the fundamental problems of the Middle East are overwhelmingly internal to the region (religion and ethnicity), that none of these were created by the United States, and that only those who live in the region can solve those problems.

Americans and the application of American military force are *not* the solution. Chapter 6 elaborates on these points, looking specifically at the American posture through the lens of American interests. It argues that the central historical American interest in assuring free access to Middle Eastern oil has had two major consequences: it has, since 1979, necessitated a permanent American military presence in the area, and it has coincided with the emergence of Islamic terrorism directed at the United States. Terrorism has supplanted oil as the central focus of U.S. Middle Eastern policy, and the text speculates on the possible connection between the American militarily activist role and the emergence of American-directed terrorism. Chapter 7 applies the observations from the two previous chapters to discrete problems: dealing with the regimes of the oil-producing states, managing currently contentious U.S. relations with Israel, and extending American priorities to places like Syria and Iraq. It suggests that one American response might be to back away from the area's problems, metaphorically erecting a change link fence around the area and forcing the countries and peoples there to work out their own problems.

Part IV consists of a single chapter that projects how American policy may change. It advocates a much less militarily activist posture and a reorientation of American national security policy around three pillars. The first is the importance of particular interests to the United States, with the principal distinction between vital and less-than-vital interests. The second is the attainability of particular goals by the U.S. military against the asymmetrical warriors who dominate the area. The third is the affordability of a "muscular" foreign policy making including generous applications of force, particularly given the paucity of results achieved in the past in places like Iraq and Afghanistan. Its conclusion is that applying these standards will result in a much less intrusive policy that will not harm American interests.

Donald M. Snow
Hilton Head, South Carolina

Part I

INTRODUCTION

Chapter 1

The Foreign and National Security Inheritance

The Cold War Paradigm

American foreign and national security policy in the Middle East appears increasingly to be caught in a conceptual time warp. Responses to ongoing problems and crises seem to be framed in understandings and frameworks appropriate to another time and set of places but not clearly to the present and the challenges a new century presents. There is a decidedly twentieth-century ring to how major actors in the decision process seem to define and propose to respond to the events, and especially the violent occurrences, of regional international relations. If, for instance, the current U.S. reaction to the Islamic State (IS) seems familiar in approach and content to past actions and reactions, it is because that is how we have reacted to Middle East crises for a third of a century or more. It is not clear that the framework fits well in the contemporary scene. Yet, it remains the dominant framework within which members of the decision-making elite operate, whether they consciously realize it or not.

The general framework has been in place for over 350 years. It emerged from the fallout of the Thirty Years' War that ended in 1648. The "Peace of Westphalia" that ended that continent-wide bloodletting between Catholics and Protestants in Europe evolved into a viable way to regulate world politics in a system where the center of power was Europe (and by the twentieth century North America) and the rest of the world was of little consequence except as a contributor to the ascendancy of the European Balance of Power. The Westphalian system arguably was shattered by Europe's self-immolation in World War II, but its remnants reassembled as the Cold War competition after 1945. The major actors and some of their dynamics changed during the second half of the twentieth century, but the rules remained much the same. They are still largely in place.

The United States was not a major part of the Euro-centered system for most of the existence of the United States. It did not exist for the first century and a half of the Westphalian evolution—indeed, the American Revolution was one of the first chinks in the armor of the values that underlay the European-dominated system. Until the twentieth century, the United States was a bit player in grand international politics, and it was not really until the United States dominated World War II that it emerged as an undeniable major player. The Soviet Union followed a similar trajectory as it rose to dominant power status. The two countries became, virtually by default, the central powers of the post–World War II world. Each preached a different and incompatible evangelical political "theology." The result was they could not cooperate in reordering the international order along mutually agreeable lines. As a consequence, they came into conflict over which vision would triumph, and the result was the Cold War.

The United States obviously prevailed in that contest. In the process of waging the competition, the Americans were forced to develop, for the first time in national history, a coherent way to think about and organize both foreign and national security affairs. The Americans and the Soviets both lacked a fresh, coherent view about how to conduct their policy, and they fell conceptually back upon principles that had organized European international politics for three centuries. For the United States, that framework became something known as the Cold War Paradigm. Because the application of this way of thinking had succeeded in overcoming the formidable challenge of communism, it created a mind-set that its practitioners were reluctant to abandon. It is still with us today.

The problem is that the paradigm provided a framework for organizing and dealing with a very different world than the one that exists today. It was born in a world that was effectively much smaller and more homogenous than the world as it now exists. It represented how a world of culturally similar and compatible independent states confined to Europe and its peripheries inter-acted with one another. At the time it was formed in the seventeenth century, all the member states had similar monarchical systems which they sought to promote and protect. By the latter part of the eighteenth century, that purview was widened with the American and French Revolutions and the gradual move toward democratization in Great Britain, but these sources of division and disagreement were mild compared to what exists today.

The Euro-centric world system was effectively ended by World War II. Most of the major players in the old balance of power were defeated (Germany and Italy) or exhausted by the effort (Britain and France). What were left were two upstart members from the peripheries of the old system. Russia had been a member of the old balance of power but had been effectively excom-municated when it became the heretical communist Soviet Union. The more conventional democratic United States had opted for "splendid isolation" from international geopolitics after World War I. In 1945, these two countries were the last standing powers, and they would have to become the pillars of a new order.

Neither was especially well prepared to take on this role. Both were evangelicals: the Soviet Union saw itself as the vanguard of the Marxist-Leninist worldview, and the United States believed with equal fervor (and still largely does) that the solution to global political woes is the gradual democratization of the world's countries. These dreams were incompatible; eventually, it became clear they were mutually exclusive, and the central theme of world politics (at least from the viewpoint of the traditional powers) was which vision would prevail and how.

From a conceptual vantage point, the ensuing Cold War was a new competition that would be conducted largely within the rules of the old balance of power. It was, in its essence, a world of traditional interstate diplomacy and interaction heavily dependent on conventional, state-sponsored military force to influence and enforce its decisions. The central players were different than they had been in the previous three hundred years, but the way they "played" was not unfamiliar to students of the past. As the Cold War evolved over the forty-plus years of its conduct, this system spawned a new class of operators who embraced those rules. When one side won, its practitioners, not unnaturally, assumed that it was the skills they had developed as "cold warriors" that caused the victory, and they were reluctant to abandon or materially alter how they did business. They still maintain those beliefs.

The problem was that the world changed too rapidly for the old paradigm to hold. The traditional European powers have not rebounded to be the prime actors they once were, meaning the Eurocentrism of Westphalia was lost forever. Two new forces, however, changed the dynamics of world politics fundamentally. The first was the advent of nuclear weapons as the ace in the hole for both the Soviets and the Americans. Nuclear capabilities and arsenals grew to staggering levels during the Cold War period. One thing became clear as these frightening weapons stockpiles grew: a nuclear war would destroy the combatants (and probably everyone else), and thus could not be won. This revelation meant that war between the two major combatants had to be avoided at all costs. This "necessary peace" (to quote the title of a 1986 book by this author) came from the gradual realization that any war between them could escalate to nuclear war. As a result, peace was indeed necessary. The "shadow of the mushroom-shaped cloud" (a 1979 title by this author) hung like a sobering sword of Damocles over the conduct of international relations.

The second, and for present purposes more consequential, change was the emergence of the developing world from colonial rule by the retreating

European powers. At the end of World War II, there were roughly 50 independent, sovereign states in the world. In the decades after World War II—when
the major powers were more riveted on their direct confrontation—largely
Afro-Asian independence movements swelled that number to over 200.
Today, it is around 220 independent states. What is important about this
dynamic is that many of these new states are different than the old states
in ways that alter how international politics is conducted. The changes they
force do not fit neatly into the Cold War framework.

The Cold War, and particularly American success in waging it, has reinforced a belief in the virtue of its dynamics and conduct in a world that does
not entirely accept or honor those values and rules. It is clear in the way the
United States does business in the world: how it thinks about and conducts
geopolitics. At this point, the foreign policy establishment, however, remains
conceptually mired in the Cold War paradigm. To understand this, the chapter moves to a discussion of the content of the Cold War, followed by a look
at the "hard men" of the foreign policy elite that continue to preach and to
enforce Cold War rules in an inappropriate environment. This problem is
exacerbated in dealing with a developing world that does not share the structure, problems, or values that underlay the Cold War framework. The result
is a curious conceptual incongruity between the paradigm and the current
environment.

THE COLD WAR PARADIGM: CONTENT AND PERSPECTIVE

The aftermath of history's greatest bloodletting created an enormous transformation in world power and hence a transformation in the way relations
between its members were conducted. As noted, neither the United States nor
the Soviet Union was especially well prepared to assume dominant leadership
roles in reordering the international political system that had been in place
and had evolved for 300 years. Both leaderships, however, were steeped in
the values of the old system and its ways of doing business, and their natural
instinct was to try to adapt those venerable practices to a new form of order.
As would prove to be the case in the 1990s, when the system was faced with
a similarly traumatic change, their efforts were not entirely successful.

The first quandary both countries had to confront was what the relationship
between them would be. The Soviets and the Americans had been wartime
allies in the fight against Hitlerian Germany and its allies, and at least the
Americans wondered if the collaboration could be continued. Most participants were skeptical, given the ideological and worldview gulf between
them, but it was only through a series of negative events (the Berlin crises,
the fall of Czechoslovakia, Soviet refusal to participate in the Marshall Plan,

for instance) that the Americans came to accept the idea that the new system would be adversarial. The North Korean invasion of 1950 was the final straw on the camel's back of cooperation.

What followed was a forty-year confrontation that became known as the Cold War. The name the competition was given is indicative of the relationship between the principal leaders. The issues that divided them were deeper than those that had divided members of the Euro-centered system prior to the twentieth century, when political democracy and fascism became the dominant ideologies between the world wars, and the result was global conflict. The differences between communism and democracy and the evangelism of both belief systems to spread their "gospel" was certainly profound enough to have justified war in an earlier era, and a reprise of World War II would not have been unexpected at all in an earlier time.

Such a war never came about, of course, because the environment had changed. The Westphalian system had relied heavily on military force to create and enforce relationships, but that force was always limited in extent and consequences. The advent of nuclear weapons during World War II and their growing possession by both sides changed the rules dramatically. Both sides came to realize that they could not fight one another directly for fear that the result might be nuclear war. The situation became less Damoclean: the sword (nuclear weapons) still hung over the relationship, but the slender string holding it in place gradually became a sturdy rope that was intended to ensure that the Cold War did not become hot.

For most of its conduct, the Cold War proceeded as if a hot war—World War III—was a lively possibility. In conventional terms, the dynamics of the situation certainly warranted a large level of military preparedness, given the adversarial nature of the relationship and the mutual desire of both sides both to spread their own systems and to frustrate the other. This competition first took place in the heart of Europe, and by the end of the 1940s an "iron curtain" traversed central Europe, with large military forces on both sides of the barrier.

The Cold War was the central reality of the international system while it was being "waged," at least in the parts of the world in which it was being primarily conducted. For Americans and Soviets, it was the central international political reality, and its conduct and management was the overarching concern on both sides. The problem was that it was also an impossible situation to resolve in a way acceptable to both sides.

The Cold War had several salient characteristics. First and foremost, it was a primarily military competition. There was a political element, in the sense that both sides wanted to convert other parts of the globe to its particular ideology, but Soviet communism—as it was practiced—had limited appeal as a standard to be emulated. At the same time, the Soviet economy was never competitive with that of the West (and especially the United States). Part of the reason was that the Soviet Union was forced to expend a much higher percentage of its economic resources in military matters to remain competitive, since the Soviet economy was much smaller than that of the United States. This burden inhibited economic growth, and the communist system as it evolved also proved to be inferior to that of the West. The economic gap widened over time, although the Soviets made great efforts to disguise it. In the end, the economic gulf contributed to the end of the competition.

The military competition dominated policy on both sides. In the early years of the Cold War, it was conceived as a very *dangerous* relationship, meaning that both sides came perilously close to elevating the Cold War to a shooting conflict. In the United States, a fatalistic political culture came to surround the competition, where people mulled not on whether war would occur, but on *when* it would break out. As nuclear arsenals burgeoned in size and deadliness, Americans foresaw a nuclear Armageddon that could only be avoided by surrender and debated "better red than dead" versus "better dead than red."

As the nuclear weapons made the competition more *deadly* (the consequences of war became more devastating), the dynamics began to change. Going back at least as far as the 1950s, American president Dwight D. Eisenhower and Soviet general secretary General Nikita Khrushchev independently declared that nuclear war was unacceptable and should be avoided at all costs, a sentiment reiterated at one time by all succeeding leaders. In fact, what nuclear weapons did was effectively to take military solutions off the table as ways to resolve differences between the dominant superpowers. It took a while for this realization to sink in, and military preparations and proposed solutions continued to dominate thinking about international problems and their solutions. The idea that military force could be the change agent was an artifact of the pre–World War II system that endured, and it remains ingrained in thinking about dealing with the world.

Although it was not realized at the time, the 1962 Cuban missile crisis was the harbinger and stimulator of change. The crisis involved Soviet plans to place nuclear-tipped rockets on the island capable of attacking and destroying most of the eastern United States. The American government discovered the preparation of missile sites in Cuba through U-2 spy flights over the island and immediately demanded their dismemberment and the cancellation of the program by Moscow. In the tense thirteen-day confrontation that ensued before the Soviets backed down and sent rockets intended for Cuba back to the Soviet Union, the world—and especially the U.S. and Soviet governments—faced the very real prospect of a nuclear war that they knew could destroy them both. It was a singularly sobering experience. It was also the high water mark of the Cold War. After Cuba, both sides slowly came to realize the unacceptability of war and to adopt, at least implicitly, what Robert Jervis called "existential deterrence" (the need to avoid war to survive). Peace was necessarily their prime goal.

It took a while for this realization to change the dynamics of the relationship. Hard-liners continued to herald the military instrument of power and its usefulness in solving the Cold War: during the crisis itself, Air Force General and Chair of the Joint Chiefs of Staff Curtis Lemay argued forcefully for war to solve the problem once and for all. Nuclear arsenals continued to grow to stunning heights, and expenditures on newer generations of yet-more-deadly conventional arms entered arsenals as if nothing had changed. In essence, the competition became more deadly at the same time it was becoming less dangerous: the consequences of war increased as its acceptability and thus likelihood decreased. It was not until the end of the Cold War that this anomaly became evident.

The political animosity of the relationship between the two countries fueled the continued arms race. Politically, the dynamics of the Cold War were inclusive, intractable, and irreconcilable. Moreover, given the consequences of a hot war, they were viewed as perpetual and unending. It was a difficult mix, and one that policy makers sought to manage in conventional ways.

The inclusive nature of the Cold War was that it encompassed all international political differences across the spectrum, and this perception gave it an absolute primacy in international relations on both sides. Virtually all interactions were viewed as part of the Soviet-American competition, and all solutions proposed were framed in terms of Cold War consequences. This mind-set permeated American thinking, and it meant that problems that were not Cold War based or relevant tended to be ignored or relegated to a lower order of concern. As argued below, this was the large tragedy of dealing with the developing world that confronts U.S. policy today.

The relationship was also *intractable*. Before the missile crisis, both sides assumed that they had nothing in common in terms of their international outlook: there were no shared values. Thus, all situations were effectively zero-sum: any gains one side made in a particular situation necessarily came at the expense of the other. The possibility of positive-sum outcomes from which both might benefit was rarely considered: indeed, among the true Cold Warriors, even considering such possibilities was viewed as a sign of weakness and naïve thinking.

The Cuban crisis punctured this assumption. As the post-missile crisis system evolved, both sides came gradually to realize that they did share at least one value, the avoidance of their mutual annihilation in a nuclear holocaust. After Cuba, arms control became the centerpiece of this new dynamic, and it spread gradually to things like cultural and athletic interchanges. Intractability slowly faded.

The conflict was also seen as *irreconcilable*. Western systems were democratic and capitalist politically (with varying degrees of purity in different countries), whereas operational communism was authoritarian/totalitarian politically and socialist economically. Some economies in Europe exhibited characteristics of both economic philosophies as measured by the degree of government participation in economic affairs (so-called democratic socialism), but the political gulf was wide and unbridgeable. To the rest of the world, the two sides offered their models as panaceas to the difficulties especially evident in the developing world, and their appeals were mutually exclusive. In the United States, communism was seen as "godless" and thus irredeemable. There was no danger that the two systems would, on their own, grow enough alike to allow reconciliation.

Because of these dynamics, the Cold War was viewed as *perpetual*—a "protracted conflict," according to Yugoslav dissident Milovan Djilas (his book has that phrase in its title)—for which there was no mutually acceptable end state. To the Cold Warriors, the only way the competition could possibly end was through World War III, an outcome that had to be avoided due to its consequences. Thus, the prime value of the Cold War had to be its maintenance—keeping it "cold" rather than letting it become "hot." This worldview, of course, precluded the possibility that one side or another might "win" the competition nonviolently. It especially rejected the ideal notion that the communist side would ever give up: the task of the Cold War was to deter military aggression by the Soviets and to avoid their successful infiltration and subversion of the United States. These perceptions gave a "hard" edge to how those officials who made policy in a world they viewed as hostile and adversarial and manageable only through the cold steel of military power.

Given this Cold War mind-set, American policy makers were flummoxed when the Cold War ended. In essence, the Soviet Union essentially gave up (I have discussed this at length in three 1990s books with the generic title *The Shape of the Future*). The end came essentially not so much because the American system triumphed as it did because the Soviet system failed. This failure was multifaceted, but two aspects stand out.

One was the utter collapse of the Soviet command economy, which simply ceased functioning in anything resembling a competitive way with the West. The Soviet leadership had maintained an elaborate hoax that the "worker's paradise" was a vibrant enterprise but, in fact, behind the veil of prosperity and success, it was a Potemkin village—a false front behind which lurked an economy that had not grown at all since the early 1970s and which had, by many standards, become stagnant or was in decline. Soviet academic economists saw this falsehood, labeled the situation as the "era of stagnation," and found in rising Soviet leader Mikhail Gorbachev (whose wife Raisa was a colleague and fellow academic at Moscow State University), someone who understood the situation and its consequences. The Soviet Union was becoming, in one popular aphorism of the time, "a banana republic with nuclear weapons." When he became Soviet leader, Gorbachev acknowledged this dynamic, concluded that the only way to rectify the situation was to join the Western economic (and especially technological) system, and that doing so meant ending the Cold War (positions he introduced in his 1986 book *Perestroika*).

Soviet economic decline was matched in the military arena. A large, imposing and apparently powerful Soviet military machine had been the key symbol of the Soviet Union's claim to superpower status, and its existence had underlay American pessimism about prevailing in the Cold War. That military machine, however, also had Potemkin characteristics, and these were revealed as the Soviet Union stumbled in its invasion and occupation of Afghanistan. That adventure proved a military disaster from which the Soviets withdrew with no semblance of success in 1988. The war demonstrated a dispirited military force liberally composed of reluctant conscripts, and their failure created an antiwar sentiment and opposition to the regime that helped fuel support for its removal.

At the end of 1991, the Soviet hammer and sickle flag came down from top of the Kremlin, replaced by the Russian tricolor. The Communist Party of the Soviet Union fell from power and the constituent republics along the periphery of Mother Russia defected and declared independence, matching defiance of communist authority that had been playing out in Eastern Europe and had been considered virtually impossible by Western analysts. The old order simply dissolved in a way that hardly anyone had predicted (George Kennan, the father of the American policy of containment was an exception). Operational communism ended with a whimper, not a bang.

After a period of adjustment to the new reality, the Cold Warriors took credit for the end of the competition. This was particularly true of conservatives who had helped President Ronald Reagan conduct a binge of American military spending in the 1980s intended to drive the Soviet economy into submission. Their efforts undoubtedly helped push a tottering Soviet system over, but the exact degree that American efforts "won" as opposed to Soviet deficiencies "losing" the competition remains arguable. U.S. policy makers, however, certainly felt vindicated that the Cold War methods had prevailed and that the basic framework of American efforts should continue.

The Cold War legacy has thus lingered on. Its primary elements have been an emphasis on the diplomatic methods of the European system, a belief in geopolitics conducted by national governments, and the ready recourse to traditional military force as the lingua franca of international conflict resolution. The central argument here is that the continuing influence of Cold War thinking has infected the way the United States views the conditions and challenges of a contemporary world order. The problems of this new order do not closely resemble those of the Cold War, rendering the approaches and solutions of dubious relevance and effectiveness for dealing with that environment.

This continuing impact is manifested in two ways. First, the cast of foreign policy decision makers who are the product of the Cold War and their orientations toward world problems remains largely in place. These analysts, what are called here the "hard men," have dominated decision-making, and the result has been conservatism and hewing to conventional, Cold War ways of thinking that have discouraged other ways of thinking about policy. Second, this emphasis has facilitated ignoring or distorting a concern about what was concomitantly occurring in the developing world. In retrospect, the emergence of the developing world from colonial rule was an international phenomenon at least as important as the Cold War, but it was not treated as such at the time. The direct Cold War competition was the first priority alongside which all other concerns paled in comparison. To the extent the developing world came into play at all, it was as an extension of the Cold War—a place where the two sides could compete for loyalty as they tried to turn the world map "blue" (supportive of Western democracies) or "red" (allegiant to Soviet communism). The developing world's problems were not reducible to Cold War logic and constructs, and treating them as if they were an exercise in irrelevance that distorted our understanding of large parts of the world.

In the post–Cold War world, the developing world has become the center of attention, and especially of violence and instability. This has partly been due to the neglect of developing world problems either out of ignorance or inattention in a Cold War-obsessed competition, partly due to the difficulty, complexity, and intractability of developing world issues. In no part of the world are these difficulties more difficult and prominent than in the Middle East. The chapter concludes by introducing some of the difficulties associated with attempting to graft the Cold War way of thinking onto an international order very different than that which prevailed in the second half of the twentieth century.

COLD WARRIORS: THE HARD MEN

Given the length of its duration and the intensity and pervasiveness of its influence, it is not surprising that the Cold War bred and nurtured a large number of people who became skilled in managing the competition. Indeed, since most of the participants in the enterprise assumed the value and likelihood of an unending, protracted conflict, developing the skills to deal with Cold War realities was a valued attribute that was nurtured in academic circles (undergraduate major and postgraduate degrees in Soviet and East Studies, Russian language, and the like), military career paths were devoted to Cold War artifacts (missile officers in the Air Force, for instance), and anticommunist strategic thinking pervaded the curricula in the war colleges and elsewhere. A claim to geopolitical understanding of the "threat" became a necessary characteristic of aspirants to serve in the military, civilian, and military-industrial sectors.

The values that were inculcated into the Cold Warriors did not disappear when the Cold War ended. The Cold War paradigm was the lens through which a whole generation of foreign and national security analysts approached the world. The problem for which they had honed their skills may have disappeared, but they did not. Rather, most of them remained in positions of authority and influence at both senior and more junior levels, many of them still remain, and the solutions they propose for ongoing situations have an eerily Cold War tone to them. Most prominent among those influences is the tendency to respond to many crises in military terms that invite the involvement of American force as a solution. The ongoing crisis in the Middle East is the most obvious example. The question is whether the advice that counsels in that direction is the most appropriate in changed circumstances.

The Cold Warriors tend to view themselves as intellectually tough, pragmatic, and realistic analysts—thus the designation "hard men." Faced with an implacable and like-minded opponent in Moscow, their orientation was effective in both understanding and countering that opponent. The hard men managed to keep the Cold War from boiling over, and in the end their side prevailed, for which they deserve at least some of the credit. Their very success reinforced their beliefs, and they have carried them over into the post–Cold War period. They remain a very potent force in shaping and influencing policy. They also tend to manifest a strong contempt for alternative ways of looking at problems, which they tend to view as generally "soft" in a world of very harsh realities.

The existence and influence of the Cold Warriors is both understandable and is invaluable in some ways. Their perspective on problems has value, and it gives them a sizable advantage in debates about policy alternatives. The heart of their advantage is experience, and it is manifested in several ways. First, it means that in dealing with a problem anywhere, they are most likely to have dealt with the physical area and problem than have others. These are the officials and commentators who have, for instance, been dealing with U.S. relations with Iran for a long time, and they have a perspective on what works and does not work that people who lack their experience do not. Their endorsement or disapproval of a particular approach to a problem—the Iranian nuclear question, for instance—is likely to carry great weight with policy makers and others with less expertise who will defer to the "experts."

This deference is understandable when the policy positions that have come from the establishment have been successful. When those positions have not resulted in particularly successful policy—Iran is certainly an example—then it is not quite so clear if the deference is justifiable.

A second advantage of experience is the knowledge of how the policy process works. The Cold Warriors have, by and large, "been there and done that" over a period of time, and they know the people and the institutional places where they can most effectively make their points. Outsiders arguing different solutions may well lack the contacts and detailed understanding of "how things work," and are thus at a disadvantage in trying to make and argue their policy alternatives.

A third advantage is experiential knowledge of the subject of any policy by virtue of their past association with other, similar policy problems and with those foreign leaders with whom one must interact. The hard men have been privy to details about situations (usually obtained from classified sources) that can provide an apparently impressive amount of understanding about the place and people involved in any crisis. Anyone who has had security clearance will tell you that the content of such information is often mundane and of marginal relevance in any given situation, but its possession endows the holder with the ability to claim that "if you knew what I know, you would agree with me." Since, by definition, the nonpossessor cannot assess the truth of the claim, the advantage is reinforced. The veteran thus acquires an aura of authority that may or may not be justified.

Some of these advantages can, however, entail limitations as well. For one thing, repeated experience within the same framework may produce a rigid way of looking at and dealing with problems that can inhibit innovative consideration of alternate perspectives in particular situations. Experience, in other words, can produce intellectual sclerosis rather than flexibility. Responses can become doctrinaire, serving established solutions and routines rather than adapting to changing circumstances. It can also produce a dulling predictability to advocacies and action. The advocacies can stifle debate before decisions are reached, and predictable responses may provide temptations to adversaries.

The hard men's counsel is clearly an important part of the decision process, and it is a vantage point that one would not want to discard. It becomes a problem in two overlapping and reinforcing ways. It can produce a rigidity and continuity in policy that is valuable when the environment is relatively unchanging conceptually—which the Cold War presented—but that is not adequately adaptive when the environment is changing rapidly or in ways that conventional doctrine does not encompass—which arguably is the case in places like the Middle East. It can also stifle healthy debate about policy alternatives, and especially alternatives that go beyond the existing paradigm for thinking about world affairs. The Cold War model of European great power politics may still have some relevance in a place like Ukraine, but it does not so readily apply to the situation in Anbar Province in Iraq. The Cold War perspective remains valuable when particular situations are analogous to Cold War events; it is not quite so obviously superior in situations that do not have those characteristics.

This criticism is particularly relevant in the contemporary environment, where the concerns of the developing world have been elevated to a much greater centrality than they formerly had. During the Cold War, attention was riveted to the bilateral Soviet-American, communist-anticommunist confrontation that all other concerns were relegated to a lower order of priority. At the top of the list of other system dynamics was the emergence of the developing world as a force in international politics.

PARADIGM BLINDERS: THE DEVELOPING WORLD

In retrospect, the attention given to the Cold War confrontation blinded the major powers, including the United States, from giving adequate attention to the other, and equally profound, dynamic of the post–World War II world— decolonization and the emergence of a developing world of new, inexperienced, and often-unstable independent states as members of the international system. While the Cold War raged, the developing (or third) world was largely ignored, other than as a peripheral, safe venue to extend Cold War politics. With the Cold War removed from the equation, the often-unstable dynamics of this developing world have gradually moved to international prominence, especially in the area of national security concern. Ground zero of this concern is the Middle East.

The developing world is different. Part of the difference is geographic: the developing world is concentrated on the peripheries of Europe: notably Latin America (the Western Hemisphere south of the United States), most of Asia, and essentially all of Africa. A map of the world distinguished by membership or nonmembership in the Organization of Economic Cooperation and Development (OECD) is a good shorthand way to differentiate the "developed" world (the OECD members) from the developing world (the nonmembers). The division is not perfect, but it is close.

For a variety of reasons, the areas comprising the developing world did not achieve the material levels of what became the OECD world (the organization is a post–World War II phenomenon). It used to be fashionable to refer to these places as underdeveloped, a term that has lost acceptability because of its pejorative connotations. Most of developed world had not gone through the developmental process of economic growth and change and political evolution into something like modern states. They remained traditional, in the sense that most social, economic, and political activity was centered on small units like villages and around tribal elders of one kind or another. Some had distinct, even distinguished, cultures. All were very different from the evolving Western world.

The Colonial Experience

The intrusion of Europe into the developing world began in the 1600s in the wake of the end of the Thirty Years' War and the emergence of the Westphalian order. It continued through the eighteenth and nineteenth centuries, formally ending with the final partition of Africa at the Berlin Conference of 1884. Most European countries took part, from small states like the Netherlands and Belgium to the "great" powers like Britain and France. Russia participated by annexing territories on its boundaries, effectively forming the parameters of the Soviet Union. A late comer, the United States joined the ranks of colonialists at the end of the nineteenth century after divesting Spain of its remaining colonies in Cuba and the Philippines in the Spanish-American War.

There tended to be two motivations for European colonialism, each of which is important in understanding the status of the new countries that emerged from decolonization. One motivation was prestige: the notion was that a great state was one with colonies; the prestige argument was particularly persuasive in the American debate about whether it should become a colonial power. In a manner similar to the possession of nuclear weapons defining superpower status in the twentieth century, it became commonplace to argue that the larger the empire, the stronger the claim to great power status. The British Empire was the clear winner by this criterion.

The other motivation was profit. It was a myth of the colonizing powers that the possession of colonies would produce profits and thereby enrich the "mother" country. The idea was that these developing countries had raw resources that the colonists could monopolize and sell or develop for profit, and that colonies provided "captive" markets for goods produced by the colonizers. In other-than-unusual circumstances, these arguments were specious, and very few colonies were economic "cash cows." Still, the fiction was necessary to justify the often-great economic burden that maintaining and controlling colonies presented. After World War II, European countries were too financially decimated to maintain the expense of empire, and this was a major factor in decolonization.

Neither of these sources of motivation suggested that colonialism had altruism as a motivating force. Prestige and profit could only continue as long as domination was maintained, meaning things like uplifting populations and preparing them for independent rule was not only an effort that most did not undertake, but was a counterproductive idea to be avoided. The more ignorant and parochial the colonial subjects remained, the better it was for the colonialists and their continuing control. In some cases, there were cosmetic activities to indicate a "white man's burden" of uplifting the native populations (like encouraging missionaries), but the heart of the colonial effort was control and subjugation. Things like educating the population or promoting integration of diverse population segments could only encourage sedition and rebellion and was thus to be avoided.

Colonial motives also contributed to the development of colonial administrative units that made no historical or political sense, often aggregating historic enemies into common political units and erecting barriers that divided and separated kinsmen. To some extent, this was the result of utter ignorance on the part of the colonialist, who had no idea of the human realities on the ground upon arrival. In Africa, for instance, it was common for colonial powers to land on the shore at a given location and claim the territory going inland as their possession—regardless of who might live there. When the Berlin Conference met and apportioned the last of the continent, there were no accurate maps of the interior of the continent that could be used to help form boundaries.

Both of these consequences of colonialism were present when decolonization occurred and have served as causes of contemporary discontent, instability, and violence. The intent to preserve colonial rule indefinitely meant that the population was not educated to a level that might inculcate insidious ideas of independence in them, and the result was that new governments lacked an educated elite to create orderly governance. Independence was generally granted to colonial units, meaning all the distortions that artificial boundaries had inherent within them were present as aggravating factors. Prior to colonialism, disputes between antagonistic groups went forward in undefined political space; after decolonization, they became the problem of new governments that would have been pressed to govern without these difficulties. Since colonial rule had been economically exploitive rather than developmental, the new countries were also generally desperately poor and lacked the tools to bring about constructive change themselves.

The Consequences of Colonialism

The European-based international order that became the basis of the Cold War paradigm did not understand of or have the mechanisms for accommodating these dynamics, but they were the central realities and concerns of the developing world. Europe had been in a similar condition a millennium earlier, and through a long, bitter, and often bloody evolution had overcome many of these burdens. The Westphalian settlement had, for instance, divided the Protestant and Catholic monarchies and helped in the establishment of what became the European state system. This same process has yet to be concluded in the developing world. The Europeans have basically forgotten their own parallel travails, and the rules and methods for regulating the relations between them are curiously inapplicable to the developing world.

Decolonization became ineluctable after World War II. The process of rejecting European colonial rule had begun in the eighteenth century with the American Revolution, which was the first successful anticolonialist conflict of the modern state system. It revived between the world wars in a few places like India, and after World War II, it became an unavoidable force. Despite the more or less systematic efforts of colonial rulers, seditious ideas of freedom spread through the colonial world, a trend accentuated because many colonial subjects had been pressed into duty during the war, saw the contrast between their statuses and conditions and those of their rulers, and demanded equality. The process began in Asia in places like India, Indonesia, and French Indochina (Southeast Asia). Success spread the phenomenon more broadly through Asia and into Africa, the last redoubt of universal colonial bondage.

The European powers by and large recognized the futility of resisting independence movements and granted political freedom as fast as they could to new countries that they had done virtually nothing to prepare for this new status. The French resisted the loss of empire for a while in Vietnam and Algeria, but finally concluded that continuing resistance was futile and domestically very unpopular. The last major empire retreated from Africa in 1976 when the Portuguese granted independence of its remaining African colonies. The problem of empire was ended; the thornier problem of post-imperial development was about to begin.

The Cold War obscured the systemic trauma that decolonization produced. To the Cold Warriors, decolonization was little more than a minor distraction from the central contest, and their only interests in the phenomenon was how it could be exploited for Cold War ends. Since the new countries were generally desperately poor and thus needed economic and military assistance from whatever sources would provide help, a competition for influence in the new countries developed between the Cold War adversaries. This competition was, however, motivated less by an honest concern for the plights of target countries as it was for gaining Cold War "points." When the Cold War ended, both sides withdrew their efforts, since they believed they had no real interests in this part of the world.

The problems the developing countries faced were enormous. Almost all these states are *multinational,* meaning there are population elements in all of them more loyal to some political entity other than the state in which they live.

Often these ethnically, tribally, or otherwise defined political entities were the result of a mindless and ignorant aggregation by colonial masters. The situation was sometimes exacerbated by colonial practice: the British, for instance, followed a practice of "indirect rule," wherein they identified one dominant group, deputized them to enforce British rule, and in the process alienated internal groups from one another more than they were before colonialism.

When the colonialists decided to grant independence to their colonies, they tended to create states coterminous with the colonial administrative units, and the result was to place subject peoples with more parochial primary identities within a single polity, where they were somehow supposed to work out their differences amicably. This represented a dynamic the colonialist had actively opposed during the colonial period. In most cases, the result was animosity and instability that is the source of many contemporary problems and underlies many of the conflicts that plague the developing world.

Put another way, multinational states are *artificial states* in the sense that they do not represent any natural political loyalty pattern of the population but instead threw together a number of national groups who had lived in some proximity to one another before colonialism and during colonial rule but had in many cases been long-standing rivals. The result, which continues to plague politics in many of these countries, is a *lack of nationalism* in terms of personal loyalty structures: on Independence day in Nigeria in 1960, the tribesmen who were aggregated in the Nigerian state remained Ibo, Hausa-Fulani, or Yoruba in terms of their primary loyalty, not Nigerians. This condition continues to plague the quality of relations among groups in many African and Middle Eastern countries.

These countries were also generally very poor and unprepared either for self-rule or for the task of improving the material condition for lot of their citizens. As already noted, colonial policy discouraged preparing native populations for an independent existence most of the colonialists sought to avoid. Thus, for instance, educational opportunities for colonial subjects were very limited, and this meant that at independence there was a severe shortage of educated citizens to organize and operate government or to provide other services. In particular, the primary need in most cases was for economic development, a priority for which most of these countries lacked the entrepreneurs, capital, and skills to undertake.

All of these conditions existed during the Cold War, but they were largely ignored or given low priority by governments like that of the United States. Given the life-and-death nature of the Cold War competition, energies necessarily had to be focused on that conflict to the point that there was little priority or resources for developing world problems. Most of the concerns surrounding the developmental needs of the emerging world were housed in academic locations and in parts of government outside the geopolitical mainstream of the Cold Warriors. Elaborate theories of development were produced by the academic community, often assisted by funding from sympathetic parts of government, but there was never adequate funding to implement them. The developing world was simply not a Cold War priority.

This neglect helps further to differentiate the Cold War hard men from the developmental advocates in ways that are relevant today. The hard men ignored, even derided, the concerns of the developmental theorists for two reasons. First, their concerns were not "hard" in the sense that they did not address the realist dictates of the Cold War. Rather, the developmental advocates were seen as somehow "soft" headed and idealistic in a hard reality. Moreover, the consequences of ignoring the academics and idealists in government were not so dire as ignoring the demands of the hard men. A call for developmental assistance could be ignored without potentially endangering the national existence, whereas the failure to stand toe to toe with the Soviets might result in exactly that danger.

The hard men never thought much about the developing world during the Cold War, and so its problems never were incorporated into the Cold War paradigm. Their worldview was constricted to the crisis at hand, and it taught a way of handling crises. The problem was that the problems of the developing world, which centered on the developmental process, neither fit that model nor were amenable to Cold War solutions. The academics had some answers, but they were ignored, as they largely are now. This gulf between elements of the expert community is especially relevant in understanding the current crises in places like the Middle East, the dynamics of which have much more to do with decolonization and development than they do with the Cold War confrontation.

THE PARADIGM IN A POST–COLD WAR WORLD

Conceptually, the Cold War would have been familiar and basically comfortable to foreign policy leaders who had managed international relations for several centuries before the end of World War II. The central players in the post–World War II period were different than those that had dominated since Westphalia, but they were both Western, espoused value systems (democracy and communism) that were Western in derivation, and were committed to conducting the new order basically by the same set of rules they inherited. Their ideological differences were deep and would have been adequate to resort to war to resolve were it not for nuclear weapons, but they both believed in a state-centered order protected and enshrined by state sovereignty as its core value and embraced state-based military force employing European methods and organization as a legitimate and effective means of conflict resolution. Internal wars fought for control of states by its members was a basically unfamiliar, peripheral concern over which little energy was expended.

There was little room for people and movements that did not accept these values, and those that did exist were subsumed within the communist-anticommunist framework. Many developing world countries saw the emergence of what are now called *sub-national groups* that challenged the post-independence order in their countries, either rejecting the legitimacy of the rulers or, in some cases, the jurisdiction of the political entity itself. Several of these organizations, like the National Liberation Front (NLF) in Southeast Asia, either were communist or were willing to associate themselves with communists to gain the support they needed to compete with governments backed by Western powers. The government of South Vietnam was an example.

Vietnam exemplifies this new phenomenon, the inability of the Cold Warriors to understand or cope with it, and the failure to incorporate this kind of conflict into managing international relations. Vietnam was fought inappropriately as a communist expansion within the Cold War framework. The rationale for American participation was based on something called the "domino theory," the idea that if the NLF was not opposed and defeated, neighboring states would fall under communist domination like falling dominos.

Although it was unrecognized at the time, Vietnam was the harbinger of the future. It was quintessentially an internal war over which population faction would rule Vietnam. It was different from most contemporary internal wars in that there were not great tribal or religious differences among the combatants. The combatants included governments as primary actors, but much of the dynamic arose from internal nonstate actors (the NLF) resisting an intervention by an outside, Western state–based force, the United States. The indigenous combatants fought the war *asymmetrically,* employing ways of fighting, rules of engagement (ROEs), and organization that were unfamiliar to the intervening Americans. Operating from the framework of the Cold War and for Cold War reasons, the United States never quite "got it" about the conflict in Southeast Asia, and the result was failure to prevail.

Conflict in the post–Cold War world much more closely resembles Vietnam than it does the World War III scenario on which the Cold War paradigm was built. The framework featured two characteristics that were crucial to its successful operation. One was traditional European state centrism: the idea that the state was the central legitimate actor on the international stage and that the operation of that system was the business of interstate relations, diplomatic, economic, or even military. Other political entities, such as nonstate actors, were considered peripheral or illegitimate. Second, the paradigm enshrined conventional, European-style military force as the basis for military decisiveness in situations where states could not settle their differences otherwise. Military forces were developed in updated versions of ways they had been prepared for centuries, armed with new and more lethal weapons but within the same chain of command, doctrinal understanding, and beliefs in military outcomes. Military force was for decisive purposes, and it was assumed that the application of that force would end with one side or another essentially capitulating.

The post–Cold War environment has progressively eroded the validity of both assumptions. An increasing proportion of the violence and instability within the global system is not interstate, and particularly in the interactions of the traditional powers. Traditional wars between states have virtually disappeared as international phenomena, and the idea that major states could come into direct conflict resolvable by force has become increasingly far-fetched. The conflict over Ukraine illustrates this well: in traditional terms, this is the kind of conflict that would have pitted Russia against the European powers—a twenty-first-century Crimean War. This prospect is not even a serious possibility, because such a war would be costly beyond any purpose for which it might be pursued—including a nuclear war.

The political movements that create instability in the contemporary world are almost all associated with non-state actors. Many are *subnational*, based on ethnic, religious, or other groups in artificial states seeking redress from their governments (or to break apart existing states that have little rationale for existing). Others are *supranational*—movements neither confined to nor willing to accept the strictures of state boundaries. Modern terrorist and religious extremist groups are good examples. The Cold War paradigm has no conceptual mechanism either to recognize or to deal with these groups except in traditional terms. Thus, for instance, the solution to the problem of IS is to destroy it militarily.

This pattern is largely the result of the pattern of colonization and decolonization. The majority of the conflicts—and especially the most violent and even grotesque—occur in countries that are almost entirely artificial and among population groups within those countries that were never reconciled during the colonial experience. They can involve Sunni versus Shiite in Yemen or multilayered ethnic/tribal and religious as in Sudan and South Sudan, these conflicts can be protracted, bloody, and system upsetting. It is not clear what could have been done during the decolonization to reduce these sources of instability, but very little was actually done in an international system virtually totally absorbed by the Cold War.

The other inappropriate aspect of the paradigm is its military predilection. Militarily, the conflict for which the Cold Warriors prepared was a reprise of World War II made more deadly by advances in the means of making war. The Cold War model was conventional interstate warfare fought by physically similar opponents adhering to basically the same set of rules. The forces preparing for this form of war were larger and more lethal than their predecessors, but they were conceptually pretty much the same.

Contemporary non-state opponents are not like the Cold War opponents. They are internal warriors, meaning they are likely to fight with extreme desperation and determination in the face of outside conventional military opponents, whom they are likely to view as returning colonizing forces. Lacking the same level of resources as the conventional forces, they are unlikely to accept or practice conventional mores and rules which, if they conformed to them, would certainly mean their decimation. They do not view war as a finite, bounded activity but as a long, drawn-out activity where the winner is determined by who is most persevering, not by some form of written peace agreement. They are classic asymmetrical warriors. As such, they represent a phenomenon that the hard men simply do not understand and tend to denigrate. Yet, the major powers (including the United States) have found *no* effective way to defeat this kind of force. The futility of countering IS by putting additional Western force in the field illustrates this futility: the Cold Warriors want to decimate IS on the battlefields and do not recognize that the military approach associated with modern asymmetrical warfare is designed specifically to avoid such a decisive negative outcome. No amount of Cold War breast beating changes that reality.

The hard men remain trapped in their vision of the world, but the world has changed. The Cold Warriors are essentially clueless when it comes to dealing with the pattern of post–Cold War conflict, because it represents a set of dynamics the Cold War did not prepare them to understand or confront. They arguably should have learned this shortcoming in Vietnam, but instead falsely blamed failure on inadequate resolve and support from the American people and not recognizing that undermining that support was a central element in the opponent's strategy. After the Cold War, their lack of understanding of the new pattern of warfare was played out by blundering into Iraq and Afghanistan, with similar predictable results. Calls for robust American military support against IS in Syria and Iraq further reinforces the hard men's attachment to solutions crafted for another time.

BIBLIOGRAPHY

Allison, Graham. *Essence of Decision: Explaining the Cuban Missile Crisis.* Boston, MA: Little Brown, 1971.

Ambrose, Stephen E. *Rise to Globalism: American Foreign Policy, 1938–1970.* Baltimore, MD: Johns Hopkins University Press, 1970.

Djilas, Milovan. *The New Class: An Analysis of the Communist System.* San Diego, CA: Harcourt, Brace, Jovanovich, 1957.

Gaddis, John Lewis. *Strategies of Containment: A Critical Appraisal of Postwar American National Security Policy during the Cold War* (Revised and Expanded Edition). New York: Oxford University Press, 2005.

———. *The United States and the End of the Cold War: Implications, Reconsiderations, Provocations.* New York: Oxford University Press, 1992.

Gorbachev, Mikhail. *Perestroika: New Thinking for Our Country and the World.* New York: Harper and Row, 1986.

Jervis, Robert. *The Meaning of the Nuclear Revolution: Statecraft and the Prospect of Armageddon* (Cornell Studies in Security Affairs). Ithaca, NY: Cornell University Press, 1990.

Kennan, George F. *American Diplomacy, 1900–1950.* New York: New American Library, 1951.

———. *Memoirs.* Boston, MA: Little Brown, 1976.

Kennedy, Robert F. *The Thirteen Days: A Memoir of the Cuban Missile Crisis.* New York: W.W. Norton, 1963.

Latham, Michael E. *The Right Kind of Revolution: Modernization, Development, and U.S. Foreign Policy from the Cold War to the Present.* Ithaca, NY: Cornell University Press, 2011.

Snow, Donald M. *The Case against Military Intervention.* New York: Routledge, 2016.

———. *The Necessary Peace: Nuclear Weapons and Superpower Relations.* Lexington, MA: Lexington Book, 1987.

———. *The Shape of the Future.* First, Second, and Third editions. Armonk, NY: M E Sharpe, 1991, 1995, 1999.

———. and Patrick J. Haney. *American Foreign Policy in a New Era.* New York: Pearson, 2013.

Stillman, Edmund, and William Pfaff. *The Politics of Hysteria.* New York: Harper Colophon Books, 1966.

———. *Power and Impotence: The Failure of American Foreign Policy.* New York: Viking Press, 1965.

Wiegley, Russell F. *The American Way of War.* New York: Macmillan, 1973.

Yergin, Daniel. *Shattered Peace: The Origins of the Cold War and the National Security State.* Boston, MA: Little Brown, 1977.

Chapter 2

Military Manpower

Who Serves His (or Her) Country

Military personnel questions are rarely discussed in discussions of the direction and content of American foreign and national security policy— particularly as a potential problem. The implicit assumption is that the current system of personnel recruitment and retention that has been in place since the end of 1972, the All-Volunteer Force (AVF), has been a great success and will continue to provide both the quantity and quality of soldiers, sailors, marines, and airmen who are needed for the future. These attitudes are largely artifacts of the Cold War and the military needs of that period. It is not clear that those assumptions and their consequences are well attuned to the contemporary environment.

The simultaneous major engagements of U.S. armed forces in Iraq and Afghanistan placed greater stress on military human resources than is usually acknowledged. One of the major arguments for a lull in U.S. combat activities—especially with ground forces—comes from a professional military that needs to be rested and refurbished. The military leadership does not make this argument publicly, but they do privately to those politicians who could place them in harm's way.

American manpower policy has evolved across time, both formally and practically. Throughout most of the history of the republic, the recruitment and retention of military personnel has been voluntary. The large reason is that for most of its history the United States has been at peace with the world or only been engaged in restrained ways that did not require a large force (e.g., the campaigns against the western Indians). When, however, the United States has become involved in large-scale commitments in major wars, that method of getting Americans has proven inadequate, and the United States has been forced to compel some of its citizens into military duty. The American Civil

War, in which both sides conscripted parts of their force, and World War II and its aftermath are the prime examples.

Military personnel policy was on a roller coaster during the Cold War period. Immediately after World War II, the United States rapidly demobilized, releasing conscripted forces from duty and did not, by and large, replace them with other involuntary soldiers. This policy exploded when the North Koreans invaded South Korea in June 1950, rapidly overrunning most of the Republic of Korea (ROK). American demobilization meant there was not an adequate force to meet this challenge, and drafting and training a new force would have taken too long to stem the tide. The United States saved the day by recalling World War II veterans to active duty. It also learned its lesson about having too few forces available.

After Korea, the draft remained in place to provide a quantitatively adequate force to wage the Cold War. There was a little bit of objection to the continuation of what was euphemistically called the selective service system—in the 1950s, Elvis Presley was inducted amid great publicity, but Cassius Clay (Mohammed Ali) refused induction, for instance. The reason was that there was, by and large, a belief in the need to make the sacrifice of involuntary service in the face of a grievous threat to the country.

The Vietnam War blew up that consensus. The U.S. buildup of forces in that conflict began in 1965, and the selective system rapidly expanded to press larger and larger percentages of the available manpower pool into uniform and off to fight in Southeast Asia. As the war dragged on and both American troop and casualty numbers increased among conscripts, the war became increasingly unpopular—particularly but not exclusively among those being forced to fight it. The unpopularity of the war convinced one sitting president, Lyndon Johnson, not to seek a second term. As Richard Nixon campaigned in 1972 for a second term, Vietnam was the major barrier to his success. To blunt antiwar sentiment, the administration announced that as of the end of 1972, the draft would be suspended. It has remained in abeyance since.

These Cold War experiences help frame the current situation regarding military manpower. The summary experience was that Americans would submit to involuntary military service if they perceived an adequate threat to make that service necessary. When there was skepticism about the nobility and necessity of making the sacrifice of service, the draft became politically unsustainable. It is speculative to suggest, but had the U.S. government succeeded in convincing the American public that the Vietnam War was a necessary part of the Cold War and that their sacrifice was clearly necessary for American security, the backlash would not have occurred. Despite elaborate efforts, the government was unable to make that argument of necessity. The answer was to free almost all Americans from the prospect of military service. It also detached Americans from the rigors of thinking seriously about how, when, and where force should be used.

This debate connects to the Cold War paradigm. A major reason that the use of force was such a prominent assumption under the paradigm was that force was, for the most part, readily available and could be expanded when the necessity arose, both consequences of the selective service method of manning. Korea reinforced the need for force availability and expansibility, and Vietnam suggested its limits when it was attached to an unpopular cause. Since 1972, these questions have largely disappeared, but their potential importance has not. The current force is both readily usable and proficient at what it does, which is fighting conventional war. It is not, however, expansible in the way a conscript-based force is, since it has no means of compulsion. The AVF produces a very good, but not very large, force. That was not a problem before the incursions in Iraq and Afghanistan. As long as the AVF remains the backbone of force size, it is a limitation on the future application of U.S. force. It is not entirely clear that the hard men truly appreciate this distinction.

Avoiding the question and potential consequences of manpower limits inherent in the AVF is, of course, politically expedient, especially in a world where the strategic consequences of raising manpower concerns can be difficult and unpleasant. Simply put, the size force the AVF can put in the field limits what the United States can do with armed forces. This may not be an altogether bad thing, as it can constrain foolish decisions. Would, for instance, the country have become as involved in Vietnam as it did under AVF constraints? The possibility that a larger-than-AVF-capable force would have been needed would have required asking some politically volatile questions about the necessity of that war, and it might have led to a critical debate before, rather than during, that conflict.

MANNING THE FORCE: HISTORIC OPTIONS

There are two ways in which military personnel can be procured into service, voluntarily or involuntarily. Volunteer systems, as the name suggests, involve manpower procurement where people join the military without coercion, generally because they want to become military members. Voluntary methods are quite popular politically, because they do not force officials to make people do things they do not want to do. The potential drawbacks of voluntary systems is whether they can produce the size force needed (a quantitative issue), the quality of force necessary to accomplish needed tasks, and costs associated with recruiting and retaining that force. The AVF is a voluntary force.

Involuntary forces are those where potential military members are chosen from the available pool of military-eligible individuals (a pool that can be manipulated) and are compelled to serve in uniform. The advantage of involuntary forces is that their size can be manipulated by changing the parameters for selection. More to the point, conscription or a draft is almost always necessary if a country needs a very large force to carry out military mandates. They are also less costly per military member than volunteer forces, since conscripts do not have to be paid competitive wages. The disadvantages include the quality of conscript forces (including higher disciplinary and morale problems) and political unpopularity, since conscription-based forces are made up of a large number of individuals who do not want to serve and are thus forced to do something they would not on their own. U.S. Cold War forces before 1972 were based on conscription, both as a means to produce military members and as an incentive to produce voluntary enlistments as a way to avoid the most distasteful military tasks (so-called draft-induced enlistment). No American male who was not at least 18 years old in 1972 (effectively anyone 61 years old or older) has been confronted with the possibility of being drafted. No American woman has ever faced that prospect. That may change.

The United States has employed both forms of procurement policy in its history. The dynamics of conscription are more complex than those surrounding an AVF system, although both forms have advantages and drawbacks.

The U.S. Experience: The Vietnam Effect

Two major political factors influence the way the United States has manned its force. One of these is an American aversion to coercive control by government over its citizens and a belief that Americans should be subject to as little governmental control as possible. This sentiment, of course, creates a generalized preference for some form of AVF and a predilection against involuntary service. The other factor is necessity. If the United States is seen by Americans to be at considerable risk that can only be countered by a very large military effort, the aversion to conscription is at least temporarily overcome.

These contradictory influences have largely defined U.S. manpower policy. For most of American history during the Cold War, the United States did not face existential threats to its existence or its independence (at least after the British gave up any hope of reimposing colonial domain after the War of 1812). As a result, most of the time the armed forces remained small enough that needs could be met by volunteers.

There were two exceptions that also speak to the special view Americans have toward involuntary service. The first conscription policy was instituted during the American Civil War. This policy was very controversial and unpopular in the Union, where the war itself was not particularly strongly supported. As a result, the conscription policy was riddled with exceptions that would allow someone to avoid the draft if he wanted to badly enough and had the resources to do so. The most blatant example was a provision that allowed young men called up by the draft system to avoid service by hiring someone else to take their place. This substitution exemption was most famously used by one of President Lincoln's sons, Todd. The need for a very large force to subdue the rebellion required conscripting a large-enough force to carry out the task, and the relative unpopularity of the war required compromising the universality of vulnerability to the draft.

The other large call to conscription came in during World War II. Once engaged, Americans accepted the necessity of the war and volunteered in large numbers to serve. The prosecution of the campaigns against Germany and Japan required a force that eventually numbered twelve million, surpassing the size force that would volunteer. A military draft was thus a cornerstone of the war effort. There was very little resistance to imposition of the system, because most Americans—including those who would be inducted—accepted the necessity of their service and potential sacrifice.

After World War II ended, the United States rapidly disengaged and returned to the "normalcy" of peacetime. In military terms, the huge American military machine shrunk to less than a million in 1946, as both conscripts and volunteers were released from duty. In the half-decade after the war ended, relations gradually spiraled downward toward the hostility between the Americans and Soviets that marked the Cold War. The invasion of ROK by the Democratic Republic of Korea (DPRK) was a wake-up call both politically and militarily. World War II veterans called out of retirement managed to halt and begin to reverse DPRK gains. By the time the war ended in July 1953, the Cold War was fully engaged, and the perception of threat was sufficient that a continuation of conscription raised little opposition. For over a decade the country's first peacetime draft continued without major controversy. Americans accepted the existence of a threat justifying their sacrifice, which was not great, since not many Americans were conscripted and those that were did not face combat.

Vietnam was the watershed. When the commitment to send large ground forces to that country began in early 1965, the public by and large accepted a major engagement of the conscription system to fill manpower needs. The reason was that Vietnam was advertised as a Cold War communist expansion—an extension of the conflict in Europe to an Asian theater. About the only segment of the population that voiced major reservations were males (especially college students) aged between 18 and 25, who were to be conscripted.

The Vietnam effort quickly became a conscript war, and as it did, it became increasingly unpopular. At its apex, over a half million American combat forces were in Vietnam (in 1970), and over 58,000 Americans perished in the war. At the same time, progress in the war toward a victorious conclusion remained elusive, and the perception that the war was really a surrogate for the "central battle" in Europe faded. Antiwar sentiment increased. The 1972 presidential campaign was largely waged over which candidate would end the war first.

Since the heart of antiwar sentiment was found in college campuses, among those who would be conscripted and shipped off to Vietnam, the draft was a political victim of the political discord the war produced. Dissent focused on two points. One was over the war and whether the sacrifice being demanded of conscripts was warranted. The other was over the conscription system: about how it worked and whether it produced acceptable outcomes. The conscription option for the future would have to deal with criticisms of the old selective service system. As a result, examining the dynamics and foibles of the pre-1972 system is a useful exercise in assessing the possibility of a return to conscription in the future. The key question is the equity or fairness of any draft-based system.

The first determination that any manpower system must confront is the extent of participation from eligible classes of citizens: should it apply universally to all members of the group from which it could draw, or should it induct only some of them? The old conscription systems have focused on young men from 18 to 26, and have excluded women. Even during its period of operation, the pool of eligible candidates numbered in the millions, far in excess of the needs for manpower in any year other than in one where the country was engaged in a major war. Thus, a draft would only require *some* members of the eligible pool to serve while effectively exempting others. The pool could be manipulated to some extent: including women in it (which would certainly be part of any attempt to revive the system) would broaden the pool and thus increase the excess. Extending service to options other than the military (such as national service) would increase the need for more people. The advantage of a universal system is that it is ultimately fair: everyone has to make some sacrifice. The disadvantage is that there are not enough meaningful jobs to put the entire cohort group to work. It is a question of equity versus efficiency.

The pre-1972 system came down on the side of efficiency. It was called the *Selective Service* system, meaning it chose the number of people from the eligible pool that were needed for military service, and did not encumber the rest. As such, it had a built-in inequity: some people were required to serve and sacrifice, while others did not. Within the decision for a selectively chosen system, however, there were other sources of inequity that fueled criticism and would have to be resolved if a successor conscript system were to be proposed.

The selective service system had two broad sources of potential inequity. The first was who from the eligible pool *actually* became vulnerable to induction. Under the old system, it was possible to receive exemptions from induction, and these benefits were, as a practical matter, more available to some potential inductees than to others. A further source of potential inequity was in who would serve and who would not. Those selected would have to make whatever sacrifices service entailed, while those not selected would not. Even if the reason for selection was randomized, the effect was not.

It is sometimes said that war is poor people's business. What this means is that the actual conduct of hostilities is by those within society who either cannot afford or do not know how to avoid service. Essentially all selective service systems have loopholes that allow those who can use them to avoid service. The selective service system during the Cold War was no exception to this rule, and the inequities inherent in the exemption system contributed to the disrepute in which the draft was held.

Exemptions took several forms. All were aimed at Americans who were either wealthy enough or well positioned enough to employ them to keep themselves or their relatives from having to endure service in Vietnam. The most usual form of exemption was education (officially 2-S). In particular, students enrolled in some form of post-secondary education were exempted for the period of their course of study. This exemption caused many young men to flock to colleges and universities, and once enrolled, to stretch out their programs as long as possible to remain "safe" from the draft. This form of exemption was obviously only available to those who could afford higher education costs (student loan programs were not widely available at the time), and over time, restrictions were placed on the kinds and durations of programs that would merit exemption. Once the exemption ended, those who had enjoyed it became prime targets of military recruiters.

There were, of course, other forms of exemption. Medical deferments were available to those who had physical ailments or disabilities that would preclude their carrying out military duties, and conscientious objection was available to those who could demonstrate that their antiwar beliefs were genuine and long-standing. Early on during the war, married men were exempt (prompting a spate of marriages that probably would not otherwise have occurred), and having children could also be the basis for exemption. For those who objected to the war but could find no alternative basis for avoiding military service, flight into exile in Canada was an option.

The largest single form of exemption was by sex. The selective service system only applied to males, and all females were exempted by virtue of their gender. This form of discrimination had largely historical and cultural bases in the belief that women should not be put in the purposeful harm's way through military service and the military's reluctance to put military members of both sexes side-by-side in combat. A few countries (notably Israel) conscript females into service; the United States did not. Should the draft ever be reconsidered, this question would certainly be revisited.

The exemption phenomenon highlights the question of equity of military service vulnerability, an issue that has two unavoidable aspects. The first is what might be called "front-end" equity, which involves determinations about who from a subject population will be vulnerable to military service. This issue is most closely tied to the exemption phenomenon. The second is "back-end" equity, which arises from the fact that in any situation where the entire eligible population is not needed for military service, some will be selected and have to endure the sacrifices of service while others will not.

Both of these sources of inequity will have to be addressed before the United States even considers the possibility of a return to conscription as one or the sole basis for military service. One can debate the virtues of any particular exemption: is it, for instance, more socially beneficial to have 19-year-olds being educated or performing military duty for their country? In essence, however, the basis for having exemption is the assertion of social privilege. In virtually all historical societies, the children of the wealthy and the elite have not been forced to do the country's fighting because of their social station. With the partial exception of World War II, the same has been true in the United States.

This frames front-end equity differently. The case for inequity resides in privilege from which the privileged class benefits. This class generally includes the wealthiest and most politically influential members of society (the two groups are not mutually exclusive). Hardly anyone wants their sons compelled into military service in which they might be killed, but if a conscription system seems necessary, the privileged class will demand ways for their offspring to avoid service. No one will, of course, phrase their support for loopholes in such open ways, but it will be present and it will be compelling for many politicians who would have to reinstate the selective service system. Perfect front-end equity is attainable by completing removing exemptions and making all members of the population equally vulnerable. Politically, this ideal is virtually impossible to attain without significant political costs for those involved in the decision to do so. As a practical matter, this means some inequity will almost certainly remain because of pressures from constituents with vested interests in one form of exemption or another.

Back-end equity is more problematic. Any selective service system means that some will serve and sacrifice while others do not—regardless of the equity of how those chosen were identified. There are only two entirely equitable solutions to who will and will not be chosen from the eligible pool. One is if everyone serves in one capacity or another, and calls for universal public service use this as part of their rationale. The problem is that some forms of service are clearly more desirable than others. Being compelled to work on public projects like road repair in the United States, for instance, clearly entails significantly fewer risks than being forced to engage in overseas combat. Perfect back-end equity requires that all participants engage in equally desirable (or undesirable) duties.

The second way to ensure equality of sacrifice is not to compel *anyone* to serve, and this is one of the allures of the AVF concept. It avoids the political minefields of forcing people to do things they do not want to do and questions of favoritism and privilege. The only people who serve are those who volunteer to do so. Critics sometimes allege that there is an indirect form of discrimination within the volunteer pool. Voluntary military service is a job decision, and it is most appealing to those people for whom the practical available options to volunteering are the least appealing. The AVF, in other words, competes for personnel with generally lower paying, less appealing work at or near minimum wage. The more educated and wealthy one is, the less likely alternatives to military service are to be the available choices. Economic and social standing do affect the attractiveness of the AVF.

The AVF versus Conscription: The Current Balance

In terms of producing different sizes and qualities of military force, voluntary and involuntary methods both have advantages and drawbacks. In times of extreme crisis where the United States requires virtually total mobilization to maintain the country's security, an involuntary system is dictated to produce the numbers needed. If the cause is viewed as sufficiently compelling by most Americans, conscription is relatively noncontroversial. World War II is the example. When those purposes are seen as less compelling, there is resistance and major public unhappiness and resistance. Resistance within the Union in the Civil War and in Vietnam caused the conscription system's fundamental commitment to equity to be compromised. Conscription is not a politically popular concept unless the need for it is compelling.

The environment of the Cold War was threatening enough to maintain a system that included drafting some young Americans without major dissent. Between Korea and Vietnam, acceptance of the draft was facilitated in that most vulnerable young Americans either were not compelled to serve or managed to serve in more agreeable circumstances like the Guard and Reserves. More importantly, those forced to serve were not thrust into combat in a war the necessity of which was not clear to them. Using the draft to fill manpower needs for the Southeast Asian war polluted the well and the political backlash caused the draft to be suspended. It has been abeyance ever since, but could be reinstated by a simple Act of Congress if the need arose.

The contemporary environment does not clearly contain situations where a massive American military commitment would require a return to the draft. There are plenty of situations where some military force might be considered, but to this point, those occasions have not exceeded the capacities of the AVF to fulfill. Moreover, those threats that do exist do not rise to the existential level of a nuclear war with the Soviets. The environment is dangerous (there are lots of small conflicts) but not particularly deadly (the existential threat to the United States is minimal or nonexistent). As already suggested, the upper limit of what can be done with a voluntary force was approached in the last decade, but it has not been exceeded to the extent that reinstituting conscription has had to be considered seriously. National politicians heave a sigh of relief over this circumstance.

Because of this reality, there is very little national political discussion of the merits of voluntary versus nonvoluntary forces, and such a debate will not occur unless the United States becomes engaged in a military situation for which the AVF is inadequate. In the contemporary debate, such an engagement would almost certainly be the result of an American choice to become so involved, rather than the engagement being dictated unambiguously by necessity. The manpower debate, such as it is, is thus about the lures and drawbacks of voluntarism, not about the AVF versus conscription.

The debate is easy to phrase in general terms. The chief advantages of the AVF concept, its allure, are basically political, and adherence to the concept exists in various political venues. The chief bases of skepticism, on the other hand, are military and centered on the adequacy and affordability of the volunteer force.

The main pillar of political support for the AVF comes from elective politicians for the reasons already suggested. As long as the AVF is in force, no politician is forced to choose among the distasteful alternatives of forcing young Americans to serve and possibly to be placed in harm's way or of possibly leaving the country physically vulnerable because of inadequate forces. As long as the AVF creates adequate forces to manage the environment, such a decision is unnecessary.

The other most prominent supporter of the AVF is the military itself. The major lures of the AVF to the professional military are its high levels of skill and proficiency, the lack of disciplinary problems it creates, and the continuity of membership it provides. The AVF becomes a truly professional force because its members have chosen military service as a job and even profession, and thus are self-motivated to do their assigned tasks as well as they can. Most of the disciplinary problems in the military historically have been committed by draftees who did not want to be there and who showed their unhappiness by breaking rules. Moreover, conscripts are a good deal less likely to reenlist than volunteers, creating more continuity (and a smaller new recruit need) in an AVF. As well, in the four decades since the draft was suspended, virtually all the personnel who could deal with conscripts have retired, and the current military lacks a well-developed capability to deal with reluctant members. The AVF is a happier and more proficient organization than a force with conscripts, and the military wants to keep it that way.

Despite this appeal, the AVF is not without drawbacks, two of which stand out. The first is quantitative: it is a simple matter of fact that military service is only attractive to a relatively small portion of the population, meaning there is a finite pool of young men and women who will volunteer for duty. An AVF of a little over two million active duty and reserves (the present size) is about as large as calls for volunteers can produce. This means that there are inherent limits on the purposes for which that force can be used because of size limitations. Iraq and Afghanistan stressed the current force, and quantitative limits forced the military to require multiple deployments for their members and produced stress on the overall force and particular members. In extreme cases, actions such as "stop loss" provisions forced military members whose enlistment was terminating to remain on duty. Were the United States to become involved in a massive war, the volunteer base would certainly have to be augmented with conscripts. It is not known (or at least not widely advertised) at what point the limits in capability are reached with the AVF, but it is certain that those limits exist and that they have an impact on national security strategy.

The military has tried to make service more attractive by adding economic and other benefits to service. The AVF, after all, competes for young men and women with the civilian workforce and higher education, and it has the drawback not shared by the others of possible combat. Thus, the military must have a compensation and fringe benefit package available that will be attractive to young people weighing their options. Doing so is expensive, and thus the second limitation of the all-volunteer concept is its expense. Publicly available estimates show that the salary and fringe benefits of service members are over $100,000 a person. Conscripts, by contrast, can be (and historically have been) paid a pittance, because there is little incentive to do otherwise.

DISCONNECTING THE PUBLIC FROM WAR: AN AVF CONSEQUENCE

The AVF concept is overwhelmingly popular, and there are currently no serious movements to abandon all voluntary accession to the armed forces.

To the extent that it thinks about military manpower procurement questions at all, the public loves the idea of voluntary forces, because it means their sons (and potentially daughters) cannot be snatched from them and forced into uniform. Politicians love the AVF concept because it frees them of the very unpopular potential task of creating regulations allowing involuntary service to be enforced. The military likes uniformed members who want to be there.

The question of manpower has not been a part of the national dialogue since 1972—over four decades ago. No one born since 1954 has been subject to being involuntarily conscripted, and that means that not only do current 18-year-olds have no experiential basis to judge alternatives to the AVF, but their fathers and even grandfathers also lack the personal experience of personal vulnerability. The military manpower debate has remained dormant for so long that it could pass for dead.

There is, however, a small minority who questions the consequences of a military force drawn entirely from a voluntary base. Part of their objection arises from the social consequences of such a force. Because of the availability of exemptions, the old conscript force was not entirely socially representative, because wealthy and well-connected Americans were able to avoid being called up altogether or were able to obtain privileged positions, such as reserve duty or officer status. Still, not everyone could escape induction, and so there was some representativeness among social and economic classes across the board. Elvis did serve, if only as a company clerk in Germany.

The AVF does not have an impact on Americans across the spectrum. Freed from the possibility of coerced service, most middle-class and upper-class Americans—and their families—simply never consider military service as a possibility. The now-famous "one percent" of Americans who are affected directly by military affairs as military members or family are the only people with a direct stake in the military and, arguably more importantly, how the military is used. To some observers, that is a problem.

The basic concern that is raised is the lack of connection between the American people and how their military is used. This concern arises in the sense that the public is not intimately involved in decisions about the use of force because they know that those decisions will not have a direct impact on them. Should the U.S. government decide to send ground forces into Iraq or Syria to pursue IS? That decision would not be accompanied by an order to conscript average Americans to fight that conflict. The AVF would do it, and since its members volunteered and presumably understood the obligations they might incur, that decision chain is acceptable to the public.

The effect is to disconnect the American public from its military and the uses for which that military is used. One of the fundamental reasons for the American Revolution was the inability of the colonists (especially in Massachusetts) to control how British military force was used to control them, and a lingering fear of those framing the U.S. Constitution was the fear of an independent military not controlled by the citizenry. The current situation clearly does not represent anything like the usurpation of authority early Americans feared, but the effect of a military in which most of the citizenry does not have a direct and intimate stake may be to free authorities of the constraint that a more personally involved populace might provide.

This sentiment first emerged as part of the controversy over the American invasion and occupation of Iraq starting in 2003. Critics of the decision argued that the thin guise for mounting the campaign would not have withstood full public scrutiny, and that public opposition might well have prevented implementing the invasion altogether had that implementation necessitated drafting the sons and daughters of Americans and sending them off to war. The American public will, as noted, support such actions when they seem necessary, but could those beating the war drums have convinced average Americans that the reasons for war were compelling enough to put *their* sons and daughters in harm's way? Under the AVF concept, war is not everyone's business in any direct way; under conscription, it is.

This line of argumentation is used in support of at least some return to the selective service system as a brake on what its proponents view as the promiscuous use of force when the public has no intimate stake in military employment. After the end of the Iraq and Afghanistan adventures, the American public were said to be "war weary," but what did that mean? Neither of the wars had created any privation nor sacrifice for most Americans, after all, so what did they have to be "weary" about? The answer, it turned out, was not much, as large parts of the American public came quickly to support American military involvement, up to and including the use of ground forces, against IS, despite the fact that it was not at all clear what such forces could accomplish (discussed more fully in Chapter 5).

The bottom line is that one aspect of the AVF experience has been to detach the American public from the use of military force. This detachment is not, of course, complete: there are clearly outlandish uses of force to which the public would react negatively, thereby constraining decision makers. At the same time, should threats become large and egregious enough, the public would almost certainly embrace a return to conscription to contain and destroy the threat.

The problem is that reality falls between the extremes. Large and compelling threats, like those involved in World War II, result in *wars of necessity,* situations in which it is clear to all (or nearly all) that the country must pick up its arms. In the contemporary world, there are none of these threats in any unambiguous sense: the case that a given situation creates (destroying IS, for instance) will always be debatable. In the contemporary environment, most conflicts will involve *wars of choice,* where the country chooses to fight a conflict which it may not *have* to fight to preserve national security. Whether situations represent threats that must be countered (wars of necessity) or threats that it would be good but not entirely necessary to counter (wars of choice) will always be debated.

The AVF arguably prejudices this debate. The prospect that one's own loved ones might be compelled to fight militates toward engagement in wars of necessity but not choice, because of the personal physical dangers involved. Wars of choice are much more difficult to sell, but the AVF facilitates this case because the public is not so concerned about the commitment of volunteers as it is of conscripts to which they might have to contribute. Advocates of a very active U.S. military policy understand this, and their advocacy of the liberal employment of American forces coincides with their support for the AVF. Because voluntary forces are likely to be smaller than conscript forces, this creates a contradiction that is the subject of the next section.

DEBATING THE FUTURE: VOLUNTEER
OR CONSCRIPT FORCES

There is a basic conundrum confronting advocates of different ways of inducting Americans into the military. Voluntary accession is by far the choice of most Americans, because it frees them of any personal obligation to participate. For the vast majority, and especially those in the age-cohort groups from which military members are recruited, war is somebody else's business, not theirs. The conundrum arises because the kind of force that can be assembled by voluntary means is too small to accomplish all the tasks that some of these same Americans believe the United States should undertake or at least contemplate.

The 2015 debate about what to do about IS illustrates this conundrum. According to figures cited by James Fallows, the "U.S. military has about 1.4 million people on active duty and another 850,000 in the reserves." Not all of these are, of course, fighting forces; indeed, the number of actual "shooters" is a small percentage of this figure. It may be recalled, for instance, that the Bush administration blanched when then chief of staff of the army, General Eric Shinseki, suggested 300,000 troops would be needed to occupy Iraq; the reason was that such a large number would engage most American combat troops and leave few for duty that might arise elsewhere.

The situation is analogous regarding IS. The IS currently occupies a territory the size of Texas, and if the United States—assisted by coalition members—were to invade and occupy the caliphate, Shinseki-sized Iraq occupation numbers would certainly be needed. The idea that ground forces could invade, destroy IS in detail, and then retreat (the essential Bush strategy for Iraq in 2003) is romantic nonsense; only a long, probably bloody, occupation would destroy IS militarily, and it would likely create all sorts of other problems in terms of alienating the residents. The current AVF is marginally capable of such an action and does not want to undertake it. Its reluctance arises from the likelihood such an action would fail in the long run. There has been a great deal of breast beating about putting "boots on the ground" in Iraq (and possibly Syria); it is not clear the country has enough of those boots or that those who wear them want to go.

Many of the same Americans who favor robust military action against IS oppose any alternative to the AVF with equal fervor, and they ignore with considerable intensity that the current AVF force is of questionable quantitative bulk for the mission and the simultaneous maintenance of an adequate size force for other contingencies. And yet that is exactly the case. One can have voluntary forces, or one can have large forces, but, in the absence of a national crisis that would dissolve reluctance to conscription, one cannot have both.

This leaves a stark question that connects manpower policy firmly to overall national security policy. The AVF concept is designed for forces operating in a nondemanding environment where large forces are not required. This is, after all, the long historical context of American reliance on volunteers to populate the force. It is also true that whenever the United States has been required to mount a significant military operation, it has been forced to abandon sole reliance on voluntary accession. The draft is as much a part of the American legacy as is voluntarism, depending on circumstances.

This frames the mechanical relationship between manpower policy and national security policy. An all-voluntary force is perfectly adequate for an environment where moderate-sized military commitments are the norm and where large-scale engagements are unlikely. At the level of policy, this means that in a situation where one relies on the AVF, it is inconsistent to advocate policies that might result in large commitments that could not be met by the AVF force levels one has. It is unfair to the members of the AVF who would have to try to meet potential requirements with forces inadequate for their size—a repeat of the last decade of overdeployment or worse. It is dishonest, even hypocritical, to advocate the potential large-scale use of force without admitting that one might have to conscript young Americans to carry out the resulting missions.

This relationship leads to a second consideration regarding the continuing validity of American reliance on the AVF concept: is it socially or politically responsible? One of the most frequent objections (admittedly coming from a minority of Americans) is that the AVF concept disconnects the citizenry from the military, and especially from its use. More specifically, a return to the draft in some form and to some degree would reengage Americans in discussions about when and whether the United States should commit to force, because the decisions to do so would have potential personal consequences that are totally missing now. It would, in Epstein's words, "make the American electorate generally more thoughtful about foreign policy."

Fallows voices the disconnection between the American people and the AVF more colorfully. The effect, he argues, is to create what he calls the "chickenhawk nation, based on the term for those eager to go to war, as long as someone else is going." In the current environment, there is an interesting, arguably perverse, relationship between the public and the military. In Fallows' words, there is a "reverent but disengaged attitude toward the military—we love the troops but we'd rather not think about them." It is perverse because the public is quite outspoken about its appall over the circumstances of returning veterans, especially the wounded and disfigured and the mentally afflicted, but show little concern about them when decisions are being made about inserting them into situations that may create those problems for them.

This perverse dynamic is lessened greatly if there is a draft. There is a rough analogy between the AVF and the old French Foreign Legion. The analogy is imperfect because officially the Foreign Legion did not include any Frenchmen, which was a convenient fiction, since French convicts were sometimes given the choice of prison or joining the Legion. The advantage of the Legion was that it allowed the French to pursue military actions without officially endangering Frenchmen, and the AVF does somewhat the same thing for American policy makers. At the same time, the regular French armed forces included both volunteers *and* conscripts that allowed the country to pursue purposes larger than those the Legion could perform, if the French public could be convinced of the wisdom of the mission.

The American tradition, as argued, is not dissimilar, except that when large forces have not been needed, the United States has not kept citizens involuntarily at arms in very large numbers. Small forces, of course, bind the U.S. government to smaller purposes than it might otherwise contemplate—arguably not necessarily a bad thing, depending on one's orientation. Since 1972, the conscription has lain fallow: the authorizations are still there and could be reactivated, allowing a return of the draft. Doing so would be inefficient and likely untimely. Gearing up selective service and inducting and preparing forces would likely take longer than the war itself. The World War I draft, for instance, inducted a very large number of "doughboys" who never made it to the European theater.

If one is to contemplate a return to conscription, what form might it take? It would almost certainly have to be different than the pre-1972 system, especially in terms of the equities involved in selection. A new draft would probably eschew or very strictly limit the practice of exemption, which would mean it would be opposed by those groups that have traditionally sought a way out for their loved ones. The elimination of exemptions would thus likely be opposed by the wealthy and well placed (who also tend to be prominent among the chicken hawks). At the same time, the failure to remove exemptions would equally be opposed by those not in a position to benefit from exemptions. The result would be politically difficult for politicians, which helps explain why so few are even willing to discuss the subject. A new draft system would also almost certainly include removing liability based on sex, which raises its own set of nettlesome problems.

A conscript system would not necessarily have to draft many people. When the country is at relative peace, there would be no need for the increased size force conscription can produce. At the same time, reinstitution could revive another dynamic from the pre-1972 environment: draft-induced voluntary enlistments. In the days when people were vulnerable to induction, they were likely to be drafted into the "combat arms" of the U.S. Army—the infantry who would fight on the ground. This was generally considered the worst form of duty and one to be avoided. When faced with the imminence of conscription into the combat arms, many young men would fervently seek out less dangerous forms of service in terms of specialties and branches of the military—draft-induced enlistments.

Reinstituting the draft would have two major advantages. The most obvious is expansibility: the draft has a very large pool of potential inductees from which it can draw, and even it takes some time to train and prepare conscripts for duty, the draft has the manpower advantage of allowing the country to size the force to its needs, rather than the vice versa. Second, if the draft does not permit discriminatory exemptions, it will be more socially representative than an AVF that only draws from a fairly narrow spectrum of society. A conscript force is, in a way an all-volunteer force is not, a people's force. The disconnection between the American people and their armed forces is addressed in the process.

The selective service system is not going to return anytime soon, making the discussion of its reinstitution and advantages at least partially academic. As long as the AVF does not fail in any way that can only be attributed to its own deficiencies, advocating a return to conscription is an exercise in tilting at windmills. That said, the chicken hawks who believe that the answer to a large number of worldwide crises is the employment of U.S. forces could create the conditions that would undercut a principle they espouse. The Iraq-Afghanistan tandem should have been a wake-up call about the all-volunteer concept. It is very effective when the country is essentially at peace—not fighting anywhere or only in relatively small ways. It cannot handle either a large-scale war (admittedly not a great likelihood) or multiple simultaneous or overlapping engagements (a much higher probability).

The dilemma is not that the AVF produces a bad product. One can accept the assertion by the U.S. military and its enthusiasts that American forces are, person for person, the best in the world and that the U.S. military is also the most powerful military force. The arguments for the inadequacy of the AVF are not qualitative: it produces a more professional, proficient force than a conscript force likely could muster. The problems are quantitative. It is a simple truth that the AVF cannot be expanded much, because there are only so many young Americans who will volunteer for duty.

The only way to expand the force is to relax admissions standards to include groups currently ineligible, but there would be consequences that are probably unacceptable. The largest pool of underrepresented Americans is female, but the military itself is reluctant to induct much larger numbers of women because it imposes limits on what roles they can perform. Notably, putting women in combat roles meets resistance on chauvinistic or performance grounds, and it is additional combat ground forces that likely would be needed where expansion is required. The other possibility would be to admit groups who are currently verboten, such as convicted criminals. The argument here is that such accessions would lower quality, because of disciplinary or intelligence concerns. Since quality is the hallmark of the AVF, this is unattractive.

The chicken hawks are thus left with a dilemma they have been reluctant to admit or confront. They can have the AVF and all its advantages like political comfortableness, but do so knowing they have a force that may not be adequate to the aggressive military policy they so often advocate.

All this boils down to a basic strategic determination. Should U.S. strategy be driven by the size and capabilities of its force? Or should the size of the force be driven by the missions to which it may be assigned? An AVF-driven strategy suggests a more modest use of American forces that is anathema to the chicken hawks. A mission-driven strategy may call for larger forces that exceed the size the all-volunteer concept will produce, and that means at least some return to conscription, an action the chicken hawks also oppose. They cannot indeed have it both ways, even if they want to—which they do.

There is an irony here that should be of some comfort to those who believe the United States should adopt a more restrained approach to the use of force in areas outside core American vital interests. As noted, the AVF has inherent limits because its maximum size is relatively inelastic: it cannot be expanded much. The reinstitution (or threat to activate) even some modest, bounded form of conscription also is restraining, because it would require advocates of force usage to prepare to a much more elaborate, detailed argument up front for that usage than they currently do. Would the Bush administration have been able to convince the American people to invade Iraq if the consequence would have been to pluck young Americans from their homes to fight that war? Since the case turned out to be factually questionable, would discovering this shortcoming have undercut the advocacy of war before the fighting and killing began?

Discussions about national security policy and strategy rarely ever include the issue of manpower. Implicit in this omission is the assumption that manpower quantity and quality are more than adequate for any needs that might be proposed for using armed force in pursuit of national interests. That assumption is not entirely correct, as has been argued. The current manpower procurement system has resulted in a magnificent military force, but it is one whose utility is limited by its size. The AVF cannot be used for large purposes such as invading and occupying sizable amounts of territory—especially territory that is or becomes hostile—without taxing its resources. As I have argued in *The Case against Military Intervention*, military occupations inevitably produce opposition and resistance, because people do not like rule by outsiders, no matter how well wishing those occupiers portray themselves to be. The folly of believing otherwise was demonstrated in Iraq. An invasion to defeat and displace IS would be even worse. It is pure sophistry to argue that American force can destroy IS without a lengthy occupation for which that force is ill prepared and inadequately sized.

Larger purposes require larger forces, and the only way to produce the size necessary is to involuntarily procure young Americans for the battle. Even the most ardent of the chicken hawks would not propose a draft to produce a conscript force to fight in Iraq and Syria. The political backlash from Americans would be more than they could bear—or politically survive. Framing the debate over what the United States without accounting for the manpower consequences of different actions is nothing short of irresponsible.

BIBLIOGRAPHY

Anderson, Martin (ed.). *The Military Draft: Selected Readings on Conscription.* Palo Alto, CA: Hoover Institution Publications, 1982.

Bacevich, Andrew J. *The New American Militarism: How Americans Are Seduced by War.* New York: Oxford University Press, 2013.

Bailey, Beth. *America's Army: the Making of the All-Volunteer Force.* New York: Belknap Publishing, 2009.

Epstein, Joseph. "How I learned to Love the Draft." *The Atlantic* 315, 1 (January/February 2015), 86–87.

Fallows, James. "The Tragedy of the American Military." *The Atlantic* 315, 1 (January/February 2015), 72–90.

Flynn, George Q. *Conscription sand Democracy: The Draft in France, Great Britain, and the United States* (Contributions in Military Studies). Westport, CT: Praeger, 2001.

Gilroy, Curtis L. and Barbara A. Bickster. *The All-Volunteer Force: Thirty Years of Service.* Washington, DC: Potomac Books, 2004.

Gold, Philip. *The Coming Draft: The Crisis of Our Military and Why Selective Service Is Wrong for America.* Novato, CA: Presidio Press, 2006.

Griffith, Robert K. Jr. and Center for Military History. *The U.S. Army's Transition to the All-Volunteer Force, 1968–1974.* London, UK: MilitaryBookshop, 2011.

Hernandez, Drysdale H. and U.S. Army War College. *The Dangerous Gap between American Society and Its Military.* Washington, DC: Penny Hill Press (Congressional Research Service), 2012.

Kenndy, David M. (ed.). *The Modern American Military.* New York: Oxford University Press, 2013.

Millett, Alan R. and Williamson Murray. *Military Effectiveness* (vol. 3), Cambridge, UK: Cambridge University Press, 2010.

Ruschmann, Paul. *Mandatory Military Service: Point/Counterpoint.* New York: Chelsea House Publishing, 2003.

Scowcroft, Brent. *Military Service in the United States.* (American Assembly Series). Englewood Cliffs, NJ: Prentice-Hall, 1982.

Segal, David R. *Recruiting for Uncle Sam: Citizenship and Military Manpower Policy.* (Modern War Series). Lawrence, KS: University Press of Kansas, 1989.

Snow, Donald M. *The Case against Military Intervention.* New York: Routledge, 2016.

Tracy, James. *The Military Draft Handbook: A Brief History and Practical Advice to the Curious and Concerned.* San Francisco, CA: Manic D. Press, 2005.

Wagner, Viqi. *Military Draft: Opposing Viewpoints.* Independence, KY: Greenhaven Press, 2007.

Part II

ENERGY AND U.S. FOREIGN
AND NATIONAL SECURITY POLICY

Chapter 3

Energy and Policy Determination

Oil Addiction and Its Consequences

Access to adequate and secure sources of energy is one of the most basic foreign and national security mandates for all states in the contemporary world. Energy provides people with both the necessities of life (e.g., heat and cooling) and conveniences and amenities such as electricity-provided services and luxuries. At the level of the state, energy is necessary to fuel economic activity and to provide the vital stuff that makes possible modern military activity. People and states are absolutely dependent on energy for their existences. Modern life is very difficult to imagine without reliable supplies of energy. Anyone who has lost their home power for an extended period of time due to inclement weather intuitively understands this importance.

Energy access and demands have steadily grown over time. For most of human history, the dominant form of energy came from the burning of wood, either to provide warmth and cook food or to allow relatively primitive activity such as blacksmithing. It was not until wood's adequacy as an energy source began to come under question in parts of the world, notably those areas undergoing the Industrial Revolution and its greater demands for energy did the dominance of wood become questionable. Prior to that phenomenon, energy was not a large public policy concern. Ever since, it has been.

The "wood era" illustrates the dynamics of energy policy. Why was wood the primary energy source for so long (essentially from the emergence of human societies until the nineteenth century and beyond in some parts of the world)? That dominance and acceptability rested on two basic premises. One was the level of *demand* for energy. For most of human history, demand was very modest, both because the world's human population was quite small and because of limits on what energy could be used for. In addition, *supply* was generally adequate, since there were trees virtually everywhere—except in extremely arid places. Moreover, wood was an abundant, renewable resource:

demands for wood generally did not exceed the ability for natural processes to grow enough new trees to replenish those cut down and burned (what is sometimes referred to as *carrying capacity*). As long as one had timber, there was little need either to look for alternate sources of energy or to explore supplies in other areas.

The Industrial Revolution upset this historic balance. Beginning as it did after the great plagues of Europe, population growth was endemic in Europe and producing increased needs for energy for traditional purposes like heating and cooking. At the same time, industrial processes increased the demands for larger and more intense forms of energy than wood could easily provide. At one level, forests could not produce enough wood to replenish given the amount of demand, and the energy produced by wood burning did not meet all the demands of modern industry. Wood fires, for instance, were not hot enough for forging steel, one of the signature products of industrialization. The overuse of wood was particularly great in the United Kingdom, which virtually denuded its supply of wood trying to provide energy for industrialization. One of the reasons for colonizing North America was as a potential source of wood. The Industrial Revolution undercut the age of wood.

When wood was the major source of energy for virtually all of the world, something like energy policy, and especially energy as a foreign policy concern was unknown. The Industrial Revolution changed that dynamic, however. The need for alternate supplies of energy meant looking for alternative sources that could outdo the performance and availability of wood. Thus, commodities like coal and petroleum that were either unknown or unexploited became policy concerns—both as questions of discovery and exploitation. Some countries were better endowed in the new resources than others. The continental United States had enough of all the new energy sources to be essentially self-sufficient until after World War II. Japan had virtually no energy resources on or under its national territory, and one of the reasons it initiated the conquests in eastern Asia that created the eastern theater of World War II was to gain and secure access to those resources.

Although the age of wood has largely disappeared, it has not disappeared altogether. Wood burning remains the principal source of energy for over a quarter of mankind, 90 percent of whom are concentrated in South Asia and sub-Saharan Africa, which subsequent energy revolutions have bypassed. As Bazilian chronicles the situation, "Some two billion people lack electricity outright or have poor-quality service, and nearly three billion rely on dirty fuels, such as firewood and animal dung, for cooking and heating." Changing this situation is a major priority for those who champion the developmental agenda, but their voices have not been prominent in policy circles, a phenomenon introduced in Chapter 1.

Energy became a foreign policy concern because of the global inequality in the national distribution of energy reserves. As the world moved toward industrialization and modern militaries became more dependent on energy sources, energy *security* became a national mandate. That security, in turn, was composed of two aspects: access to energy supplies, and a reasonable and sustainable price for those supplies. Energy security first emerged as a major national security concern in the two global conflicts of the twentieth century, and especially World War II. As energy demands have increased worldwide, control over energy has become a major geopolitical tool of the states that possess energy reserves, and a major geopolitical imperative for those who rely on foreign sources of energy.

Energy policy has become effectively *intermestic* (to use a term Patrick Haney and I among others employ in *Foreign Policy for a New Era*). This means energy policy has both *inter*national and do*mestic* aspects. For the United States in the contemporary era, the international aspect has centered on secure access to the petroleum reserves of the Middle East and has been a leading driver of American policy in the region and toward the world. Domestically, it has led to a policy debate over various forms of energy and correlated concerns such as the ecological impact of various energy technologies.

The energy policy nexus is also changing rapidly, which is one reason for an emphasis on energy policy in this volume. As suggested in the last paragraph, a good deal of American foreign and national security policy over the past 35–40 years has been directed at Middle Eastern oil and has caused the United States to engage in policy actions—up to and including the dispatch of American armed forces—to affect regional disagreements. These initiatives are often not framed in energy terms—which seem crass (e.g., "American blood for Middle Eastern oil")—but securing access to that petroleum is the only clearly compelling geopolitical explanation for the concern with the Middle East. That calculation, however, may be changing, as new sources of energy have been discovered in the United States and are widely potentially available worldwide. These raise the prospects that the era of Middle East oil supremacy and its broader impact on world politics may soon be on the wane.

Framing energy in this manner is not entirely conventional and requires some explanation and justification. The explanation must begin with a brief review of the historic evolution of energy concerns and policy leading to the rise of petroleum to its current position in energy terms, with an emphasis on the emergence of the Persian Gulf littoral as the global energy cornucopia and the United States as a petroleum "junkie." It also includes a discussion of the global ecological challenge to the supremacy of fossil-fuel burning as the world's energy underpinning. The result of this process has been an oil addiction with significant geopolitical implications.

THE EVOLUTION OF ENERGY USES
AND POLICY: FROM WOOD TO OIL

One common way to think of the dynamics of energy use is in cycles, where one form of energy is dominant over others for a period of time before its dominance wanes and another source becomes supreme. The cycles can be depicted as falling on a normal curve, where a particular form is introduced, grows in popularity until it reaches a peak, and then it begins to recede, either because its availability declines or proves inadequate or because a new and apparently superior form enters the equation and begins its own bell curve of dominance. The bell curves can be shorter and steeper or longer and flatter. Normally, as dependence on one form of energy goes into decline, its bell curve overlaps with the ascent of the successor energy form. Even as one source loses dominance, it may remain critical for some people, as in the case of wood in Africa and South Asia.

There have been a limited number of energy use cycles. For most of human history, as already noted, the burning of wood from trees and bushes was the dominant form. Increases in human populations and activities for which energy was needed began to exceed the utility of this source in the eighteenth and nineteenth centuries with the advent and spread of the Industrial Revolution. In places that had available supplies, coal became a substitute, and for a relatively short period, coal became the dominant source, at least in those parts of the world undergoing industrialization. In most of the developing world, which did not enjoy the fruits of industrialization, wood remained the dominant fuel until well into the twentieth century. Coal's dominance was never complete because of limits on its availability geographically, the technology to mine it and bring it to where it was needed, and even the predecessor of ecological concern over the pollution that coal burning produced in some places (Charles Dickens' London, for instance).

The second significant energy cycle has been petroleum. It began with the discovery and exploitation of oil in places like Titusville, Pennsylvania (where the first American oil field began production in 1859) and has continued to the present. People disagree where on the normal curve current levels of petroleum dominance resides, but most estimates suggest the cycle is at its zenith or slightly beyond, based on availability and depletion of reserves and the undesirable effects of energy usage. Whether "peak oil" (the apex of availability and use) has been reached is a matter of debate. There is an ongoing debate about what energy source may supplant petroleum in the next cycle.

One of the major characteristics of dominant energy usage to date is that it has exclusively involved the burning of carbon-based fossil fuels. These sources generally share two characteristics that limit their desirability as long-term solutions to global energy needs. For one thing, most are not renewable, or they cannot be renewed quickly enough to meet energy demands. Wood can be replenished, but not quickly or in adequate supply as demand increases; oil cannot be replenished at all. Only more reserves can be found.

The point at which the use of a particular energy source exceeds the ability of the environment to replenish it is known as *carrying capacity*. The basic premise of carrying capacity is the sustainability of a resource, and this requires a balance between its natural production and its exploitation. This idea, first publicized widely in the nineteenth century by Thomas Malthus, applies mainly to wood in terms of energy usage, because wood is the only sources that is depleted but that naturally regenerates itself by growing new trees. It does not apply to other fossil fuels, which do not regenerate: the ecosystem is not producing more petroleum or coal, and these resources only become elastic and increasing through the discovery of previously unknown supplies. Renewable sources like wind and sunlight are not "consumed" by their conversion to energy, so that carrying capacity is not threatened by their exploitation. The depletion of wood (exceeding of replenishment ability or carrying capacity) is not apparent to most Americans (particularly those living in the heavily forested eastern parts of the country), but the overuse of wood has contributed to desertification of parts of sub-Saharan Africa such as the Sahel where wood continues to be the major energy source.

The second negative characteristic of fossil-fuel burning is that it pollutes the atmosphere. Fossil-fuel burning releases carbon dioxide into the atmosphere, and it is the increasing injection of carbon dioxide beyond natural abilities to absorb and convert it into harmless compounds that have been the root cause of global climate change. Some fossil fuels are worse than others in this regard. The "dirtiest" fossil fuel in terms of noxious residues is coal, which not only emits carbon dioxide but also particulates that produce extremely unhealthy levels of smog (Beijing, China is a prime example). Ironically, it is also the most abundant fossil fuel in terms of global reserves. Natural gas is much less of a polluter, emitting about half the carbon dioxide of coal. This difference is the major reason American power plants are rapidly being converted from coal to natural gas as part of the shale gas and oil revolution (discussed in more detail in Chapter 4).

Petroleum, which has become the twentieth and early twenty-first centuries' energy source of choice, illustrates both of these points. Petroleum is, of course, a fossil fuel, and that means its burning introduces carbon dioxide into the atmosphere that would not otherwise be there. The use of petroleum for transportation and energy production has been the focal point of environmentalists' efforts to improve the atmosphere. Used in large amounts, petroleum can create noxious, even deadly levels of smog, as it did in southern California until environmental limits were put in place late in the last century.

Petroleum remains the centerpiece of global energy generation, however, both because it is still widely available (and known reserves keep getting augmented by new sources) and because the world's economy is so closely tied to its use as an energy source.

Petroleum addiction and fossil-fuel-based pollution are the pillars of the energy debate, both domestically and in foreign policy. The addiction is the result of the decisions made during World War II to rebuild war-torn economies using petroleum as the major fuel source. This decision is accentuated by the rising demands for energy that are a cornerstone of economic prosperity. The debate geographically centers on the Middle East, because the most important known oil reserves in the world have been there. Without oil, the Middle East would be far less important in the world than the oil-besotted Persian Gulf littoral has been for over half a century.

Conscious Oil Addiction and the Middle East

The quest for access to petroleum began in earnest early in the twentieth century. One of the interesting sidelights of World War I, as described in detail in *Lawrence in Arabia,* involved the competition between the major powers for the remnants of the Ottoman Empire at the end of that conflict, and the areas where oil had been discovered or was suspected were high on the list of concerns for countries like Britain, France, Germany, and to a lesser extent, the United States, which already had its own vibrant and growing oil industry in the American Southwest (notably Texas and Oklahoma). The exploits of T. E. Lawrence (*Lawrence of Arabia*) in assisting the Arab rebellion in what became Saudi Arabia was part of these dynamics.

Oil became a major geopolitical factor during World War II. The second global conflict of the century was the first fully mechanized war, with the tools of war in all media dependent on propulsion by internal combustion engines powered by petroleum products: ground forces with tanks and personnel carriers, navies using diesel powered submarines and surface ships, and propeller-driven (and later jet) aircraft, for instance. World War II was also a war of factories, meaning the countries that could produce the wherewithal of war had great advantage, and factories required energy for their operation. Moreover, petroleum was also used to produce the lubricants that made the weapons usable. POL—petroleum, oil, and lubricants—were a major factor in the war.

Given the dependence that war machines had on petroleum, its control (and denial to the enemy) was a major strategic goal of all sides. Obtaining a monopoly on Middle Eastern sources was the major unachieved concern of Germany (whose only other source was in Eastern Europe), and the Western allies managed to keep Germany from attaining access to Persian Gulf reserves that could be refined into the liquid of war. Indeed, Western champions of airpower argue that their success in interdicting petroleum headed for Germany and in destroying German refining capabilities were the key elements in defeating the Nazis, whose war machine literally ground to a halt for lack of gasoline and lubricants. Although it was not widely depicted as such at the time, the geopolitical emphasis on petroleum control was the harbinger of an emphasis on *energy security* as a major factor in more contemporary global politics.

Among its other effects, World War II largely shattered the European power system, which had been largely based on coal burning before the war. Led by the Americans, the decision was made to rebuild the power grid in Europe using petroleum as the primary energy source. This calculus was based on what was presumed to be exclusive, secure access to Middle East petroleum and a reasonable, controllable cost for the oil. Petroleum was cheap and reliable.

The reason for this optimism was that most of the Middle Eastern oil fields were effectively controlled by Western oil companies. The "seven sisters," as they were known, had long-term, renewable leases on most of the region's reserves at very low prices, an arrangement that decision makers assumed could be extended essentially into perpetuity. The countries whose oil was being exploited were paid a relatively small fee for the oil that was taken from their soil, a condition they eventually—and predictably—came to resent and reverse.

On this basis, European energy grids became dependent upon Middle Eastern petroleum, and cheap, available petroleum became the basis for European recovery after the war. As subsequent studies have amply demonstrated, the single best indicator of economic productivity and thus prosperity is energy consumption, and the result was that energy demands increased rapidly, especially when Western European economies began to compete with the United States, the only country in the world that had essentially escaped the physical ravages of World War II. In the United States, economic expansion and the exhaustion of relatively cheap oil fields in Texas and elsewhere also caused the Americans to look for alternate sources, and their gaze also fell on the Middle East.

The cozy relationship between the Western oil companies and their Middle Eastern hosts did not endure, as host governments came to realize they were not getting very much for their one valuable commodity. The first reaction to the "sweetheart" deal the seven sisters had negotiated came in 1953, when the democratically elected Iranian government of Mohammed Mossadeqh announced its intention to take control—to nationalize—Iranian oil fields so that Iran would have control over the revenues it would receive. This proposal was, of course, viewed as apostasy in Western capitals, because it threatened both pillars of the arrangement on which oil dependence had been premised: cheap and secure access to petroleum. As a result, the American CIA and others conspired to overthrow Mossadeqh and replace him with the exiled Shah of Iran, Reza Pahlevi. The successful coup occurred in 1953 and bought the Western powers some time to continue their exploitation of Iranian and other regional oil fields. The CIA's prominence in the coup also helped create an animosity between the Iranians and the American government that still exists today.

The Iranian action was also only a temporary stopgap to Middle Eastern determination to take control of the exploitation of its only economically viable resource. In 1960, the Organization of Petroleum Exporting Countries (OPEC) was formed as a counterweight to the Western oil countries. Saudi Arabia and Venezuela were the leaders in forming the organization, membership in which now includes twelve countries (Algeria, Angola, Ecuador, Iran, Iraq, Kuwait, Libya, Nigeria, Qatar, Saudi Arabia, the United Arab Emirates, and Venezuela). The organization includes all the major oil producers employing traditional means except Russia and has members in the Middle East (6), Africa (4), and South America (2). Its constitutional mandate is "to coordinate and unify the petroleum policies" of its members and "to ensure the stabilization of oil markets in order to secure an efficient, economic, and regular supply of petroleum to consumers, a steady income to producers, and a fair return on capital for those investing in the petroleum industry." OPEC's primary activities include setting global oil prices and supply levels. At heart, OPEC undercut the control of the petroleum companies and the governments of the countries where they reside and transferred that power to the producing countries. The power equation thus shifted effectively to the Middle East, where the largest producers were located.

As OPEC has evolved, it has thus undercut both premises of the move to Middle East oil: secure access to energy, and especially a low price for that resource. It also resulted in the rise of the region to the center stage of global politics, a position that it has occupied virtually unopposed since the end of the Cold War.

Among those caught in the spider's web of Middle East dynamics has been the United States, in two ways that helps define much of the current malaise of American foreign policy. First, the United States became the world's premier oil junkie. As American oil fields became exhausted (or at least mined out of easily—and cheaply—recoverable reserves), the United States became increasingly dependent on foreign sources. At the center of those sources was Saudi Arabia and, to a lesser extent, other producers on the Persian Gulf littoral (e.g., Kuwait). Second, the Shah of Iran was driven from power in 1979. The Shah's government had been America's most reliable partner in the region, especially providing military force that guaranteed that oil flowed unimpeded from the Gulf to the United States. When the Shah was replaced by a wildly anti-American regime nominally headed by the Ayatollah Khomeini, this protection was withdrawn, and the United States felt the need to fill the void by committing its own forces to Gulf petroleum security, a mission it still carries out.

Choking to Death? The Ecological Challenge to Fossil Fuels

The dynamics of petroleum addiction are clearly intermestic both in supply and demand terms, but the question of adverse ecological impacts of exploiting various energy sources is even more so. On the domestic side, supply issues include the availability and exploitability of reserves of various kinds on American soil (e.g., the Alaskan oil fields) and getting raw resources to market (e.g., the Keystone pipeline). Demand-side issues encompass all claimants on energy, but are most popularly associated with transportation uses by individual Americans (e.g., gasoline for automobiles). Most of the international issues are supply side, with access to petroleum at the top of the list for Americans. They intersect on questions such as the extent to which energy conservation domestically (e.g., more fuel-efficient cars) reduces dependency on foreign sources of petroleum.

All these questions are redoubled when the question of the ecological impacts of using different energy sources is added to the mix. Once again, the issue is intermestic. The major sources of demands to reduce carbon dioxide emissions from fossil-fuel burning have been domestic in the United States and in other advanced areas such as Western Europe and Japan. The burning of fossil fuels, however, is the most cost-effective way by which many developing countries can increase the access to energy that is necessary to uplift them economically, and often the most polluting are the most attractive: overwhelming Chinese dependence on coal to support its manufacturing sector is a prime example. The intersection point between domestic and international aspects is symbolized by international efforts to fashion a global follow-on agreement to the Kyoto Accords of 1997.

The energy problem as an ecological concern is familiar. As noted, the burning of fossil fuels releases carbon dioxide (CO_2) into the atmosphere in varying amounts depending on the fuel source. Natural processes for converting carbon dioxide into harmless compounds is supposed to occur through photosynthesis, which occurs when the carbon dioxide traverses tropical rain forests that serve as carbon "sinks" that breakdown CO_2 into its natural elements. Historically, these dynamics have kept carbon dioxide in the atmosphere at unthreatening levels. Two modern phenomena, however, have upset this balance. On the one hand, fossil-fuel burning to produce energy has increased (and continues to increase) exponentially, resulting in more carbon dioxide injection into the air. On the other, countries (especially those along the equator) with large rain forests have been cutting down the trees that absorbed and transformed carbon dioxide into harmless substances.

The result of these two phenomena is that more carbon dioxide is being injected into the atmosphere than can be absorbed. That excess, in turn, ends up in the upper reaches of the atmosphere, where it serves as a "greenhouse gas" that holds the heat from sunlight in the atmosphere that would radiate back into space in the absence of this effect. In turn, the result is a gradual warming of the atmosphere and other ecologically undesirable impacts such as the melting of polar ice caps and the subsequent rising of sea levels, all courtesy of "global warming."

This phenomenon is controversial in the United States, where there are a number of mostly self-interested critics who argue that climate change science is flawed. Such defenses generally come from people who are either ignorant of the science or who have a vested interest in denying it—supporters of the American Petroleum Institute or apostles of "clean coal" (a classic oxymoron), for instance. For present purposes, such arguments will be dismissed or ignored; global climate change exists, and the science is clear on the topic. Moreover, the burning of fossil fuels is the primary villain in this phenomenon.

Ecological damage is a factor in energy cycles and should become a factor in the international politics of energy. The clear path to reducing carbon dioxide damage to the ecosphere is the gradual movement away from carbon-based fuels and their replacement with energy sources that do not pollute. This is a formidable task, because the mandate to speed the conclusion of the petroleum cycle occurs in a hostile physical climate, for two reasons.

The first reason is pressure from the developing world to enter the prosperity enjoyed by the richest countries. Countries like China and India that were not part of European and North American development revolution fueled by fossil fuels now demand the same availability for themselves. Given the enormous population in those two countries alone (over 2.5 billion), even modest demands for energy provided by burning oil or other fossil fuels could have enormous ecological effects. It is ironic that the cheapest fossil fuels generally are also the most polluting. Advertising campaigns by its producers (clean coal) notwithstanding, coal is generally the dirtiest fossil fuel in terms of pollutants, and it is the mainstay of Chinese energy usage: in 2012, China used nearly half (47 percent) of all the worldwide coal used for energy generation. Less polluting sources are generally more difficult to exploit and thus more expensive, although advances in shale gas and oil are changing that calculus. The technology for such exploitation in economically attractive terms is, for now, basically limited to North America.

The result is a bind that confronts developing world government directly and developed world countries as well. Developing world governments by and large recognize the problems their entry into the fossil-fuel energy cycle creates and want to cooperate in its alleviation, but their populations also yearn for and demand the kinds of economic growth that requires energy. They are thus drawn to exploit the cheapest and dirtiest forms of energy production possible, even though they recognize the undesirable ecological effects such use produces. On the other hand, while developed world countries argue vigorously for the developing world to eschew fossil fuels, they also recognize that their own development, a century or more ago, was based on exploitation of these same fuels—a source of some hypocrisy on their parts in the eyes of the developing world.

The other problem is the absence of an obvious and compellingly attractive alternative to petroleum as the basis of the next energy cycle. The movement of developed economies from wood to petroleum energy usage was reasonably seamless, and the physics of creating energy by burning such fossil-derived fuels was not overwhelming. There is currently great ecological pressure to condense the current petroleum cycle and move to an alternate base that does not create the same environmental challenges that fossil-fuel burning does. The problem is that there is not a clear new form of energy production that meets all the criteria that the next cycle must attain to provide the needed results.

There are several frequently mentioned possibilities of varying promise, both individually and in combination. If one eliminates fossil-fuel variants as no more than interim solutions (e.g., shale oil and gas), all share the common characteristic of not burning and emitting carbon into the atmosphere, thus avoiding the CO_2 problem and thus contributing to a lowering of the greenhouse gas/global climate change problem. The most appealing in terms of minimal environmental impact are the renewables: solar power and wind. Their principal limits, of course, is that they can only produce adequate energy supplies in places that either have prolonged sunny conditions or are located where it is windy. Storage is also a problem to provide solar power at night and wind power when it is calm. A semi-natural form of alternative power is hydroelectric: power produced by water cascading through dams on rivers and the like. The problem with this source is that virtually no one believes it can make a sizable impact on overall energy needs.

Nuclear power is another alternative. One form is fission reactors, which are currently in service in the United States and especially in France, where a majority of electricity comes from nuclear generation. This traditional nuclear power generation has the advantage of not introducing pollutants into the atmosphere, but nuclear power facilities are very expensive to build, are potentially vulnerable to disruptions, leaks, or even sabotage, and create nuclear waste the storage of which is highly controversial. The other, and arguably ultimate, form of nuclear power is fusion (the process by which the sun produces energy), but containing a fusion reaction so that it can produce energy remains problematical.

There are at least five criteria that a new fuel must provide. The first, and overwhelming most important, is *feasibility*. This criterion contains two elements: it must work, and it must be capable of providing large amounts of power. No current alternative unambiguously meets this criterion. Second, the next source must be *abundant*. Given that energy demands are likely to grow greatly in the future, a nonrenewable source that cannot regenerate itself adequately is clearly undesirable. Oil supplies, for instance, will eventually be exhausted. The energy technology that most clearly might meet this criterion is fusion, since it would be based on the fusing together of deuterium and tritium molecules found abundantly in sea water. Fusion, however, is not yet feasible (if it ever will be).

Third, the next energy source must be *nonpolluting*. This criterion is most damning for traditional nuclear power generation. Fourth, the next source must be *economical*. For energy use to expand worldwide, it must be affordable in the places where it will be used, and this primarily means in the developing world. The next source must, in other words, be measurably cheaper than current prices of fossil fuels. Unfortunately, the most polluting of these fuels like coal also tend to be the cheapest and thus the most appealing currently to developing world economies.

The fifth criterion is that access to the next energy source must be *secure*, meaning that access must not be threatened by natural or political obstacles. This criterion, if met, would remove energy from the list of geopolitical concerns. All countries have sunshine and wind some of the time, for instance, and only landlocked countries lack direct access to the ocean water that has the building blocks (deuterium and tritium) for fusion power. A world where energy is both available and secure would be very different than the world today.

Oil is currently the centerpiece of global energy production, and the petroleum picture is changing for countries like the United States, largely because of the exploitation of shale oil and gas, a dynamic discussed in Chapter 4. The gist of the preceding discussion, however, is that petroleum, and especially the discovery of new petroleum sources, offers no more than an interim solution to global energy needs and problems. A decade or so ago, it was fashionable to predict that the apex of the oil cycle had been reached (something known as peak oil), and that due to depletion, the sway of oil was on the wane. Peak oil was generally thought of as the point at which half the world's reserves had been used, suggesting that availability would gradually decline, meaning a new energy source needed to be identified and developed. Subsequent discoveries have stilled most of those discussions, but the dynamics of the petroleum cycle will run their course. The time is now further in the future than the doomsayers predicted, but oil will be depleted at some point.

With specific reference to petroleum energy, there is an additional complicating factor. Petroleum is critical not only to global energy supplies, but also to the plastics industry, which relies almost exclusively in the conversion of petroleum to the various plastic products that dominate many industries. This raises the possibility that as petroleum supplies begin to decrease, there may be greater pressure from the chemical industry to curtail its burning to preserve remaining reserves for more vital uses. Pressure could mount to phase out the use of petroleum as a fuel may be phased out before supplies dry up because oil becomes too valuable to burn. The late Shah of Iran Reza Pahlevi (quoted in Fleischman) raised this issue early in 1979 before his fall, noting the necessity of oil in making plastic and concluding that "Oil is too valuable to burn. When we run out, what will we do? Fight each other for the last drop?" Things like shale oil and gas simply provide a little more breathing time for the transition away from the petroleum cycle. The point, however, is that the discovery of additional sources of petroleum may prolong the time to reach and pass peak oil, but it will be reached eventually. Pressure to preserve what is left for other purposes may combine with ecologically based concerns to hasten the point at which the transition begins.

Changes in the energy situation have major implications for the geopolitics of energy, and especially oil-rich and oil-dependent areas like the Middle East. The conscious choice to move to petroleum as the prime source of energy elevated the Middle East to a position and prominence in the world that it had previously not occupied, that it would not have enjoyed in the absence of that transition, and which could dry up as the transition to an alternate energy model evolves. What this might mean to geopolitics more generally requires looking at how oil thrust the Middle East into such prominence and, in the process, elevated a formerly and otherwise obscure part of the world to such prominence in American policy.

THE GEOPOLITICS OF OIL ADDICTION

The petroleum energy cycle has obviously moved geopolitical emphasis to the Middle East. For many Americans, this movement and the degree of emphasis and concern that the United States has upon the international relations of that region seem almost perpetual, but that has not historically been the case at all. Before the latter quarter of the twentieth century, the Middle East remained a foreign policy backwater for the United States and much of the rest of the world. Decisions made in the years after World War II that were not intended to highlight the centrality of the region inadvertently elevated its importance to what today seems "normal." Put simply, before the world worried much about secure access to petroleum, it paid little attention to the Middle East. When the growing worldwide addiction to petroleum began to appear after World War II, the Middle East muscled its way onto the geopolitical map. Should a new energy cycle supplant the world's reliance on traditionally recovered petroleum, the region could easily slip back into the backwaters again.

There are two basic timelines that define the American level of involvement in the Middle East. The first centers on petroleum energy security and has 1979 as its critical point. The second has its origins in the Cold War, and has the end of that confrontation in 1991 as its seminal event. These events in 1979 and 1991 impelled the United States to assume a prominent, personal, ongoing military role in the region that it had not previously had and which remains the most prominent and, to many area residents, most irritating trademark of continuing U.S. policy.

Like the crisis in the developing world, this growing prominence was a less-than-compelling sidelight during the Cold War. The end of the Cold War fixation removed the historic post–World War II emphasis on the Soviet-American confrontation, left the American national security community no clearly compelling geographic or functional focus, and thus allowed the redirecting of American national security thinking to Middle Eastern events, especially after the terrorist attacks of September 11, 2001.

The Critical Events

The seminal events of 1979 and 1991 were not the result of careful, concerted American direction and coordinated effort. As noted in Chapter 1, the United States did not anticipate and was virtually blindsided by the disintegration of operational communism in Europe, and it had placed secondary concern on the political dynamics of the developing world, including the Middle East, a part of the globe that was developing in all senses except for the monetary riches afforded by oil revenue. It took virtually all the 1990s to absorb the reality of the demise of the Cold War and to conclude that it was basically a good thing. This process of adjustment, and especially its military implications, was still ongoing when the attacks of 9/11 occurred and created a new threat environment on which the national security community could refocus. Since the source of the new threat was the Middle East, the questions of terrorism and energy policy became intertwined. They still are.

The decision to rebuild European energy systems around petroleum had elevated the Middle East status in global politics to levels it had never previously achieved. Before oil became a major concern to virtually all the world's countries, the region had been a decidedly marginal player in world affairs.

The fact that it was the birthplace of three of the world's great religions provided it with some notoriety and concern among the various faithful populations, but this was not enough to engage the major powers to any great extent. The Middle East was simply a very dry, sandy backwater. Its transformation into a central competition ground for the world's powers was a post–World War II phenomenon.

The Middle East as the global energy solution met four of the five criteria identified in the last section as crucial for a follow-on fuel. Oil was a feasible commodity on which to base a new energy source, because it was available in generous supplies not far from the European countries in which it would be used (in the early postwar period, the United States was largely self-sufficient, a condition that would erode). There appeared to be an abundance of petroleum, particularly given demands at the time. Under the control of the seven sisters, that supply was available at economically attractive prices that would remain stable as long as the private European and American oil companies maintained their stranglehold on the leasing and royalty rates paid the host countries. Once Soviet attempts to gain influence in Iranian Azerbaijan were thwarted in 1946, no hostile party threatened interference with the flow of petroleum from Persian Gulf oilfields to European and later North American markets.

All of these conditions would change for the worse across time. While the feasibility of exploiting the oil domes under Middle Eastern sands remained (and remains) technically feasible, political problems have gradually made access more problematical. The original major source of tension was growing displeasure at the rents the oil producers were receiving from the oil companies. The governments of the oil-producing countries came to realize that oil was their only fungible commodity, and that unless they maximized their revenues from that resource (which their arrangements with the seven sisters did not allow them to do), they were in danger of virtually giving away their national treasure and being left with very little in return when the oil was gone, as they knew it eventually would be. The fact that the two major producers were dominated by different, and competing, sects of Islam—Sunni Saudi Arabia and Shiite Iran—came to be a growing problem as well.

The abundance question also developed gradually, with two bases. One was an exponential growth in worldwide demand for oil beyond 1940s projections, fueled by high modernization and thus energy consumption and by populations growing very rapidly and demanding energy for their sustenance and prosperity. This growth was the result of greatly increased demands that arose from rapid and increasingly universal movements toward economic modernization and rapidly growing global populations. Both required more and more energy, which meant oil. This meant there were increasing demands on Middle East oil supplies, and one of the increasing suitors was the United States, where economic productivity and the depletion of domestic sources made the United States the world's largest importer on petroleum, chiefly from the Middle East. This problem was made more difficult because virtually all the oil consumers underestimated the degree to which their demand would grow.

The economics of petroleum also changed for the worse after the formation of OPEC. It is unclear whether those who made the initial postwar decisions to move the world's energy economy to the Middle East anticipated that those producing the oil from beneath their soil would eventually rebel and assert a greater demand for control over their sole important resource, but in 1960 they did. The result was twofold. Middle Eastern governments gradually nationalized their oil assets, thereby wresting control from the private oil companies and forcing them to renegotiate oil leases on much more favorable terms. At the same time, nationalization allowed regional governments to exert control over the price of their oil, and the days of cheap oil were gone forever. The seven sisters and the governments of the countries in which they were located resented and opposed the birth and growth of OPEC, but there was little they could do about it that did not threaten their ongoing access to petroleum—the greater priority.

The security of access to the oil was not initially challenged by the formation of OPEC. The United States had a very close and mutually advantageous relationship to ensure security. The Shah wanted to modernize the Peacock Kingdom and in the process to reassert the historical predominance of Persia/ Iran. To accomplish this goal, he allied himself with the Americans, who provided the training, education, and materials for Iranian development, and this included providing the Iranian military with state-of-the-art equipment and training that made Iran clearly the premier military force in the region and that nurtured the White Revolution (the name the Shah gave to his program of modernization). In return for this assistance, the Shah employed his military to guarantee the free flow of the oil tankers through the Persian Gulf and thus on their way to markets in the West.

This arrangement worked well for a time, but it was based on two false assumptions that eventually led to its undoing in Iran. One of these was that Westernization could occur peacefully in the largest Shiite country in the world. The vast majority of the country's population consisted of Shiite peasants. Deeply conservative, these peasants did not benefit from the Shah's modernization efforts, and they deeply resented the practical implications of that process, which included secularization and the adoption of a Western, consumer-driven lifestyle. Secularization, one of the hallmarks of Western development, was simply anathema to the Shiites. Believing they would accept or embrace it was naïve on the part of its advocates. Equally conservative Shiite mullahs were another source of opposition to the Shah and provided voice and leadership to the disconsolate masses. At the same time, the Shah's regime was both despotic and tyrannical. The excesses were highlighted by the alleged atrocities committed by the Shah's secret police, *Savak,* which added to internal opposition and made external support more difficult. In the late 1970s, the American administration of President Carter insisted that the Shah's security forces be reined in; when they were, there was no force to suppress anti-Shah activism.

The house of cards in Iran began to teeter in the mid-1970s. The catalyst was a leading Shiite cleric, the Ayatollah Ruhollah Khomeini, who demanded the overthrow of the Shah from his exile in Paris. The situation deteriorated as demonstrators began to call for the Shah's overthrow. Much to the West's surprise, the Shah did not demand disruption of the demonstrations. In early 1979, the Shah went into exile, never to return. After a brief succession struggle, Shiite militants emerged as the victors in the Iranian Revolution. Their violent anti-Shah emotions extended to hatred for his chief sponsor, the United States. The United States became the Great Satan, militants captured the American embassy in Tehran, kidnapped its personnel, and held them for 444 days. The days of U.S.-Iran collaboration were over. The geopolitics of the region was transformed, and so was the American perceived role in Middle Eastern affairs. The consequences are still being felt, for better or worse.

The major impact was on energy security. One of the first acts of the new religious regime in Tehran was to expunge all evidence of the old order. Operationally, this meant the so-called Revolutionary Guard roamed the country virtually unimpeded, arresting, trying, and punishing (usually executing) officials and supporters of the Shah's regime, and this prominently included members of the Iranian military. As many members of the officer corps as could do so fled the country (often with the help of American friends). In the end, the old military order that had enforced freedom of navigation (particularly for Western oil tankers) was gone. What remained was a potentially hostile vacuum, since the eastern banks of the Persian Gulf, including the critical Gulf of Hormuz (a classic naval "choke point" that traffic traversing the Persian Gulf in either direction must negotiate), wash onto Iranian soil.

There was another significant Middle Eastern event in 1979 that is rarely connected to the petroleum equation but which, at the time, seemed it could become part of it. Over Christmas in 1979, the Soviet Union invaded neighboring Afghanistan. Their purported reason was to prop up a faltering, inept communist regime in Afghanistan, but there were other, more geopolitically ominous possibilities that gave Western, and specifically American, analysts pause for concern. The most ominous possibility was that the Soviets would subdue Afghanistan and use the captured territory as a launching pad to move southward along the Iranian-Pakistani border to the Gulf of Oman, from which they could harass and potentially interrupt petroleum flows out of the

Persian Gulf. On close inspection, these possibilities turned out to be overly inflated, even hysterical (they badly overestimated the likelihood the Soviets could subdue the Afghans and underestimated the difficulty of traversing very harsh terrain to reach the Gulf).

These Soviet "horror" scenarios never came to fruition, and it is not entirely clear the Soviet leadership ever seriously entertained them. Even if they did, the first premise of the scenario, the subduing of Afghanistan, never reached fruition, a fate it shared with numerous historical outsiders who have tried—and failed—to conquer and occupy that country. The invasion did, however, cause the United States to invest clandestine CIA assets in ridding Afghanistan of the Soviets and thus developed an American interest in that country that had not truly existed previously.

The Impact on the United States

These two major events helped frame current American interests and actions in the Middle East. The Iranian Revolution had three broad effects. First and most prominently, the Revolution meant that Iran would no longer be available to guarantee the safe transit of regional oil to market and would, if anything, become a potential barrier to such movement. Since no other state in the region had major naval assets it could commit to maritime freedom against possible Iranian attempts to interrupt commerce, the United States decided it would have to do so itself. As a result, the United States established, for the first time, a military presence in the Middle East that has become essentially permanent. Driven virtually exclusively by petroleum access, this presence has been resented by some in the region, who view the Americans as unwelcome intruders—Crusaders, neo-colonialists, or worse. It is arguable (and will be argued in Part III), that this presence forms much of the animus that many regional actors, including terrorist organizations, have for the United States and which provides much of the reason for their fierce anti-Americanism.

Second, the replacement of the modernizing Shah by a militantly Shiite government reanimated the historical split between Sunni Arabs and Persian Shiites that had remained largely dormant under the Shah's program of secularism. Sectarian divisions within Islam have existed since the succession process after the death of Muhammad in 632 AD. A militantly Shiite Iran and an equally militantly Sunni Saudi Arabia—both awash in petroleum reserves—were bound to clash, creating internal and international strife in the region that continues to the present. Third, that militancy was manifested almost immediately when the Iran-Iraq War broke out in 1980, pitting the new Iranian regime against the minority Sunni Iraqi government of Saddam Hussein (the population of Iraq was, and is, majority Shiite). The United States became involved in the latter stages of that war, providing material support to the Iraqis. The two countries had minimal prior relationship, but their common bond was activated by the principle that "the enemy of my enemy is my friend." That friendship survived until the end of the war in 1988. It was severed entirely in 1990, when Saddam Hussein's forces invaded and conquered neighboring Kuwait. Iraq, which previous to 1979 had been at most an afterthought in U.S. policy, has been center stage ever since. Without oil, there would have been little reason for an intimate U.S.-Iraq relationship.

American involvement in the Afghan resistance to the Soviets was more oblique but certainly equally consequential. Prior to the Soviet invasion, American relations with and interests in Afghanistan were decidedly minimal. The Soviet invasion created an interest no so much in Afghanistan per se, but it did provide what appeared to be an opportunity to create difficulties for the Soviets by aiding those who opposed the Soviet intrusion. Initial American interests and efforts in Afghanistan were an extension of Cold War politics, not the result of any particular interest in Afghanistan. To this end, the CIA began to funnel assistance to the *mujahidin,* the rough coalition of tribal elements and outside "freedom fighters" resisting the Soviet incursion. The introduction of American Stinger shoulder-mounted antiaircraft missiles was especially critical, since these weapons were particularly effective against Soviet helicopters that were the primary means by which Soviet elements in the country communicated with one another.

Aid to the *mujahidin* had two long-term effects that are distinguished by the fact that neither is directly associated with petroleum. First, the Afghan resistance formed the seedbed in which two hostile movements were formed. Some of the native Afghan *mujahidin* became the core of the Taliban, which has been the primary U.S. opponent in the Afghan War. The other hostile outgrowth, primarily consisting of foreign fighters who joined the resistance, was Al-Qaeda. In fact, Osama bin Laden initially rose to prominence as a recruiter of foreign fighters in the Afghan cause.

These outgrowths provided a direct link to American direct military involvement in Afghanistan beginning in late 2001. After the 9/11 attacks, the United States sought to pursue, capture, and punish the Al-Qaeda perpetrators of the brutal attacks. At that point, Al-Qaeda's primary haven was in Afghanistan, and the government was controlled by their anti-Soviet partners the Taliban, which had offered safe haven to Al-Qaeda after their expulsion (at U.S. insistence) from Sudan in 1996. The American government asked the Taliban to turn Al-Qaeda over to them, but the request was denied. As a result, the United States began planning and executing a strategy to enter Afghanistan and capture or kill Al-Qaeda members.

At the time, the Taliban was locked in one of Afghanistan's perpetual civil wars with other elements from the anti-Soviet resistance. The United States had no particular stake in this contest beyond the Al-Qaeda connection, but Taliban protection of Al-Qaeda was enough for the United States to begin assistance to the so-called Northern Coalition, of which Hamid Karzai was a prominent leader. American air strikes against Taliban locations helped turn the tide against the Taliban. The American efforts were ultimately unsuccessful in capturing Al-Qaeda leaders, who snuck successfully across the border into Pakistan, but the United States became partnered with the Karzai government that emerged at the end of 2001, presumably as part of its ongoing efforts to destroy Al-Qaeda or to keep it from returning to Afghanistan. This link was the closest thing the United States ever made to a commitment to engage in the longest war in American history.

The picture that this review provides is of a growing American presence in the Middle East that did not result from some long-term set of interests or any coordinated strategic determinations. The depiction portrayed here is admittedly skeletal and arguably incomplete in more or less consequential ways, but it does suggest some of the important, if sometimes ignored or denied, bases for American policy.

The overarching theme of growing American involvement after 1979 is energy, which is to say petroleum, security. During the Cold War, it was often argued that the United States had three sometimes contradictory interests in the Middle East region. These were access to petroleum, security protection for Israel, and geopolitical exclusion of the Soviet Union. The basic reason for keeping the Soviets out was to prevent their becoming a threat to regional petroleum reserves. Excluding the Soviets was less directly related to Israel in the sense that one of the Soviets' few bases of support in the Middle East region was based on its willingness to supply weapons to Israel's enemies, an emphasis that had limited success. Seeking to frustrate Soviet designs in Afghanistan created some linkage to that policy goal. Since the Soviet Union no longer exists, that priority has disappeared from contemporary calculations. The question of support for Israeli security is a separate matter that does not fit neatly into U.S. regional efforts in the oil-rich part of the Middle East beyond the fact that American support of Israeli policy (e.g., the Palestinian state) creates some friction between the Americans and the Arab states that do possess the petroleum. Israel-U.S. relations are discussed in Chapter 7.

The common denominator that runs through the gradual increase in salience of the Middle East in U.S. foreign and especially national security policy is the question of energy security. Before the recent combination of conservation efforts and the exploitation of new sources (like shale gas and oil featured in the next chapter), the United States was truly the world's biggest petroleum junkie, importing from Middle East (especially Saudi) petroleum sources about half of the 20 million barrels a day the country consumed, slightly less than one-quarter of a global consumption of around 85 million barrels a day. When combined with the addiction most of America's clos-est allies also had to foreign oil—a dependency that the United States had, of course, helped create after World War II—energy security was indeed a major dictate of U.S. policy. When dealing with arguably the most volatile, unstable part of the world, that interest inevitably had a major potential mili-tary component.

The events of 1979, and especially the traumatic changes in Iran, upset what had been the reasonably tranquil consequences of oil addiction. American active military involvement in the region prior to that year was not inconsequential. The United States was the principal source of arms for Iran and Israel, sold military equipment to other deep-pocketed regional states like Saudi Arabia, and supported friendly states (e.g., Jordan) and a NATO ally on the northern border of the region, Turkey. American Marines had landed on the beaches of Lebanon in 1958 to help quell sectarian violence there, but direct, continuous, and prominent American military presence was not part of the geopolitics of the Middle East as long as the Shah was in power.

The Iranian Revolution and Soviet invasion of Afghanistan began the flood of events that changed that situation and transformed the Middle East into the primary theater of American geopolitical concern. When the Shah was replaced by a fiercely anti-American regime, the security "architecture" providing energy security from the Persian Gulf collapsed with it. In a short time, the guarantor of oil flow became the primary potential barrier to that flow, and there were no regional actors capable or willing to guarantee secure access to petroleum.

In this circumstance, an American decision to supplant Iran as the guardian of freedom of the high seas in the Persian Gulf seemed natural and necessary. It was natural because the United States had the only true global blue-water navy capable of performing this critical mission, and American personal presence would discourage the Soviet Union, with smaller and inferior but not negligible naval assets, from trying to intrude. It was necessary because of American addiction to regional oil. An interruption of oil flows from the Gulf could make the oil crises of 1973 (when OPEC oil was withheld from the American market) seem like child's play.

The 1973 crisis was particularly traumatic for Americans. Because the United States (and the Netherlands) supported Israel in the Yom Kippur War of that year, the six Arab members of OPEC declared a boycott on their oil to both countries. The result was to create massive shortages, especially of gaso-line for cars (the most vivid symbol of the crisis was long lines of cars waiting to get gas at service stations). The Nixon administration was powerless to get OPEC members to rescind the boycott and instead responded with a series of intended conservation measures, including a 55 miles per hour speed limit on the country's Interstate highways, year-round daylight savings time, calls for lowering home thermostats and buying more fuel-efficient cars, and a greater reliance on coal to provide fuel for industries. The crisis also helped trigger a worldwide recession and helped convince many Americans that helpless dependency on foreign oil producers was unacceptable.

It also began the process of redefining the Middle East as a national security concern for the United States, particularly when taken in conjunction with the fall of the Shah. In his 1980 State of the Union address, President Jimmy Carter announced that freedom of access to the Persian Gulf was a vital interest of the United States. This assertion, which represented a fundamental change in the historic American relationship to the region, was accepted by the American public virtually without a dissenting voice. That same year, the Rapid Deployment Joint Task Force (RDJTF) was established to provide the United States with a viable vehicle for Middle Eastern military action. In 1983, that effort was upgraded to the U.S. Central Command (CENTCOM), the first time the country had established a unified or specified command to that part of the world. In the 1980s, CENTCOM was viewed as more of an oddity than as a major operational part of the armed forces. Today, it is the operational hub of actual U.S. military employment.

The implications of the Carter Doctrine included a permanent American military presence in the oil-producing regions of the area. One, and occasionally two, American carrier-based battle groups (CVBGs) began permanent patrol in the Gulf, a deployment that flew in the face of naval doctrine (the Gulf is relatively narrow, and the navy preferred a much wider swath of open ocean to operate its task forces, thereby minimizing the danger that ships would be attacked by shore-based weapons). The assignment was also accepted as necessary. To help protect those assets, American airmen and soldiers also became permanent residents and presences in a growing number of countries. The Carter Doctrine seemed vindicated when the United States led the eviction of Iraq from tiny but oil-rich Kuwait in 1990–1991. The ubiquity of the American military in the Middle East was cemented by the Afghan and Iraq operations.

The creation of a permanent American military presence changed fundamentally the quality of U.S. relations and thus policy in the Middle East. This theme is developed more fully in later chapters (as well as *The Case against Military Intervention*), but that presence has inevitably been resented by some regional peoples. Americans *are* racially distinct outsiders in the area, and they are different: hardly any are Arab, and even fewer are Muslims, for instance. Because they are different, they are naturally viewed, at least in the minds of some residents, as suspicious intruders who need to be expelled.

The importance of petroleum in creating the rationale for all this cannot be overemphasized. The overthrow of the Shah in 1979 was important to the United States for one major reason: it threatened to pull the Middle East oil needle out of the arm of an addicted America, a trauma the United States was unwilling to countenance. Without that dictate, the fall of the Shah might have been little more than an unfortunate event that the United States regretted but accepted. Oil made it different. It set in motion the chain of events that leads to the presence. Simply put, Middle Eastern oil got us into the mess in which we find ourselves today in the region. The question is whether alternative energy futures can reverse that condition, a matter to which the discussion now moves. If oil got the United States into the current morass in the Middle East, can oil or other energy sources help get the country of this predicament?

BIBLIOGRAPHY

Anderson, Scott. *Lawrence in Arabia: War, Deceit, Imperial Folly, and the Making of the Modern Middle East.* New York: Anchor Books, 2013.

Ansolabchere, Stephen, and David M. Konisky. *Cheap and Clean: How Americans Think about Energy in the Age of Global Warming.* Cambridge, MA: MIT Press, 2014.

Bazilian, Morgan D. "Power to the Poor: Provide Energy to Fight Poverty." *Foreign Affairs* 94, 2 (March/April 2015), 133–139.

Johnson, Ben. *Carbon Nation: Fossil Fuels in the Making of American Culture.* Lawrence, KS: University Press of Kansas, 2014.

Jones, Christopher. *Routes of Power: Energy and Modern America.* Cambridge, MA: Harvard University Press, 2014.

Kalicki, Jan H. and David L. Goldwyn. *Energy and Security: Strategies for a World in Transition.* 2nd Edition. Washington, DC: Woodrow Wilson Center/Johns Hopkins Press, 2013.

Kinzer, Stephen. *The Brothers: John Foster Dulles, Allan Dulles, and Their Secret World War.* New York: Times Books (Henry Holt and Company), 2013.

LeVine, Steve. "Battery Powered: The Promise of Energy Storage." *Foreign Affairs* 94, 2 (March/April 2015), 119–124.

Madrigal, Alexis. *Powering the Dream: The History and Promise of Green Technology.* Boston, MA: De Capo Press, 2013.

Maugeri, Leonardo. "Two Cheers for Expensive Oil." *Foreign Affairs* 85, 2 (March/April 2006), 149–160.

Muller, Richard A. *Energy for Future Presidents: The Science between the Headlines.* New York: W. W. Norton, 2013.

Nye, David E. *Consuming Power: A Societal History of American Energies.* Cambridge, MA: MIT Press, 1999.

Pinner, Dickson, and Matt Rogers. "Solar Power Comes of Age: How Harnessing the Sun Got Cheap and Practical." *Foreign Affairs* 94, 2 (March/April 2015), 111–118.

Pirages, Dennis, and Ken Cousins. *From Resource Scarcity to Ecological Security: Exploring New Limits to Growth.* Cambridge, MA: MIT Press, 2005.

Roberts, Paul. "The Seven Myths of Energy Independence." *Mother Jones* 33, 3 (May/June 2008) 31–37.

Shaffer, Brenda. *Energy Politics.* Philadelphia. PA: University of Pennsylvania Press, 2011.

Snow, Donald M. *The Case against Military Intervention: Why We Do It and Why It Fails.* New York: Routledge, 2016.

———. *Issues in International Relations.* 6th Edition. New York: Pearson, 2015 (especially Chapter 2).

———. and Patrick J. Haney. *American Foreign Policy for a New Era.* New York: Pearson, 2014.

Yergin, Daniel. *The Prize: The Epic Quest for Oil, Money, and Power.* New York: Free Press, 2008.

———. *The Quest: Energy, Security, and the Remaking of the Modern World.* New York: Free Press, 2011.

Chapter 4

A Return to Energy Independence and Its Consequences

Shale Oil and Gas

The age of fossil-fuel burning as the dominant way to produce energy is by no means over or even in danger of disappearing. There is still a very large amount of fossil fuel in one form or another that can be exploited globally, the world's power production capabilities and power grids are based upon fossil fuel energy production, and there are powerful political forces that favor its continuation. Domestically, these political forces are generally tied to energy producers (the American Petroleum Institute and its sponsors and large coal companies, for instance) and the places where the energy sources exist (e.g., Appalachia, the American Southwest). Internationally, the large producers of energy, and especially petroleum, have a clear vested interest in maintaining global dependence on their reserves. The Middle East is, of course, the prime example.

Petroleum accentuates this continuing dominance. Hardly anyone worries excessively anymore about whether peak oil has been surpassed and that the world is consequentially on the downward slope of petroleum availability and usage. Instead, new sources of petroleum are regularly discovered, and new techniques for exploitation redouble the world's available supplies and reinforce dependency. Some projections, for instance, indicate that the continental shelf off South America could be the source of major new supplies of both traditional and shale oil and gas and could become globally significant as a result. Petroleum geopolitics is not going away anytime soon. Shale oil and gas exemplifies the impact of new technologies in expanding the availability of this most fungible of fossil fuels.

There is comfort and concern in all this. The comfort is that the world is not on the precipice of having to make a major, cataclysmic change in energy sources because of the depletion of petroleum. Dire predictions about running out of oil that were commonplace twenty years ago are hardly heard at all. This elongation of the petroleum cycle due to increased supply of the resource provides breathing space in the discovery of the "fuel" for the next energy cycle. At this point, it is not clear what form of energy propagation will be dominant in that next cycle. Discovering more reserves and means to exploit petroleum takes some of the pressure off these efforts.

The concern is equally apparent and arguably compelling. Stretching out the petroleum energy cycle also increases the period of time in which the harmful residues of fossil-fuel burning will be injected into the ecosystem. As noted in the last chapter, one of the apparent requisites of a follow-on fuel source is that it be nonpolluting in terms of CO_2 release into the atmosphere. Global climate change is underway, and at some point it may reach a tipping point at which time the effects become permanent and possibly cataclysmic. Some of this harmful effect can be mitigated by using less noxious fossil fuels—substituting natural gas for coal in power plants, for instance—but these efforts only partially mitigate environmental effects. The simple fact is that all fossil-fuel burning puts CO_2 into the atmosphere, and the only way to stop this consequence altogether is to quit or greatly reduce the burning of fossil fuels.

Patterns of fossil-fuel exploitation have geopolitical consequences both for producers and for consumers chasing the holy grail of energy security. Production changes due to new discoveries or the exploitation of new extraction technologies can have the dual effects of increasing the independence and importance of those places where discovery or innovation occurs. Because it has both significant off-shore petroleum reserves and deposits of shale gas and oil, Argentina and Brazil could become much more important world players than they have been in the past. American technological predominance in shale oil and gas recovery is already changing the geopolitics of its petroleum needs and thus affecting its calculation of energy security, and these changes have ripple effects worldwide.

The goal remains energy security, a condition that has remained problematical under a regime in which Middle Eastern petroleum is a prominent source. The most desirable form that energy security could take would be of energy independence. Taken literally, total independence would require that all needed supplies were located in territories under sovereign American control, a situation that has not been approached for nearly a half century. If it could be realized, however, it would have a dramatic impact on the calculation of energy security and thus national security policy, notably in the Middle East where the quest for secure energy is the bedrock of American regional interests.

The practical commercialization of shale gas and oil reserves in deposits under American and Canadian soil has changed the basic calculation. The exploitation of shale deposits has reduced greatly the need for the

United States to import petroleum, especially from the Middle East. The technology that has allowed this to occur, hydraulic fracturing or, more popularly fracking, is not especially new, but only the United States and Canada have developed it adequately to make it commercially possible and economically viable. There are huge shale reserves in a number of other countries of the world, notably China and, to a lesser extent, Russia. There is essentially *no* shale oil or gas in the parts of the Middle East from where petroleum has been extracted. The geopolitical prospects and implications are clearly monumental.

The shale boom has been both lauded and assailed in the United States. Like energy more generally, it is clearly an intermestic resource. Domestically, it is a mixed bag. On the one hand, the exploitation of shale deposits has created great prosperity in a number of places where it is mined. The state of North Dakota, where the so-called Bakken field is located (named after the farmer on whose property it was first found) has led the boom. Because there are exploitable deposits of shale in 30 American states, the economic impact could be widespread. At the same time, however, there are questions about the ecological impacts of fracking. Spokespersons for the industry have declared fracking to be "safe" and not environmentally harmful, but many in the environmental movement find these claims unconvincing in a variety of ways. The jury is still out.

The international dimension represents the most positive interpretation of what shale promises, at least from an American perspective. The chief threat to American energy security has been its reliance on foreign sources of petroleum. Reserves are generally abundant, but they are often located in unfortunate places: areas that are remote from the United States (the long transit of Persian Gulf oil on tankers) or in places that are politically hostile (Venezuela) or unstable (Nigeria). Petroleum from shale deposits in the United States and Canada is replacing some of that dependency and could reduce it to very low levels. Such a change would allow the United States to be more selective in the places from which it obtains its petroleum imports, thereby increasing energy security and reducing dependency. These kinds of advantages tend to underlay much of the enthusiasm of oil producers in their public defenses of the shale gas and oil revolution.

The shale revolution has a differential appeal within an intermestic outlook for the United States. The international side is almost entirely positive. The United States possesses some of the largest and most exploitable reserves of shale energy, as does its neighbor Canada. As the shale oil and gas industry expands and produces more petroleum products, this growth reduces dependency on foreign sources and thereby increases energy security. Global exploitation may have some negative geopolitical innuendos, but for the foreseeable future, shale is an international positive.

Domestically, the ledger is more balanced. Energy security and the emergence of the United States as a global energy leader certainly contain domestic advantages, and that exploitation will create jobs and wealth widely in the United States. Who exactly benefits the most is not so certain, but the overall American economy surely will. On the other hand, the environmental impact of fracking is largely unknown, and projections about it are both highly conjectural and often self-serving. The highly toxic, adversarial nature of the political dialogue in this country tends to make this discussion more volatile than it might otherwise be.

It is possible to wax too rhapsodically or apocalyptically about the impact of the shale boom. The petroleum geology of shale suggests that it represents a very significant American and global source of energy for some time in the future, but the practical ability to exploit it is still largely confined to North America. Enthusiasm for the exploitation of shale is particularly high in areas where there are known reserves, but reaction in these same areas also includes some of the greatest statements of concern over possible deleterious impacts. Promise and danger are both part of the constellation of reactions. Because the shale phenomenon is still in its relative infancy, the outcome of the debate over the desirability of this new "revolution" can only be predicted by going beyond the known science on the subject.

FRACKING GOOD (?): THE GEOLOGY AND CONSEQUENCES OF THE NEW PROCESS

Hydraulic fracturing has burst onto the public policy radar very forcefully in the past several years, but, as already noted, neither the name nor the process it represents is especially new. The first experiments in the area were conducted in the years immediately after World War II, and the first successful applications were in 1950. The early investigation and engineering were not aimed at shale deposits, but at recovering relatively small residual pools of petroleum in traditional oil fields where almost all the oil extractable by conventional means had been obtained. What is now known as fracking was a way to force these residues out of the pockets in the oil domes where they were located and to bring them to the earth's surface.

Modern hydraulic fracturing represents the application of techniques initially designed to milk the last residues of oil fields in places like Texas and Oklahoma to the capture of petroleum imbedded in shale formations. That there was a significant amount of oil in the shale formations had been known for some time; what was not known was how to capture that oil in commercially and environmentally acceptable ways. Fracking has been the answer.

The basics of hydraulic fracturing are simple and straightforward enough. The basic process involves the injection of sand and chemicals suspended in water into underground seams of shale formations. In most operations, a single vertical shaft is drilled through the earth's crust until it arrives at the strata where the shale and its petroleum are located. At this point, additional shafts are radiated from the central shaft, and the fracking solution is forced into these appendages (this process allows multiple recovery pipes to be radiated from the central shaft, thereby minimizing the number of needed vertical wells). The solution fills the seams in the shale and literally squeezes the oil and natural gas out of the shale formations and forces it to the surface.

Two phenomena were necessary to bring hydraulic fracturing to commercially acceptable levels. One was the perfection of the mix of ingredients that are injected into shale formations. The "cocktail" of chemicals mixed with sand and suspended in the water that squeezes the petroleum products out of the formations is extensive and complex, because it must accomplish several duties. "Hydraulic Fracturing 101" from Earthworks describes the chemicals in some detail. These chemicals have controversial environmental and potential public health consequences that are a bedrock concern of opponents of fracking.

The other phenomenon is cost. One of the major factors in petroleum exploration and exploitation is how much it costs to extract the petroleum from wherever it is located. Producers are acutely attuned to how much the cost per barrel of extraction is, particularly in terms of the overall price that oil brings. Oil sources are attractive for exploitation when those costs are enough lower than prices to allow a profit from the extraction. They are unattractive when costs of extraction are at or above the price of oil on the market. Extracting petroleum from shale is at the higher end of costs among various sources, meaning that shale gas and oil extraction is most economical when the price per barrel of oil is relatively high. When prices dip (as they did in 2015), the profitability of shale becomes more problematical; at some point, profit versus energy security becomes a factor.

The United States as Fracking King

American hydraulic fracturing technology has made the United States the unchallenged leader in energy production from shale sources. This exploitation includes both the release of natural gas and oil from shale formations, and each of these has different energy impacts. One of the first effects of the U.S.-led revolution has been to make the United States the world's leading producer of natural gas. Unlike petroleum, natural gas is primarily beneficial for domestic consumption due to the difficulties and economic barriers to overseas shipping. The only currently available means to ship natural gas over long distances is to liquefy it, so that it becomes somewhat equivalent of petroleum for transportation purposes. Liquefied natural gas (LNG) is normally reconverted to a gaseous state before use. All this is expensive, therefore the domestic uses of natural gas produced in shale fields is currently its primary use. The "flood" of natural gas made available through fracking has, however, facilitated the process of moving toward the substitution of natural gas for coal in power-generating plants, which in turn leads to reduced emissions of CO_2 into the atmosphere and helps move the United States toward environmental goals established in the Kyoto climate change process.

The more symbolically important impact has been on the distribution of petroleum production. The United States has already cut its need to import foreign petroleum by half, and that reduction will continue, particularly if Canadian shale oil is part of the mix. Current projections call for the United States to be energy self-sufficient around 2020. This does not mean the United States will not still import some foreign energy for cost purposes and because of special properties of some imports; what it does mean is that when American energy imports and exports are balanced out, the ledger for the United States will be positive.

The Beneficial Consequences of Shale for the United States and Beyond

The shale revolution in petroleum extraction is so new and undeveloped that almost any projection one can make about it could prove false. At this point, it is almost entirely a North American phenomenon, because the operational technology for shale extraction is almost completely held by Americans who developed the techniques for depleted oil fields in the southwest a generation or more ago. Shale formations can, and eventually likely will, be utilized worldwide, although the distribution is by no means uniform.

Much of what happens globally will depend on the American experience, the outcomes of which are by no means preordained. Shale gas and oil has already had a dramatic effect on American energy supplies and the American position as a global energy power. Lineal projections of the impact could place the United States in a dominant energy position for some time to come. That position could, however, be attenuated as other large repository countries like China begin to exploit their reserves. At the same time, there may be as-yet-undiscovered negative impacts of shale exploitation that will make it a less desirable source of energy. Any beneficial impact must be assessed, as well, in the context that shale oil and gas are fossil fuels, their exploitation does contribute to the injection of CO_2 into the atmosphere, and thus they only represent an interim step in the energy equation.

Those rejoinders noted, the exploitation of shale offers a number of energy and geopolitical advantages for the United States. The United States (along with Canada) has some of the world's largest shale formations suitable for exploitation, and those supplies are mostly located in accessible places where the oil and gas can be captured and transported to market for processing in technologically feasible and economical ways. China, by contrast, has much larger potentially usable reserves, but that country lacks the technology for extraction. In addition, most of the reserves are in remote, largely inaccessible locations in China, meaning the Chinese would have a difficult time getting the fruits of fracking to market and thus into the energy cycle. The upshot is that the United States and Canada have a virtual lock on the shale industry, and this advantage is likely to continue for some time.

A monopoly of extraction technology is also an important American advantage. Since the technology has existed for over half a century, some of it can probably be obtained openly or surreptitiously in the United States, but countries hoping to develop their own reserves are going to need American help to maximize their efforts. That situation provides the United States with geopolitical leverage by allowing us to negotiate whether or on what terms countries gain access to hydraulic fracturing technology. The modern equivalent of wildcatters who now operate in American shale fields will undoubtedly be highly valued in the development of foreign oil fields, providing the prospect of profit and prosperity as well.

There are clear international benefits as well. At the most obvious level, every barrel of oil that is squeezed from a shale formation is a barrel of oil that does not have to be obtained from other sources, notably overseas sources where energy security and cost are always implicit, if not explicit, concerns. If shale oil exploitation is maximized, the United States will be the world's leading natural gas producer, and if claims by the American Petroleum Institute are to be believed, the largest producer of energy overall in the world. The country will not be entirely self-sufficient, but it will be a net exporter of energy.

This possibility offers two positive prospects. One is economic: the United States' balance of trade with the rest of the world has been negative for most of the last half-century, and the large reason is that American foreign exchange has had to be transferred to Middle Eastern countries to pay for oil imports. This necessity has made the globalizing international economic market more cutthroat than it might otherwise have been, because virtually all countries must compete for foreign exchange to pay for their own petroleum addiction. Shale-driven energy sufficiency changes that: the United States will still have to buy some foreign energy, but it will be able to pay for it with larger profits from energy sales. Uncle Sam will once again have foreign exchange cash in his pockets.

The other, and ultimately more important factor within the purposes of this book, is geopolitical. The oil-producing states of the Persian Gulf, and especially Saudi Arabia, have effectively been the drug dealers for American petroleum addiction, and the constant American need for the liquid narcotic of Middle Eastern petroleum has provided enormous leverage for the Saudis (and others) in their dealings with the United States. If the United States no longer needs the petroleum of the oil sheikhs/dealers, it is effectively liberated from the compromises it has had to endure because of the need not to offend the source of its petroleum "fix." The prospect of going through foreign oil "detox" is itself an intoxicating possibility, explored more fully in Part III of the text.

Shale oil and gas also have domestic attractions. For one thing, a great deal of the American shale deposits are in remote, lightly inhabited, and less than prosperous parts of the American west, and the boom caused by the arrival of the oil industry provides a great boost for the economies of many places. The Bakken formations are located in North Dakota, for instance, and are part of a large area that includes locations in western states like Montana and Wyoming, as well Canadian provinces like Manitoba. The shale oil business has transformed the North Dakota economy into one of fastest growing in the United States, bringing jobs, new housing projects, and oil lease payments to a large number of people. Oil produces wealth.

Minable shale deposits have been identified in 30 of the 50 U.S. states, meaning the prospects for economic stimulation will spread broadly across the country. The fact that shale is found in so many parts of the country also bolsters its political appeal. Exploitable deposits of traditional petroleum are only found in five U.S. states, thereby limiting overt support for them politically. Since shale oil and gas are found in 60 percent of the states, the prospects for exploration and development support within the Congress are much more widespread on geographical grounds alone. Because people in so many constituencies benefit, opposition to fracking is more difficult than if the political constituency were narrower. It is not, however, missing altogether.

The Not-So-Positive Side of Shale: Possible Ecological Effects

Not everyone agrees that fracking is a good idea. The most vocal objections come from ecological advocates, who contest the assertions by proponents that fracking is "safe," which generally implies that it is ecologically neutral, beneficial, or minimally harmful. Most of the objections, ironically enough, come from people living in the same physical areas where exploitation is underway or proposed. The confrontation is politically combustible, pitting generally liberal ecologists opposing fracking because of the dangers it may pose against generally conservative developers who downplay those objections and emphasize the energy and economic benefits.

The ecologists argue that the absence of damaging effects is not as well established as proponents maintain. Most defenses of ecological neutrality, they argue, are based on limited fracking in southwestern oil fields, where the volume of fracturing and recovery does not approach the levels involved in full-scale shale mining. The ecologists fear that a headlong rush into shale operations could produce irreversible ecological damage and should be suspended or slowed until natural effects are better known. Developers argue there is scant evidence to support the ecologists' claims and that the economic and geopolitical advantages outweigh those dangers.

This confrontation forms the parameters of the intermestic debate over shale. There is virtually no disagreement between the ecologists and the developers over the geopolitical desirability of loosening dependence on foreign, and especially Middle Eastern, oil. On the other hand, opponents question whether that benefit is worth the possible deleterious effects that exploitation could have on the American ecosystem. Indeed, some even argue that should the anti-fracking ecological arguments prove true and serious damage occur in the American ecosystem as a result, exploitation could prove harmful to the United States: the United States would be saddled with the burden of repairing or coping with fracking disasters, while others would view the American experience and avoid it.

There are a number of specific concerns raised by the ecologists. A major thrust of criticism has focused on water usage in fracking operations. In order to create enough of the mixture of water, sand, and chemicals to free shale gas and oil from formations requires an enormous amount of water. The Earthworks study, for instance, quotes Environmental Protection Agency (EPA) figures indicating that in 2010, 70–140 *billion* gallons of water were used to fracture 35,000 wells in the United States. Shale wells "can use anywhere from 2 to 10 million gallons of water to fracture a single well," Earthworks reports. Much of the fracking occurs in relatively arid parts of the west, where this level of activity can threaten delicate underground water supplies and often requires that much water be trucked to sites to provide enough water for the fracturing process. There is a danger: water tables could be lowered critically in a number of places by shale operations.

A related concern surrounds the "cocktail" of chemicals mixed with sand that is injected into wells to release the oil and gas deposits. The number of chemicals involved is extensive, and, as Earthworks points out, "Many fracturing chemicals are known to be toxic to humans and wildlife, and several are known to cause cancer." In many cases, these liquids are sealed in the sites after mining is completed on the premise that they are at great depths and separated from human water supplies by great amounts of impermeable material. Those who are concerned about possible ecological impacts are concerned that some of these noxious chemicals might leach their way back toward the surface, enter groundwater, and cause significant health crises when they do. Methods are available to treat most of this problem, but are expensive and generally opposed by developers as unnecessary and making the economics of fracking prohibitive.

Fracking also has potential environmental effects beyond water pollution and over-usage of existing water. One of these concerns is air quality, and the "villains" are both seepage of one kind or another from wellheads, and the exhaust from the many tanker trucks that transport shale oil from drilling sites to refining capabilities. In turn, these trucks produce much wear and tear on roads in parts of the country like North Dakota and Montana where roadways are subject to much degradation due to weather, thereby increasing road maintenance costs that drillers do not want to underwrite.

There is also seismic uncertainty that surrounds fracking. The shale seams in which shale oil and gas exist are very deep underground, with thick layers of very hard and impermeable material between them and the surface. These rock layers, according to proponents, provide adequate protection against any seismic activity that might be caused by creating what are essentially empty or aquatic layers in the earth's crust after shale products are removed. Skeptics, however, argue that the evidence available is not adequate to support these claims of a neutral effect. The question is whether shale exploitation weakens the earth's crust. Nobody really knows.

As a study reported in the April 2015 *Economist* suggests, the earthquake possibility illustrates the debate over negative ecological consequences particularly clearly. The study shows that the instances of increased numbers of small earthquakes is indeed occurring mostly in eight generally arid western states (Alabama, Arkansas, Colorado, Kansas, New Mexico, Ohio, Oklahoma, and Texas), and there is little disagreement that the cause is a reaction to inserting the fracking cocktail into old faults.

While these data are generally matters of agreement, their meaning and implications are not. Earthquakes are quite small (generally, around three or less on the Richter scale), so there is disagreement about how much damage they can do in the short or long terms. Moreover, there will be a debate over how acceptable any damage is. The science (on either side) notwithstanding, a long and continuing debate is possibly the most predictable outcome of this disagreement.

What worries the critics is that the hollow seams created by fracturing will result in underground vacuums that will promote earthquakes as the earth's subsurface shifts to adjust to the new vacant spaces caused by the fracturing phenomenon. There have already been instances of small earthquakes in places like Oklahoma and North Dakota and elsewhere where hydraulic fracturing has occurred. The causal evidence, however, is not yet complete enough to determine whether or not the earthquakes are the result of extraction of shale products or from other causes, leaving a debate between the developers (who deny any connection) and the environmentalists (who argue that development should proceed very cautiously until the causal link can be established one way or the other).

There is also a demographic effect that is not generally included in discussions of shale oil and gas but probably should be. Unlike traditional oil operations, the productive "life" of shale wells and fields is quite short. Estimates suggest that once a shale formation has been successfully "cracked," it is only a matter of a couple years before it has yielded almost all the oil and gas that can economically be recovered. At that point, the specific operation is closed down, and the wildcatters move on to new sites. Sometimes these new sites are not terribly far from abandoned sites, but sometimes they are.

Because most of the shale sites are, as noted, in fairly remote locations, there is a demographic problem that development in places like North Dakota illustrates. In most cases, the shale industry is present at sites where there is very little prior infrastructure development: inadequate housing, transportation facilities, and public services like schools, hospitals, and the like for an expanding population of oil field workers and their families. The boom effect of shale money being pumped into the economy results in a rush of construction and development: schools, parks, and public buildings are built alongside new housing units to service the population imported to work in the new oil fields.

What happens after the boom passes in particular locations? In most cases, the absence of preexisting infrastructure was the result of the absence of much economic activity, so if the oil industry moves on, those employed in it are going to leave as well—mostly to newer sites. If that occurs, which it may well, the old localities may be left holding the bag: abandoned housing and public facilities with large debts to repay but not enough people to service or make the payments. The question is, how many contemporary ghost towns will the shale boom create? It is a question that has not been addressed or answered, but it is one that seems inevitable in the long run.

Despite these potential problems, the movement toward the shale revolution in gas and oil has considerable momentum because of its clear benefits. It does offer an alternative, much more secure source of fossil fuel energy than was available previously, specifically a source on Western Hemisphere soil (there is also a lot of shale in South America). At the same time, there are uncertainties about the effects of exploiting this new energy source. It is, after all, a fossil fuel, and thus it does not address the ecologically desirable movement away from the petroleum cycle in energy production. Domestically in the United States, it may decrease reliance on foreign fossil fuels; globally, it stretches the bell curve of petroleum dominance. As noted, it is an interim solution to global energy over the long haul. At the same time, whether or to what extent shale gas and oil will have deleterious ecological and other physical effects on the planet remain uncertain but potentially important.

The other piece of the shale oil and gas puzzle is its geopolitical impact. Energy security is a major part of the equation of national security throughout the world, and the consequence of the dominance of traditionally extracted petroleum energy has been to tilt the geopolitical focus on one of the most unstable parts of the world. Shale gas and oil could level the playing field by redistributing world production and thus reducing the stranglehold the Middle East has over global energy. What differences could that make? Are they good or bad?

The intermestic element of the equation is fairly clear. Supporters of shale development loudly argue the geopolitical advantages of greater energy independence. This argument may be slightly disingenuous given that shale extraction is also very profitable for those who undertake and defend it—a case of narrow self-interest that has little to do with national interest or security. Which motivation really activates proponents? The domestic opposition, however, comes mostly from grassroots sources, and especially from communities directly affected by proposed shale operations on their environment and health. As Mufson points out, local communities in a number of states have passed or proposed regulations banning or limiting fracking. These states include New York, New Jersey, California, Colorado, Michigan, Ohio, Pennsylvania, and Ohio. The most common thread in these objections centers on water usage and contamination.

The Obama administration weighed in on the issue in March 2015, issuing regulations on hydraulic fracturing operations on public lands (less than a quarter of all shale enterprises in the United States). The regulations were issued by the interior department and publicly championed by Secretary of the Interior Sally Jewell, a former petroleum engineer with experience in the shale industry. The interior department standards include requirement on well construction, the storage of liquid wastes, and transparency measures to force companies to disclose the chemicals they employ in fracturing. The petroleum industry predictably opposed the regulations, arguing they were unnecessary and threatened the economic viability of their industry.

THE GLOBAL ENERGY EQUATION AND
AMERICAN ENERGY DEPENDENCE

The geopolitics of energy dependence has been an especially important concern for the United States for two related reasons. One is that the

United States, as the world's biggest petroleum junkie for so long, has been particularly exposed and vulnerable to the implications of energy dominance on the Middle East, both to satisfy its own addiction and to protect the security of others—notably in Europe—whose addiction was also influenced by the United States.

The other source of interest is more traditionally geopolitical. The United States, especially since the demise of the Soviet Union, has also been the predominant country in world politics. The result of the collapse of Soviet communism was a global power vacuum that has been described as a "unipolar moment" of American preeminence (in Krauthammer's term), "the end of history" (in Fukuyama's book title), or slightly more modestly, then Secretary of State Madeleine Albright's observation that the United States is the "indispensable nation." By whatever description, being *the* global superpower has meant the United States has had interests everywhere in the world.

Because of its stature in the world, the United States is the remaining superpower. Despite a challenge from China, it is the world's preeminent economy and possesses by far the world's most potent traditional conventional armed forces and the globe's largest arsenal of nuclear weapons. Economic factors alone mean the United States has some self-interest in what happens everywhere, and its military forces are the only resource that could quell a major conventional armed conflict anywhere in the world. What the United States will or might do is necessarily a part of the calculus for any government or movement around the globe.

This burden means the United States cannot avoid being a world leader, even if there are different interpretations of what that means. The United States is the only true global power, and it cannot avoid having some level of interest in problems that occur around the globe. Global leadership is a given; the variable is how it is exercised.

Because of America's long-standing foreign energy addiction, the Middle East stands at the center of the second part of the global geopolitical agenda. Global political leadership means the Middle East, which has historically not been part of the sphere of major concern for this country, now occupies a central position. Part of the reason is geopolitical in the same sense as American concern for the rest of the world is. Under any circumstances, the Middle East would be unstable because of ethnic, religious, and historical rifts (discussed in the next chapter) that make it unstable and volatile. Regional turbulence makes the area interesting and a concern as well. Thus, what happens in the Middle East today has clear global implications for other regions as well. The most dramatic and publicized of these stem from global terrorism emanating from the region; the more profound implications come from the effects of conflict on the flow of oil. Were it not for petroleum, the world—including the United States—would probably treat the Middle East the same way it treats violence and instability in much of Africa: decrying it but not doing much about it. Oil elevates everyone's attention and concern.

The energy equation, however, represents a complicated mandate. At its base, it has meant developing a sensitivity to and level of involvement in a part of the world in which the United States has not historically been heavily invested, about which its knowledge is imperfect, and toward which there is considerable ambivalence. The United States has been stuck in the Middle East because it needs its oil and because there has appeared to be no one since 1979 to secure access to that resource. It is not a relationship born of affinity, but one based on necessity. Remove the necessity, and what happens to the relationship? Oil has mandated a permanent military presence and has coincided with the rise of terrorism, part of which is directed at the United States and forms a further rationale for the military presence. How are they related? If oil security decreases as a worry, can the United States reduce its Middle East military presence? What effect would that have on U.S.-directed terrorism emanating from the region? These questions could not meaningfully be raised a decade ago. They can be now.

This is where the shale revolution comes in. The United States may not be able to retreat meaningfully from its global leadership role, but under the right conditions, it could reduce its dependency on the Middle East. The shale revolution can have quite opposite effects on the two dynamics of American geopolitical concern. As the United States becomes a more dominant energy producer and exporter, its global leadership role is enhanced. This is particularly true in Europe, which desperately needs to break its dependence on natural gas from Russia. The United States can play a dual role in this quest. If it can find a commercially attractive way to export natural gas (e.g., through economic conversion to LNG), it could become an alternate source. It can also help Europeans develop their own shale industries, although most European shale is in Eastern Europe. At the same time, the shale revolution has the potential to loosen the bonds of American dependence on Middle East sources, possibly even to approach severing them.

The delicious prospect of the shale revolution is to free the United States of its relationship of necessity to the most unstable part of the world. It is by no means a done deal. As suggested in the last section, the environmental battle over the impact of shale exploitation has by no means been resolved and probably will not be for some time to come. In the meantime, that battle will slow the exploitation process, reduce the volume of shale gas and oil entering the marketplace, and therefore slow the geopolitically desirable movement toward energy independence from the Middle East. At the same time, the shale industry is growing and will continue to do so, if possibly not at maximum rates. The real question is only about the pace of change the shale revolution will bring.

This possibility makes it feasible to think about the impacts that American petroleum independence could have on American national security and specifically on its relations with the countries of the Middle East. The discussion is necessarily conjectural and hypothetical. It rests on a condition of independence that does not yet exist and may not ever. The question is indeed indeterminate, and in this case, the variables include the pace and impact of the shale revolution in the United States, the reactions of the oil-producing Middle Eastern states, and the responses of other countries who have developmental goals for which they lack energy sources and who would thus be very interested in reduced American demand for Persian Gulf petroleum.

Speculating on the impact of reduced American dependence may be hypothetical, but some of the impacts can be identified and examined, both as an exercise in alternate futures and as a model of what American policy might be in the absence of a dire need for that scarce resource. That examination in turn can be applied to possible future American policy and presence in the Middle East, the subject of Part III.

Oil Security and American Interests

As a driver of foreign and national security policy, American dependence on foreign petroleum is this country's "dirty little secret." That condition has had real consequences for the United States and its national security policy, and not all of them have been favorable. The United States has supported a Saudi religious monarchy that is medieval in structure and policies and some of whose citizens openly fund anti-American groups, yet the United States only mildly (and mostly privately) rebukes the Saudis. Would a country on which the United States did not rely on for petroleum receive such benign treatment? Before the 1990 invasion of Kuwait, most Americans were only vaguely aware of the existence of Iraq. In 2003, the American political leadership bought the incredibly flimsy arguments of the Bush administration that were used to justify invading that country. Was it because the Iraqis have the world's fourth largest reserves of traditionally recoverable reserves of petroleum, access to which had been denied by Saddam Hussein since he came to power in 1978? The Bush administration adamantly denied the connection. Were they to be believed?

Since 2001, oil addiction as the motivating force of U.S. policy has been sublimated, as the "war on terror" has supplanted the crassness of oil-for-blood as the mantle of a vital national interest in avoiding terrorist actions against American citizens. An emphasis on the anti-American content of most Islamic terrorist groups is undeniable, but is countering terrorism an adequate linchpin for American security policy in the absence of oil addiction? And why does this hatred of the United States exist?

The answer is complex, and any interpretation necessarily goes beyond hard evidence (or cherry-picks the available evidence). Flowing from the Carter Doctrine of 1980, the cornerstone of American policy has been that secure access to Middle Eastern oil is vital to American interests in the region. That statement was at least honest about motivations. Coming as it did on the heels of the fall of the Shah, it justified a continuing American military commitment to the oil-rich areas of the Middle East, an emphasis that did not predate 1980. The Carter Doctrine remains the signal policy statement on American military presence in the region, even if current levels of forces and military actions are not justified in its name.

The importance of establishing the justification of a continuing U.S. military presence in the area arises from the definition of vital interests. A vital interest is conventionally defined either as preventing a condition that would be intolerable if not present (a denial of access to oil would violate a fundamental American interest) or as a condition over which one would go to war. In either case, the key element is that American force is usable (and thus should be available) where vital interests are involved. Whether such forces should be available otherwise is more debatable.

Walking the logic backward, the continuous presence of American military forces in the Middle East since 1979 suggests that there are American vital interests that must be protected. But what are they? There was no terrorist threat against the United States in 1980 (other, arguably, than the Iranian occupation of the American embassy in Tehran), so that terrorism could not have been the instigating interest. The terrorist threat, after all, evolved out of the resistance to the Soviet occupation of Afghanistan and began growing in the 1990s. The events of 9/11 may have reinforced the need for an American military presence in the Middle East, but it certainly did not create it.

Access to petroleum, however, spans the period from 1979 to the present. As such, it is a much more durable reason around which to justify a continuing military presence than terrorism, a kind of "Johnny-come-lately" among reasons to keep American forces in the region. Thinking of the problem in that manner, rather than the currently more popular emphasis on terrorism, clarifies the causal justification for force and suggests how that causal change could be affected by the shale revolution.

In its most basic, simplified form, the impact of the shale revolution is to reduce American dependency on foreign petroleum. Depending on how the shale boom evolves, this decreased dependence could mean something close to oil independence (adequate supplies of petroleum available under American or adjacent Canadian soil), or a reduction of needs for foreign oil to the point they can be met from non-Middle Eastern sources. At that point, the American vital interest in Middle East petroleum would be greatly reduced to basically three considerations.

The first of these is the maintenance of secure access as a hedge against a failure of other sources. The exploitation of shale reserves changes the relative availability of potential oil from traditional sources like the Middle East, but the Persian Gulf does remain the location of, by far, the largest reserves of traditional oil. Can the United States afford to abandon access to that source? The second consideration is the continuing dependency of American allies and friends on petroleum from the region, access to which is currently secured by the American military. Can or will these countries (notably in Europe) provide security if the United States recalculates the strategic vitality of the Persian Gulf? Third, these oil reserves are located in or adjacent to countries in which terrorist organizations like AQ and IS are active. Would a changed U.S. calculus embolden these organizations to put pressure on the countries that produce oil? There is precedent: one of the early sources of funding for IS was the exploitation of the relatively small oil industry in Syria.

A lessened dependency of the United States on foreign petroleum has obvious benefits in terms of American energy security, and these benefits potentially extend to whether the United States needs to maintain the large, expensive military profile it now projects into that reason if the vital interest on which that presence is premised is no longer so compelling. As suggested in the last paragraph, there may be other, derivative reasons to continue the American military profile. Breaking the hold of the addiction does, however, allow one to think about whether the dictates of the Carter Doctrine are so compelling in a world where the U.S. military does not need the area to supply its energy.

Is a reduced United States presence in the Middle East feasible? Since 1979 and especially since the massive infusion of American forces into the Persian Gulf region in 1990 (the first Persian Gulf War over Kuwait), 2001 (Afghanistan), and 2003 (Iraq), a robust American military presence has been an essentially unquestioned tenet of American national security strategy. Part of the reason is to protect what has been accomplished already (the independence of Kuwait), part of it remains freedom of the seas in the Persian Gulf, and part of it is to provide a platform for other U.S. actions in the area, most of which are ostensibly tied to the terrorist threat in its changing permutations.

When Jimmy Carter announced the original rationale for that presence, the core interest to be protected was access to oil, and the shale revolution could greatly reduce or eliminate that rationale, leaving the modulation of political instability and violence in the region as the continuing bases for an American presence.

In a very real sense explored from various angles in the next part, the purpose of American continued presence is to protect the Middle East from itself if one removes oil security from the primary position in the policy equation, and doing so could have broader effects. Ongoing calls for inserting American advisors or forces in Iraq to blunt the advances of IS, for instance, are justified to defeat terrorists, but their local impact is on the Sunni-Shiite power balance in that country. Calls to keep troops in Afghanistan are premised on the need to keep a stable government in power there (which may be a chimera under any circumstances). All boil down to and are justified in the United States as theaters of the war on terror: the fear of AQ returning to Afghanistan, IS in Iraq, and IS and AQ in Yemen, to cite three examples. The rationale, hardly ever seriously questioned, is the validity of the need to contain the terrorists at the source, so that they do not wreak havoc on American soil. It is, nonetheless, a narrative into which an astonishing number of Americans have bought. A reduced American military presence changes the possibility of such discussions.

There is an alternative hypothesis, the testing of which was not possible as long as energy security remained the bedrock of policy, but which can be pursued as shale renders that mandate less compelling. That hypothesis is that the large continuing, and arguably permanent, American military "footprint" in the region may be a large part of the *reason* for animosity toward this country, and that forcing the United States to leave may be the big motivation that Middle East terrorists have for declaring the United States as the enemy.

There are, of course, more conventional arguments made for why the terrorists consider the United States an implacable foe, and if these are the actual reasons for animus, a reduction in American presence is inadvisable. The terrorists have uniformly espoused fundamentalist ideologies which westerners consider bizarre, even medieval, and these are certainly incompatible with worldviews in the developed world. They are also at odds with the philosophies of various modernizing state in the Middle East, and these countries (Turkey, for instance) have a much more intimate interest in countering them than do Americans. These incompatibilities exist and will continue to be highlighted as long as there is consistent physical interface between Americans (and especially military forces) and the peoples who are vulnerable to terrorist appeals. The current policy calls for eradicating the problem; an alternative is to remove the irritant from the equation and to see if the animosity diminishes. That irritant is the continued high-profile American presence in the region. It amounts to changing the animosity question from "Do they hate us for what we are?" to "Do they hate us for *where* we are?"

Is the idea of reducing greatly American military presence in the Middle East a naïve will-o'-the-wisp? The hard men would certainly deride even the possibility on the grounds that an American military presence is necessary to keep the regional situation from deteriorating any further than it already has and that, if anything, a greater American military presence is the only way to enforce stability in the area. In their view, a reduced American presence would promote even greater chaos and likely more anti-American outcomes. This position comes to the forefront often when the question of putting "American boots on the ground" is raised.

Does this argument stand up to the facts? Implicit in the argument that American force is needed to stabilize has to be the assertion that it has been effective in the past. That assertion is warranted in regard to the eviction of Saddam Hussein from Kuwait in 1991, but has it been true elsewhere? The Iraqi and Afghan experiences certainly do not reinforce the idea that adding American forces to the mix—especially in a lead role—makes a favorable outcome more likely. The basic reason is that these forces are obviously *foreign* and are generally only acceptable if their presence is short enough that the indigenous people do not begin to wonder if they are not neo-colonists rather than liberators and that they may do things that do not serve the perceived interests of the indigenous population. Since the United States overthrew a Sunni regime and allowed its replacement with a Shiite regime in Iraq, for instance, it is not at all clear that the Sunni residents of Anbar Province in Iraq (an IS stronghold) would welcome "liberation" by the U.S. Army or by Iraqis obviously in cahoots with the Yankees. In fact, the insertion of American troops into Middle East conflicts is at least as likely to produce anti-Americanism as it is to spur opposition to whomever the Americans oppose. Nowhere is this problem greater than in the Iraqi areas controlled by IS. The hard men would argue things would be even worse without Americans on the ground.

It is also possible that American military presence in this area is less stabilizing than a roiling influence. It is a fact that American forces are so "popular" in Saudi Arabia that the regime hides them in remote desert bases where the average Saudi does not have to see them on any regular basis. Could that be because the Saudis really do not like that presence? Is it possible—just possible—that a *reduced* American military presence in the Middle East might serve American interests better than the current large footprint?

Even if the most compelling U.S. vital interest is in secure access to Middle Eastern oil, this does not mean that the shale revolution preordains a shift in American policy away from such a large degree of direct, occasionally military involvement in the region. If the United States does not currently need that petroleum, it may in the future, and so may its allies. What a reduction in dependence caused by the availability of shale oil and gas does do, however, is to make it possible to contemplate different policy positions and force postures. These, in turn, offer some fascinating possibilities.

Although it is rarely discussed in this direction, the reduction of U.S. dependency on Saudi oil leaves the Saudis in a particular national bind. The Saudis have played a leading geopolitical role in the region not because of their traditional military power or because people "like" the Saudis. Saudi power has derived from the need for its oil and what it could buy them. The way they have wielded the oil weapon has not endeared them to anyone except hard-line anti-Shiites.

A reduction in the salience of the oil "weapon" thus leaves the Saudis potentially very vulnerable, and they know it. An interesting manifestation of this self-awareness appears in a 2015 edition of *The Atlantic* featuring a look at the Saudi plan to build a solar power program. Its ironical that the work-aversive Saudis have mounted an international effort to bring together scientists and technologists from other countries to build this initiative rather than doing it by themselves.

Some Geopolitical Consequences of a Reduced Presence

A reduction in U.S. physical commitment arising from a lessened need for regional oil would address one of the two apparent reasons for a large and continuing American presence in the area. If the United States no longer needs personally to secure access to Middle Eastern oil because it has enough of its own, what does this mean for the military component of American policy in the region?

The oil mandate has two physical manifestations. One of these is freedom of the high seas in the Persian Gulf that guarantees the unfettered ability of oil tankers to traverse the Gulf and out into the Indian Ocean without fear of interference. Protection of the Gulf itself has been the province of the U.S. Navy, which has nervously assigned carrier-based battle groups there for decades. These flotillas serve the dual purposes of controlling both the Gulf itself and of being a mobile platform for inserting carrier-based airpower into the region. Because the Gulf is a fairly narrow body of water (125 miles across at its narrowest point) and exit from it requires traversing a classic naval choke point, the Straits of Hormuz, this mandate extends to assuring that countries onto whose shores the Gulf washes do not seek to interfere with that transit (effectively, Iran).

If the United States no longer buys oil from the Persian Gulf, two things occur. One is that oil shipped from the Gulf no longer heads to American destinations, and Gulf oil producers will have to develop relationships with other countries, both to buy their oil and to get it to market. At the same time, the question of freedom of the high seas takes on a somewhat more abstract, less compelling importance to the United States, since it is no longer our oil that might be imperiled.

The question of changed markets symbolically can be thought of in terms of which way tankers turn when they exit the Gulf. Going back to the days when commerce in Middle Eastern oil was controlled by the seven sisters, oil tankers made a right-hand turn out of the Gulf, heading west toward European and North American markets, either via the Suez Canal or around the Cape of Good Hope at the southern tip of Africa. Ships bound for the United States used to dominate this traffic, but American-bound ocean traffic has decreased as energy conservation and shale production have reduced American needs. If shale mining surmounts environmental barriers and continues to expand, that traffic will further diminish, and almost all the traffic will be headed toward Europe. This could mean that European navies will have to bear increased responsibility for ensuring the safety of Gulf-originating supplies to their markets.

If the Gulf no longer provides much of the petroleum needs of the United States, countries like Saudi Arabia will need to nurture other markets. Fortunately for them, in Asia, rising powers like China and India and established but energy-poor powers like Japan provide ready markets for the petroleum. These markets are all east of the Gulf and require a left turn out of the Gulf for the tankers. They also represent a whole new set of potential barriers to free transit. With the exception of petroleum heading for India, almost all the markets requiring shipping petroleum products through the Straits of Malacca and even possibly the South China Sea, both contested strategic locations in which the Japanese and Chinese are both active.

The United States retains some residual interest in both redirections. The American fleet is active in the South Atlantic and has an important interest in European access to Persian Gulf oil, since an interruption could force American allies to rely even more on Russian sources until they can bring their own shale deposits into production (which the United States will doubtlessly assist with—for a price). Likewise, the U.S. Navy has always been active in the west Pacific and, to a lesser degree, in the areas surrounding the Straits of Malacca. The growing Chinese navy poses a major competitor in the Pacific, and Chinese air forces can operate over the Straits of Malacca.

The direction the oil tankers turn is relevant to the question of *how* important the transit routes are to the United States if it does not personally rely on Gulf oil, and this question is particularly germane to patrolling the Gulf itself. It is no particular secret that the U.S. Navy does not particularly like having to keep a carrier battle group (or sometimes two) in the Gulf. U.S. naval doctrine is based upon the composition and spacing of battle groups, with the aircraft carrier as its centerpiece to be protected. Support ships are arrayed around the carrier to protect it from attack, and the ideal swath of water that the battle group should occupy to protect the carrier is over 700 miles of open water, thereby maximizing the likelihood that incoming attacks against the carrier can be deflected. The Gulf is much too narrow for implementing this strategy, and the problem is made worse because a carrier in the Gulf is at least theoretically vulnerable to attack from the surrounding littoral—Iranian cruise missiles, for instance. The flip side of this is that the naval air assets on the carriers give the navy a combat role in the modern world which it otherwise largely lacks. There are, after all, no other navies in the world in which to engage in classic naval warfare.

A drastic reduction in American-bound oil flowing out of the Persian Gulf could logically raise the question about what vital American interest is served by keeping a dominant naval presence there. If the answer is negative, the freedom of the high seas question revolves around who might supplant the United States as the guarantor of that condition. The country that would almost certainly perceive the greatest interest in supplanting the United States is China. China has a growing navy of its own, it is a regional power, and it has a claim to access to Middle Eastern oil (how great that need is depending partially on the disposition of the oil reserves under the South China Sea).

One possible outcome of an American naval reduction in the Persian Gulf would be to turn what has been effectively an American "lake" into a Chinese lake. Most Americans and other Westerners would recoil at this prospect, because of the leverage it would give the Chinese over global energy resources. It is always possible that the West (including the United States) might have a future need to return to the Gulf for energy, and China might not be hospitable to that return if it were in control of the Gulf. The question is how likely a Chinese incursion would be and how much effort the United States should undertake to avoid it. These are questions that did not arise when the United States depended heavily on Persian Gulf oil; they become concerns as that dependence declines, with implications for the burdens and responsibilities the United States retains for an area the vitality of which to American interests has shrunk.

The other reason for the American military presence is the terrorist threat. It is indirectly connected to the question of oil in the sense that a number of oil-producing states have interests in the terrorist problem. Saudi Arabia is the most obvious example, although its interest is ambivalent. Officially, the Saudi government deplores the destabilizing impact of the terrorists, especially in places like Yemen that border on the kingdom. At the same time, the state religion of Saudi Arabia is Wahhabism, a fundamentalist interpretation of Sunnism not dissimilar to the doctrine propounded by IS. It is a scarcely denied fact that a number of oil-rich Saudis contribute to both IS and AQ. Osama bin Laden, the founder of AQ, was a Saudi, and 17 of the 9/11 bombers were Saudis. The Saudis thus walk a terrorism tightrope, and the United States nervously watches in fear that they may fall off.

Terrorism is an American interest—argued as vital—because religious terrorists regularly threaten the United States, and all the major terrorist groups emanate from the Islamic world, and especially the Middle East. This line of concern has nothing conceptually to do with petroleum, but there is an indirect connection that is tied to petroleum. That commonality is that the oil connection created the sustained military obligation. It is accurate and arguably causally true that most of America's military involvements—and woes—are artifacts of the maintenance of visible American force in the region.

Is it possible that a major reason for the levels of anti-Americanism in the Middle East do not arise from some atavistic hatred for Americans (George W. Bush's famous "they hate our freedom") but instead because what they hate is our physical presence? The American military has been very active in the Middle East, after all, and while one can argue that the American presence has in balance been for the good, the actions that the United States has taken have not all uniformly benefited everyone. Even if this country inadvertently helped bankroll the creation of Al-Qaeda, it opposed this creation consistently. It was U.S. insistence that got AQ evicted from Sudan, and the United States did pressure the Afghans to throw AQ out or turn them over to the Americans. IS anti-Americanism has become much stronger since American air forces began attacking and killing IS fighters. Is it any wonder that either group might want to fight back against us?

The shale revolution changes the structure of American vital interests in the Middle East and thus creates the possibility of a different kind and quality of dialog about what American policy in that region can or should be. Given the centrality of the Middle East in operational foreign, and especially national security, policy in the contemporary world, such a dialog is not a bad idea. Despite other objections one can raise to the shale revolution, opening that possibility is a positive thing.

BIBLIOGRAPHY

Ball, Jeffrey. "Why the Saudis Are Going Solar." *The Atlantic* 116, 1 (July/August 2015), 72–80.

Central Intelligence Agency. *CIA World Factbook 2015.* Washington, DC: Central Intelligence Agency, 2015.

Fleischman, Stephen E. "Too Valuable to Burn." *Common dReams Newsletter* (online), November 29, 2005.

Faulkner, Chris. *The Fracking Truth: America's Energy Revolution: The Inside, Untold Story.* London, UK: Platform Press, 2014.

Fukuyama, Francis. *The End of History and the Last Man.* New York: Free Press, 1992.

Gold, Russell. *The Boom: How Fracking Ignited the American Energy Revolution and Changed the World.* New York: Simon and Schuster, 2014.

Graves, John. *Fracking: America's Alternative Energy Revolution.* Asheville, NC: Safe Harbor, 2013.

Heinberg, Richard. *Snake Oil: How Fracking's False Promise of Plenty Imperils Our Futue.* Santa Rose, CA: Post-Carbon Institute, 2013.

International Energy Agency. *World Energy Outlook 2012.* Paris: International Energy Agency, 2012.

King, George E. "Hydraulic Fracturing 101." Society of Petroleum Engineers, Paper 152596, 2012 (reprinted by Earthworks online, 2015).

Krauthammer, Charles. "The Unipolar Moment." *Foreign Affairs* 70, 1 (Winter 1990/1), 23–33.

Maugeri, Leonardo. "Two Cheers for Expensive Oil." *Foreign Affairs* 85, 2 (March/ April 2006), 149–160.

Mufson, Steven. "Here's the Grassroots Political Story behind the New York Fracking Ban." *Washington Post* (online). December 18, 2014.

"Oil and Gas Drilling Triggers Manmade Earthquakes in Eight States, USGS Finds." *Associated Press in Los Angeles (online)*, April 23, 2015.

Prud'homme, Alex. *Hydrofracking: What Everyone Needs to Know.* Oxford, UK: Oxford University Press, 2013.

Rao, Vikram. *Shale Gas: The Promise and the Peril.* London, UK: RTI Press, 2013.

Roberts, Paul. "The Seven Myths of Energy Independence." *Mother Jones* 33, 3 (June 2008), 31–37.

Snow, Donald M. *National Security for a New Era*, 5th edition. New York: Pearson, 2014.

———. *What after Iraq?* New York: Longman, 2008.

United States Energy Information Agency (Department of Energy). *Annual energy Outlook 2013.* Washington, DC: Energy Information Agency, 2013.

Warrick, Joby. "Obama Administration Tightens Federal Rules on Oil and Gas Fracking." *Washington Post* (online). March 20, 2015.

"World Fossil Fuel Reserves." *The World Almanac and Book of Facts, 2015.* New York: World Almanac Books, 2015.

Part III

THE UNITED STATES
AND THE MIDDLE EAST

Chapter 5

The Vexatious Middle East

There is no question that the Middle East is a mess, and this observation permeates the analysis in this book. The politics of most of its countries are unstable and anachronistic by Western standards, and many of the region's countries have little reason to exist within the borders they occupy. Fratricidal sectarian violence is rampant and provides the cause of a good deal of the slaughter that seems a regular part of the landscape. One is reminded of the Kingston Trio's 1950s hit, "The Merry Minuet," where the narrator declares, "And we don't like anybody very much."

As a number of internal and external observers are coming to agree, the situation in the Islamic Middle East is not dissimilar to the religious chaos and bloodletting in Europe three centuries ago. Outsiders could not solve those problems then, and there is no reason to believe we can do any better now. But we keep on trying—and failing.

America's need for oil caused us to get dragged into this situation that we did not really understand, and that same oil may allow us to slide off the hook. Petro-politics was compelling until recent events like the shale revolution, and these events and dynamics are changing the relations considerably. We needed the Middle East and its oil before. We need both a lot less today. As a result, we can begin to think about national security policy alternatives we could not have considered before.

Understanding the pattern and trajectory of change in U.S. policy is a two-step process. The first step is identifying and analyzing basic underlying regional dynamics that permeate the Middle East conflict from a regional perspective and which adds measurably to both the intractability of situations and the impossibility of solving them. Historically, the United States' record of analyzing regional conflicts at this level of analysis has been particularly abysmal. The second problem has been analyzing and responding to individual manifestations of broader conflicts in specific places. The latter is really two problems: we have spent less than an adequate amount of time understanding individual places—Iraq, for instance—and we tend to particularize events that are actually parts of broader phenomena. There is little indication, for instance, that many in the U.S. government saw Iraq as part of the Sunni-Shia divide rather than as sui generis.

This introduction suggests what follows. Chapter 5 looks at general structural problems and how they apply to specific problems, notably IS. Chapter 6 presents an overview of patterns of U.S. policy in the Middle East, and Chapter 7 looks at some of the specific problems and solutions—in effect applying distinctions made in this chapter to other aspects of the Middle East conflict identified in Chapter 7.

A COMPLEX PROBLEM

The Middle East seems to be in a constant crisis state, with multiple violent conflicts going on in different locations with different competitors over different issues. In March 2015, for instance, a partial list would include Syria, Iraq, Tunisia, Libya, and Yemen. Trying to find common threads that would help define what Middle East conflicts are about and what can be done to influence them is very frustrating, because of their idiosyncratic nature. The Middle East is confusing, and understanding its problems is difficult and, in some cases, futile. That recognition, for better or worse, has not kept American policy makers from dabbling extensively in the briar patch of Middle Eastern violent politics. It probably should.

In March 2015, Yemen effectively blew up. That fact was not particularly unusual either for a country in the region or for Yemen. In some ways, Yemen symbolizes the travails of the entire region. It is, for instance, an artificial country that was cobbled together in 1990 from two competing regions: Yemen (Sana) to the west and north along the coast of the Red Sea and Yemen (Aden), a British colony that forms the southern end of the Arabian Peninsula. The marriage between the two areas was never natural or complete; the divisions that preexisted merger never went away and are now the bases of violence. It is not an unfamiliar phenomenon in the region.

That is, of course, not all. A desperately poor piece of land at the southern and western extremities of the Arabian Peninsula, poverty alone assured its isolation and its status as a basically failed or failing state. Its importance in the world was mostly geographic, since it juts into the naval choke point of the Bad al-Mandeb, a strategic point connecting the Red Sea to the Straits of Aden and the Arabian Sea, through which oil tankers using the Suez Canal must pass. It also shares a long border with Saudi Arabia.

Governance of Yemen has always been problematical. Rural tribes have always resisted control and influence from the capital of Sana, with divisions along both tribal and religious grounds. About 65 percent of the population of 26 million (2013 estimates in the *CIA World Factbook*) are Sunni, with the rest mostly Shiite. The largest and most activist Shiite group is the Hauthis, who formed the majority in northwest Yemen Sana, and were not heavily represented after independence and merger occurred. They overthrew the government in Sana in 2015, and helped ignite the ongoing chaos. Yemen also became the headquarters for one AQ spinoff, Al-Qaeda on the Arabian Peninsula (AQAP). More recently, IS joined the mix. The government has been too weak to effectively counter the AQAP, which in turn has created an American interest and drone campaign in the harsh Yemeni countryside. The major accomplishment of that campaign was to kill American-born AQ leader Anwar al-Awlaki in 2012. IS and AQAP both compete for leadership of the Sunni majority and occasionally talk about cooperation. Neither, quite rightly, really trusts the other.

The Yemeni economy is weak, with a per capita GDP of about $2,500, ranked 187th in 2013. Yemen is hardly a major oil-producing country, but 25 percent of its GDP is derived from oil, as is 63 percent of governmental revenue. By virtually any measure, Yemen is a failed country.

What gives Yemen its prominence in the mid-2010s is terrorism and its status as a surrogate battleground between Sunnis and Shiites. Amid anarchy in Sana, the Saudis, who back the majority Sunnis, attacked in late March 2015 to weaken the Hauthis, who in turn are backed by Shiite Iran. AQAP remains in control of a good bit of the forbidding hinterlands, and as a Sunni-based group, it is at odds with the Hauthis. Reports of IS activity in the country only add to the volatility, both between IS and AQAP and between Sunni and Shia.

How extensive the "battle" over Yemen will become remains to be seen. In late March 2015, Saudi Arabia was hobbling together a coalition of like-minded (i.e., conservative, fundamentalist Sunni) states to oppose the Hauthi incursion, and Saudi bombing raides and a possible Saudi-led ground incursion were possible not out of the question. This possibility in turn caused rumblings in Iran of more overt assistance to their Shiite brethren in Yemen. The crisis had the potential of leading to a broader Sunni-Shiite conflict in the region, with the Saudis and Iranians toe to toe. This dynamic, also present in the IS-controlled parts of Iraq and Syria, volatility is endemic to regional conflicts but generally peters out. The United States has largely limited its role to decrying violence on both sides.

What Yemen does is illustrate the complexity and intransigence of Middle Eastern problems and the frustration of trying to deal with them. The problems that fester in the Yemen have been ongoing for a long time, dating back well before the establishment of Islam in the seventh century. The basis of conflict is very old and its bases are cross-cutting along both ethnic and religious lines. It is not clear what, if any, actions outsiders could take to affect the problems positively, and American investment in trying to rid the country of AQAP continues to be frustrated. Can the United States do anything about the situation? It is not clear.

Middle Eastern conflicts are made complicated by the complex of factors that can come together in any particular situation. There are at least four of these that can be identified for introductory purposes. One or more of these are present in almost all situations, but generally in a unique enough way to make generalization perilous. The list is not definitive, but it does serve as a kind of a checklist when one of the inevitable conflicts flares in the region. Two of the criteria are about characteristics of the region (and the states in it), and two are about American reactions to particular areas and crises. In terms of a guideline for the likelihood of a reasoned and reasonable response to crisis, each is important. The more concerns arising from the four is present in any given situation, the more cautionary the prospects are for a successful American involvement and the more suspicion one should show toward an American effort to "solve" a problem the principals apparently cannot solve.

The first factor is *political and nationalistic.* The simple fact is that almost all the countries of the Middle East are artificial states, and the bases of their artificiality makes them politically dysfunctional, thereby creating the seedbed in which conflict and violence can emerge. The map of the region is ill-defined, and is largely the result of European finagling as they retreated from empire. Most of the region does not break down into natural national units, because primary political loyalties are so often attached to smaller tribal or clan affiliations, rather than an attachment to a modern state. In most cases, it is probably impossible to draw "natural" political boundaries for states (boundaries in which essentially all people were loyal to the same political authority and in which essentially everyone holding that affiliation were part) without extreme Balkanization. Politics and states do not align very well. This problem is not so great in a few places that have long histories of existence. Iran and Egypt represent two of the world's oldest civilizations, as does Turkey, and there is some historic continuity in North Africa.

The problem is most serious in the historic Levant area and the Arabian Peninsula. Three of the ongoing hot spots exemplify this dynamic. Iraq is an absolutely artificial state, with loyalties based on both tribal and religious differentiations. These differences have impeded the development of any kind of strong Iraqi nationalism among large segments of the population and have led many analysts to conclude that Iraq will eventually balkanize into at least three states. Syria, the other site of the struggle with IS featured in the next section, is similarly a state with a number of tribal groups that vie for control over the state. In Syria, the minority Alawite tribe has ruled for nearly half a century, and the minority Sunnis from Anbar Province in Iraq ruled that country until the United States overthrew their leader, Saddam Hussein, in 2003. The civil contest in Yemen has tribesmen from former Northern Yemen (Sana) pitted against tribes from former Southern Yemen (Aden).

The result is the second factor, the existence of *cross-cutting cleavages* among people and groups within many regional states. As suggested immediately above, these sources of division and enmity have several bases. One of these is clearly religious and is reflected in the rivalry between Sunnis and Shiites that is the source of conflict in most countries and prominently features in the most contentious situations. The poles of leadership in this source of conflict are Sunni Saudi Arabia, which bankrolls Sunni movements, including terrorist organizations that are assisted financially by rich Saudi citizens, and Shiite Iran, which bankrolls Shiite minorities and terrorist groups in a variety of regional states. The current focus of this source of conflict is Yemen, where the Shiite Hauthis (from the North) compete with Iranian assistance against the Sunni Southerners who are supported by Saudi Arabia. This situation is complicated in Yemen by the rivalry between and mischief caused by both AQAP and IS, both of which are Sunni and neither of which is openly embraced by the Saudis.

Religious cleavage is often reflected in and accentuated by ethnic differences. The basic split is between Arabs and non-Arabs. Those who claim to be Arabs believe themselves to be superior to others because of their common heritage with the Prophet. The chief rivals of the Arabs are the Persians of Iran, who are Semitic and descended from people indigenous to the Asian subcontinent. Other ethnic minorities are also present, notably the Kurds in recent regional instability. Being Arab or non-Arab often overlays more basic tribal differences that form more basic loyalties. In places like Afghanistan, tribal loyalties are so overwhelming that the historic form of "national" governance was a series of tribal meetings (*loyo girgas*) where tribal leaders met and hammered out solutions to common problems that preserved their autonomy. Because of their fundamental distrust of one another, however, one of the matters they regularly sought to agree upon was how to keep the central government weak enough that it did not pose a direct threat to any of them by allowing too much power to be achieved by any group.

This cleavage is also manifested in both economic and political ways. Economically, there are essentially two kinds of state in the Middle East: the wealthy and the poor. The basic difference between the two categories is the possession of oil reserves under their soil. The conditions of the two categories of state is often quite stark and creates a sense of dependency of the poor states on the rich, who dole out what amounts to charity to the poor. Inevitably, this relationship is strained and resented by the poor states.

Politically, the differentiation is between the so-called "moderate" Islamic states and the "conservative" states. In terms of form of government, the difference is a matter of degree. There are no full-blown political democracies in the region except in Israel, only relative degrees of authoritarian rule. The moderate states tend to be less oppressive, less sectarian, and relatively more tolerant of the positions of other groups within their societies. Jordan (despite being a monarchy) and Lebanon are examples. The more conservative states tend to be more oppressive, more sectarian (including fundamentalist) and less tolerant of the rights of other groups. Many are sectarian monarchies or the equivalent. Saudi Arabia and several of the other Gulf states, as well as revolutionary Iran, fall into this category. There are also hybrids: Jordan is a monarchy but is otherwise quite progressive by regional standards, whereas Egypt is fairly secular but has generally had governments that are more oppressive than one might expect in what is generally thought of as a progressive state by regional standards.

All of these sources of differentiation are distinctive within and among the various states of the Middle East, and each characteristic individually and in various combinations creates different obstacles both to a coherent general policy toward the Middle East and its individual states. This leads to a third factor: the degree of American understanding of the situations when, as is so often the case, circumstances deteriorate to violence and the need for some American policy response seems to be dictated. It has become common for American analysts—notably the hard men—to declare an American interest in virtually every situation in the region, usually without specifying what the interest is and the degree of effort that should be expended to realize it. All too often, suggested policy responses tend to be driven by the situations (which usually deteriorate) and not by American interests. Most notably, some form of American military activism generally is suggested early on, regardless of whether the United States has sufficiently important interests to justify an American military response. One way to do this is simply to declare that interests exist but not to specify what they are. A perusal of American-proposed responses to the 2015 chaos in Yemen offers a pretty good depiction of this phenomenon.

The problem is that American understanding and expertise tend to be limited and shallow in terms of dealing with these problems. The reasons are real and understandable enough. Unlike some of the European powers, the United States has only been involved in the Middle East in any systematic way since the post–World War II period. Prior to that, the U.S. perception of interest was in what lay below the Middle East (the oil), not in what was on or above the surface (the people and their enormous problems). As a result, the United States did not develop or accumulate a large store of expertise or experts on the Middle East region in the first half of the twentieth century, and during the second half, the Cold War dictated that the emphasis would be on Russian or Chinese studies, not the Middle East. Most universities offered majors in Russian language and Soviet affairs, for instance, but there was very little on Arabic language or Middle Eastern history, culture, or politics. The consequence was that there was a very small number of experts in the region to be parsed out to diplomatic or national security concerns, and the government was forced to rely on immigrants from the region, most of whose knowledge was to some extent influenced by their particular backgrounds, a subtlety that was not always realized by American officials.

Some of the results are familiar. Leading up to and after the 9/11 terrorist attacks, the U.S. government made a concerted effort to intercept communications among Al-Qaeda figures. They were quite successful in gathering this information clandestinely through electronic means, but there was a catch. Almost all the communications were in Arabic, and the U.S. government did not have enough Arabic speakers to translate the traffic received. In a kind of Catch-22, they had difficulty reaching out to the Arabic-speaking community in the country, because much of the community was viewed as security risks (whether they were or not) and were precluded from this process. When the Bush administration began to contemplate invading Iraq, one of its sources of political advice was Dr. Ahmad Chalabi, an Iraqi expatriate who hoped to use the invasion to improve his goal of becoming the successor to Saddam Hussein and who was a convicted felon in Jordan.

This thinness of expertise has not chastened policy makers from reaching conclusions on how to deal with what are generally extraordinarily complex, nuanced situations in Middle East countries. Given the historical insignificance of the area in U.S. policy, it is not surprising or inexcusable that the United States would not have a deep expertise pool on the Middle East and individual countries of the region. There is a small base of true experts in the government, but they are mainly Foreign Service officers within the State Department, and their advice is often not solicited or heeded by those with a predilection toward military solution to problems. What is inexcusable is that American officials in both the executive and legislative branches of government ignore the limits that exist, propound policy positions that are based on misperceptions or ignorance, and end up sending the United States into situations where it would not be involved if it had and acted upon better understanding of regional dynamics. Nowhere is this faulty dynamic more evident than in proposed U.S. actions in the contest with the Islamic State in Iraq and Syria.

IS: THE PERFECT STORM

The existence and nefarious activities of the Islamic State (IS) became a central obsession of the U.S. national security policy community in 2014, as IS fighters emerged from a welter of opposition groups to the regime of President Bashar al-Assad of Syria and went on a rampage of highly publicized, exceedingly cruel violence both in Syria and neighboring Iraq, all in the name of establishing a new Caliphate (successor) to the reign of the Prophet Muhammad in the seventh century. At first blush, its activities did not seem central to American interests in the world and seemed simply the most recent demonstration of the barbarity of a region that demonstrates a great deal of inhumanity to its fellow men. When IS burst onto the world public screen, the American policy community (and virtually everyone else) had very little idea what this complex, bewildering, confusing (and in some cases confused) movement was all about. What Americans thought they knew was that IS by whatever name (also known as the Islamic State of Iraq and Syria—ISIS— and the Islamic State in the Levant—ISIL) is bad and that it poses a threat to the United States. Beyond that, knowledge and agreement tend to fade.

The problem is that IS (the designation it chose for itself in 2014) is a microcosm of the Middle East region. It is a religious movement in a part of the world where religious disagreement is somehow central to almost all conflict. It is a political movement that seeks to rearrange the terribly imperfect boundaries of the Middle East in order to create the caliphate. Its means is a conquest of territories that are unhappy parts of Syria and Iraq. It is also a terrorist organization that revels in the hideous murder of large numbers of people that it considers apostates and thus its enemy. In Max Boot's phrase, it "functions both as a government and as a sectarian killing machine." Its original enemies and victims were mostly within the region. When the United States became interested in defeating it, the Americans were added to the enemies list.

Now that the United States has engaged itself in the anti-IS movement, the organization presents two different, and possibly contradictory and unachievable, challenges to U.S. policy makers. First and originally, it is an adjunct of the Syrian civil war, in which the United States has been a concerned party since that conflict broke out in 2011 as a loose part of the Arab Spring. Second, IS has become a problem in and of itself, since it menaces both Syria and Iraq and makes threatening, antagonistic gestures toward the United States, including overtures to American youths to join the organization, be trained by it, and even to return to American soil to carry out its terrorist bidding.

Was American involvement in this regional brouhaha a natural or inevitable adjunct of U.S. foreign policy? The current structure of the conflict from an American viewpoint (the U.S. dedication to destroying IS) was essentially an accident of American involvement in the Syrian civil war, of which IS was part of the resistance. The American role in Syria has been oblique, limited to condemnation of the Syrian regime and calling for its removal, demands that the Syrians end atrocities (especially the use of chemical weapons) against its own citizens, and the imposition of sanctions against the Syrians. Much of this base was and is humanitarian, a reaction to atrocities that almost certainly reach the level of war crimes and which apply equally to both the Assad regime and to Abu Bakr al-Baghdadi (the self-proclaimed IS caliph). A strong international case can be made for efforts to end the war crimes and to bring the perpetrators within Syria and IS to justice at the International Criminal Court (ICC). Decision makers—and certainly the hard men in Washington and other capitals—are seldom motivated by such concerns, which they tend to view as "soft" and naïve. IS is clearly a regional and arguably a global problem.

The question is why it is an *American* problem. Beyond the fact that the United States, as the leader of the air campaign against IS in Iraq, has killed a significant number of IS members, it is not clear the United States should be a particular concern to those who want to establish a caliphate other than in retaliation for American actions against it. The caliphate is not going to extend to Europe or North America (despite the End of Days prophecy to which dedicated IS members subscribe). Others in the region who are potentially victims and part of an expanding caliphate have every reason to oppose the religious fanatics who would lead the Islamic world back fourteen or more centuries in time, but their efforts to date have been less than all-out. Why? What does that mean for the United States? Understanding the dynamics requires looking first at the nature of IS and then at American interests and options in opposing it.

IS as a Unique Phenomenon

Part of the difficulty of dealing with IS arises from the fact that it is a unique organization that poses both a unique problem and challenge. There are organizations and movements that have had all the characteristics of IS, but what makes the organization unique is that it is the first to combine all of its attributes. It has become conventional to describe IS as a terrorist organization, and it is. But it is also much more. As Audrey Kurth Cronin sums it, "IS is not really a terrorist group at all. . . . If IS is purely and simply anything, it is a pseudo-state led by a conventional army." Even that description by one of America's leading civilian terrorism experts only gets at a part of what IS represents. Understanding its nature is crucial to portraying what kind of threat it poses to the region and the United States.

Although the list is probably arbitrary and arguably incomplete, there are seven characteristics of IS that cumulatively capture its nature, its uniqueness, and why it has been so difficult doing anything decisive about it. Other problematical organizations have displayed some of these characteristics, and each of the characteristics is associated with some national security threat. What distinguishes IS and baffles many Western decision makers is that the Islamic State displays all of them. This makes it sui generis.

The first characteristic of IS is that it is indeed a *terrorist organization*, in at least two senses of the term. It had its origins as the terrorist group Al-Qaeda in Iraq (AQI), and it clearly uses acts of terror as a prominent part of its campaign against its many (and often richly earned) enemies. The origin of the organization was as an affiliate of bin Laden's parent AQ organization, organized among displaced and out-of-power Sunnis in Iraq by a Jordanian freedom fighter from the Afghan mujahidin named Abu Musab al-Zarqawi. AQI operated mostly in the Sunni areas of the country after the Sunni government of Saddam Hussein was overthrown. They were eclipsed when an American bombing raid killed al-Zarqawi in 2006 and by the Anbar Awakening of 2007, when Sunni tribesmen were convinced by the Americans (some argue essentially bribed) to turn against the terrorists. At that point, AQI essentially went dormant, not reemerging in public view until 2012 as part of the Sunni resistance groups to the Syrian regime. Much of the coalition of Sunni opponents had been fragmented, disorganized, and mutually antagonistic, and the remaining leadership of AQI was better organized and had a more coherent message than many of them. As a result, they out recruited the other opposition groups and became a leading component in the coalition. Along the way, they changed their name to ISIS and broadened their appeal and reached out to potential recruits in the region and elsewhere. From this rising fortune, ISIS was born. It began as a terrorist organization, but it was destined to be much more.

Its terrorist roots are still apparent in many of its actions. The root of the term terrorism is the Latin word *terrere*, which means to frighten, and clearly much of the IS campaign against religious minorities (including Christians) and even what it considers apostate Muslims is designed to terrorize them and other similar groups who might get in their way in the future. The beheadings of captives and the hideous burning alive of a Jordanian pilot were also warnings of what happens to opponents of the Islamic State. The suggestion that IS could engage in attacks in Europe and the United States clearly would be in the form of terrorist attacks.

As a number of terrorist experts (see, for instance, Jessica Stern) have pointed out, the reasons for engaging in these atrocious actions include frightening opponents, dissuading others from opposition, demonstrating potency to believers and followers, providing morale boosts to active members, and as a recruitment device for attracting new members from disaffected populations. This multiplicity of benefits likely guarantees that IS will not abandon terrorism as part of its arsenal. Ironically, if its opponents succeed in weakening the organization, their recourse to terrorist actions might actually increase, since terrorism is historically the tactic of the weak, organizations and causes that cannot compete successfully by any other means.

This terrorist heritage and continuing recourse to terrorist actions colors and distorts the way the West, including the United States, views the organization. Certainly, part of the problem IS poses arises from its terrorist aspects: it is impossible to imagine, for instance, that IS could ever pose more than a limited terrorist threat to Americans on U.S. soil, for instance. Likewise, the major reason IS apparently is trying to recruit young members into its ranks is to train and return them to carry out terrorist attacks. Countering these actions is important national security business, but it is not conceptually adequate to form the basis for a comprehensive strategy against IS, since the IS is so many things in addition to being a terrorist organization.

The second characteristic that IS possesses is that of a *criminal organization*. By definition, of course, terrorist organizations are criminal in nature, because terrorist actions break laws (e.g., murder, property destruction) in the pursuit of their goals. Different terrorist movements have broader terrorist portfolios, such as the kidnapping campaigns of Boko Haram in Nigeria or random violence to destroy tourism in Bali, but all terrorist groups break laws.

Two things stand out about the criminal activities of IS. The first is its systematic nature and the purposes for which it engages in crime. In many ways, crime is an organic part of the very fabric of the organization, because it is the way that it finances itself. As an example, Peter Von Drehle points out, "its armies are supplied from captured arsenals and paid from money from looted banks." Crime bankrolls the IS and gives them an expanded financial independence that other groups have not had in the past. This allows IS to have a much more ambitious agenda than other groups have had. It also means that IS must be an ever-expanding phenomenon that finds new places it can effectively loot. An IS that can steal the spoils of war remains a potent force; an IS that is static or in retreat is confined to the territory it has already denuded. It becomes more vulnerable to being defeated if it can be contained or shrunk in territorial terms.

Criminality is a main element of IS success, but it is not its only financial base. IS has multiple sources of funding, and they cumulatively define its third characteristic, which is its *affluence*. The multiplicity of sources from which IS can draw for funding makes it much more independent of outside assistance than other terrorist-based organizations and also eliminates some of the traditional levers that are used to strangle and shrink or destroy the ability of such organizations to thrive. The economic instrument of power simply does not have the potency to coerce the IS that governments like the United States might like to wield as an alternative to using their military forces to defeat the IS.

Three broad sources of wealth have been particularly evident in supporting and enriching the IS. It has been possible to attack, and to some extent, to dry up two of these sources, but not the third. Until or unless some method is found to impoverish the IS to the point that it can no longer engage in large-scale military operations, it will remain a force and a problem. Traditional means of drying up its revenues have not succeeded; new variants of the instrument of power must be found.

The first source of funding has been revenue from the small oil industry in parts of Syria that are occupied by IS forces. Early on in their campaign of conquest and territorial occupation, the IS took over and began to operate a trade in low-quality fuels (e.g., gasoline, heating oil) from Syrian sources that it was able to transport clandestinely and illegally across a loosely enforced Turkish boundary, where it was sold to Turks. This practice was lucrative but vulnerable to counteraction, which took two forms. One of these was a campaign of aerial bombardment against refining facilities and transportation routes and carriers (trucks) that greatly reduced production and interrupted the commerce in what product there was. The other was bringing pressure on Turkey to increase its border patrolling and control, thereby reducing the flow of that oil that survived destruction to Turkish markets. The result of these efforts has been essentially to shut down the sale of oil products as a meaningful contributor to the IS war chest. Unfortunately, IS has been able to replace its oil revenues with funds from other sources.

The second, and among the most controversial, sources, has been from private contributions from other Muslims. The Muslims who are most likely to support IS are those who are sympathetic to the IS movement on religious grounds. Sunnism is the religious orientation of the IS, and more specifically, IS propounds a form of fundamentalist Sunni faith that is not dissimilar to Wahhabism, which is the state religion of Saudi Arabia and is widely adhered to by residents of a number of the Gulf monarchies. The controversy arises because these sources are in countries that have close ties to the United States—economically through the sale of oil and militarily in terms of U.S. supply of military equipment and guarantees of their security.

The United States wants the Saudis and others to cut off these private donations, of course, and has brought pressure to bear on the Saudi government to rein in the giving by its citizens. The Saudi monarchy itself is sympathetic to American demands and understands the logic that if the Saudis expect American help in maintaining their security, they need to reciprocate in their opposition to American enemies. This reciprocity is particularly strong given that Saudi Arabia and Iran may be headed toward a regional confrontation based on faith that has the caliphate as a major theater and in which the Saudis on their own are severely disadvantaged.

The Saudis are, however, reluctant to rein in their Wahhabist citizens. The monarchy rests on an agreement between the Wahhabis and the House of Saud that has lasted for over a century, the essence of which is that the Wahhabis will support the Saudi monarchy in return for the elevation of Wahhabism to being the state religion of the kingdom. The monarchy is reluctant to confront the fundamentalists frontally for fear of breaking the bond. Domestically, this is manifested in very slow and sporadic expansion of human rights. It is also evident in the reluctance of the government to come down as hard as the Americans would like on deep-pocketed Wahhabis supporting the IS. The United States recognizes this pressure on the regime, but it still results in an inconsistency in policy: the Saudis support the United States and its enemies in the conflict with IS. Some progress has been on reducing the flow of private funding to IS, but it has not been eliminated. The Saudis must realize that if they really need American help again, as they did when Saddam Hussein stood menacingly on their border from occupied Kuwaiti soil in 1990, their pleas may be compromised by their lack of enthusiastic support for the United States in the IS crisis.

Receipts from criminal activities constitute the third, and most lucrative, funding base for IS. The sources of ill-gotten gain are numerous. They include a variety of criminal activities from a number of sources. Especially in its early campaigns in Iraq, for instance, much of the purloined military equipment it used was American weaponry abandoned by the fleeing Iraqi Army. IS routinely "liberates" all the money from banks in towns that it conquers. The organization also acts as an extortionist, charging what amounts to protection fees to shopkeepers in occupied areas and converting formerly free roads into toll roads for those traversing them. It also acts as a kidnapper, demanding ransom for the release of people it captures as it advances either from their government or relatives. It also, of course, kills some of those it captures for a variety of effects already suggested. It has also engaged in well-publicized lootings of antiquities housed in captured locations, either selling them on the open or clandestine antiquities markets or destroying them if their origin is sufficiently apostate and thus, in their view, barbaric.

The cumulative effect of its criminal activity is to provide a large and reasonably stable source of funding for IS activities. Its size has been estimated at as much as $1 million a day, and it is a steady source for which outside pressures are ineffective. This base in the occupied territories is, however, potentially its Achilles Heel. Part of the IS problem is the nature of the occupied lands which are, in Graeme Wood's term, "mostly uninhabited and poor." This means that IS must expand physically to new territories to extract funds, suggesting that a policy of military containment might work against them. If they are contained and forced to plunder and thus bleed ever drier present areas of occupation, they stand the danger of alienating the populations, largely Sunni like themselves, who have been basically supportive of the Islamic State. Ultimately, this dependence also suggests that if the Islamic State is attacked and dispossessed of the territory it now holds, its most important funding source could be dried up, possibly leading to its shrinkage. Doing so would require a concerted military invasion to drive IS out of its Iraqi and Syrian bastions. It is not clear that other Muslim states have the will or ability to carry out such a military campaign or that Western states—notably the United States—are interested in such a campaign.

The fourth major characteristic of IS is that it is a *religion-based movement.* When it was reborn out of the ashes of AQI, IS, under the charismatic leadership of al-Baghdadi, fashioned itself as part of the fundamentalist religious tradition that is present in both the Sunni and Shiite branches of Islam. The call for religious purification, a return to the purity and virtues of the original rule of the Prophet, has been a recurring theme within Islam, and, as Wood points out, "derives from a coherent and even learned interpretation of Islam." At the heart of this revival is a return to the model of rule of the seventh-century caliphate and a belief in the End of Days, which Wood describes as a "leitmotif of its propaganda."

This interpretation of the Quran is shared by conservative Muslims, and it contains elements of *salafism* (which translates as "pious forefathers" and is often used to justify violence), literal and extreme interpretations and enforcement of *sharia* law (which derives much of its definition of crime and punishment from seventh-century sources in the Quran), asceticism that it shares with the Wahhabis of the Arabian Peninsula, and even the *takfiiri* (which "proclaims people to be apostate because of their sins," according to Wood). The takfiiri doctrine is widely defined by IS and justifies killing members of other religious beliefs and other Muslims who do not agree with its views of pious Islam. This faith represents very much a minority position within Sunni Islam.

Because of the extremely violent behavior associated with the evangelical aspects of *takfiri,* many Westerners have had a difficult time accepting that there is an honest religious element to IS and that its pretensions of aspiration to establishing the caliphate are insincere and callously political. As Wood describes it, "much of what the group does looks nonsensical except in light of the sincere, carefully considered commitment to returning civilization to a seventh-century legal environment and ultimately bringing about the apocalypse." Most Muslims do not share the IS vision, just as most Christians do not embrace similar interpretations about the apocalypse held by some Christian sects. Mainstream Muslims, who are moderate in their beliefs and in literal adherence to the Quran, are equally astounded and appalled at the Islamic State's interpretation but recognize that it does have a base in the Quran and are thus reluctant to denounce it as vigorously as nonbelieving Westerners wish they would.

The fifth characteristic of IS, which flows from the fourth, is its *territorial ambition*. The caliphate is not, after all, an abstract idea, it is a physical place—a state. The stated and often repeated goal of IS is to establish such a state—the caliphate—over unspecified parts of the Levant. Since the caliphate is a physical territory, IS can only succeed if it gains, holds, and administers territory as a sovereign state. This central mandate may be the most starkly distinguishing difference between IS and other terrorist organizations. Terrorist organizations normally lack the wherewithal—size and appeal, most notably—to aspire to controlling territory and exercising governance over that real estate. In effect, they act as violent, renegade interest groups whose purpose is to convince governments to do (or not do) things of which the group approves or disapproves. Taking over an existing state or creating a new one is simply beyond their reach and ambitions.

By declaring the caliphate, IS has gone beyond that level. To some extent, this simply reflects that IS possesses greater coercive resources than other groups have had: creating a new holy state is not necessarily beyond its reach. At the same time, creating and defending a new state carries additional burdens and criteria of success and failure than more modestly defined terrorist groups propound.

One major difference is that possession of a defined territory creates a target for those combating terrorist organizations that are not so easily available against more "conventional" terrorist groups. Rather than trying to take over governments, traditional terrorist groups typically occupy territory in weak countries that lack the resources to evict or suppress but which are also so weak and unstable that they cannot afford to invite outsiders in to evict the unwanted guests. Pakistan and Yemen have been good examples. The advantage this creates is that it means there are no ready, obvious places on which to retaliate without alienating the host government and damaging relations with it.

When IS declares that a piece of Syrian or Iraqi land is now part of the caliphate, the injunction against attacking IS in that territory disappears. In effect, IS has declared that piece of territory fair ground for retaliatory attacks. The problem this creates is that the states whose territory has been annexed to the caliphate may not recognize the annexation, meaning they consider retaliation an act against them. That situation is clearly the case in caliphate-occupied areas of Syria, where the Syrians vehemently oppose United States or other bombing raids in IS-held lands. At the same time, the IS intrusion is an occupation that many indigenous people oppose, and these people may be allies in helping to kick IS out. Thus, retaliation efforts must be very careful not to alienate these potential allies.

The other unique influence that being a territory possessor creates is the standard for success and failure it entails, and this is particularly true for IS. When faced with overwhelming opposition and the imminence of defeat, traditional terrorist organizations historically have simply quit the field and laid low for another day when their opponents become less diligent against them. Ironically, AQI is an example. Having declared their intention to be a sovereign state, however, means that IS cannot abandon its territory without implicitly admitting defeat. This problem is particularly great when the state is a special, religious place. As Wood explains, "If it (IS) loses its grip on its territory in Syria and Iraq, it will cease to be a caliphate. Caliphates cannot exist as underground movements, because territorial authority is a requirement." By fashioning itself as a state with the obligations and structures of a state, the caliphate also is encumbered with all the vulnerabilities of defense that any other state has.

The sixth characteristic of IS has been its *apparent success*, a factor that appears but does not really diminish the burdens of statehood. Particularly in the early going, IS military efforts were spectacularly successful: they drove across eastern Syria into northwestern Iraq, ultimately nearly reaching Baghdad before their progress was halted. A map of IS-controlled territory in the two countries was impressive, incorporating large chunks of both Syria and Iraq into the caliphate. Al-Baghdadi and his associates began to hint at spreading their control into other parts of the Levant, including Jordan and Lebanon but pointedly stopping short of specific threats against the Israeli-occupied West Bank, site of the proposed Palestinian state. Most ominously, IS began to talk about attacks against the United States, thereby spiking interest in the IS "juggernaut."

Some of this success was almost certainly illusory and overblown. The military success of IS forces, which for most of the offensive thrust numbered less than 10,000 fighters, looked good when projected on a map of the region, but when one looked more closely, the successes were not so impressive. Most of the territory was nominally populated by Sunnis who felt they were being liberated from Shiite governments in both states and at least initially saw IS more as liberators than invaders. As Von Drehle puts it, "Al-Baghdadi's forces raced through northwestern Iraq . . . not because they were an unstoppable military force, but because no one wanted to stop them. In city after city, they met seething citizens eager for a champion. It was a cakewalk." The most shocking success came against the much larger and better supplied Iraqi Army, which dissolved in front of the advancing IS drive, usually without firing a shot and abandoning their American equipment as they fled. The problem in this case was the extremely poor quality and morale of the Iraqi forces (and especially its leadership) as much as it was the invincibility of IS. This image of IS as a juggernaut took hold in the United States, and despite reversals in IS fortunes, it is the image that still motivates many of the hard men in the decision process. This is not to dismiss IS as a military threat; it is more precisely an entreaty to understand the nature and extent of the threat—a problem, but not as great as some would maintain.

A number of IS successes remain, although they are shrinking. The Iraqi armed forces have been regenerated under new and more competent leadership and have, along with Kurdish *pesh merga,* managed to push IS back away from Baghdad and partly away from Sunni Anbar Province. A symbol of that progress was the liberation of Tikrit, Saddam Hussein's hometown, by Shiite-dominated Iraqi forces. In the process, the chinks in the IS armor are being revealed. Von Drehle puts it colorfully: "ISIS is only as strong as the power vacuum it inhabits. Where anarchy reigns, its small but fanatically ruthless units can pile up rapid victories. But against disciplined and well-supplied forces, ISIS fades." While IS may not be as formidable as its initial successes made it appear, they have been very successful, he believes, "at marketing the illusion of its invincibility."

The seventh characteristic has been the *international appeal* of IS. The core appeal of IS has been among disaffected Sunnis in both Syria and Iraq, where regimes have been controlled by the Shia and have discriminated against the Sunnis. Since IS represents a distinctively minority element within Sunnism, however, their appeal for actual members and fighters is only directed at the most oppressed and fellow fundamentalists who share their beliefs in extreme sharia law and the prophecies of doom it preaches. This appeal cuts both ways. It means that those it recruits tend to be true fanatics, but it also narrows their appeal base. It has been suggested, for instance, that its fanaticism will eventually turn those Sunnis who originally supported the arrival of IS as liberators into opponents. As Wood says, "Properly contained, the Islamic State is likely to be its own undoing. No country is its ally, and its ideology guarantees that this will remain the case." The transitory nature of its appeal is a factor to be considered in action against IS.

The more troublesome aspect of the IS appeal has been its effective outreach to disaffected youth in the West, and specifically in Europe and the United States. That appeal has been based on a very sophisticated campaign largely on the Internet and through social media that has glamorized the movement to vulnerable youth. Following the appeal that is typical in recruiting "foot soldiers" to other terrorist organizations, it has been most effective among teenagers who are frustrated and experience both low self-esteem and negative views of their future, and who find glamour, excitement, and a sense of purpose in joining the renegade group. Many, but by no means all, of these recruits come from Middle Eastern backgrounds and are alienated from either their families or their new environments. The fear is that those youth who do make it to IS training facilities in Syria will be both radicalized and trained in terrorist methods and then returned to the United States and Europe to carry out terrorist activities. This possibility, it should be noted, is the only direct physical threat that IS poses to the United States.

The IS Problem for the United States

When the world first became aware of IS sometime in 2013, it was not a particular problem for the United States, and the United States was not especially high on the list of IS concerns. Such mutual interests as the two had centered on the anti-Assad effort in Syria, since IS was part of the coalition of organizations seeking to overthrow Assad, a goal the United States shared. Having effectively ruled out a direct combat role for itself in Syria, the United States was mostly concerned over whether or who among the opposition groups to back with arms transfers, which brought IS to its attention.

One chastening consideration for the United States was the recollection of the effect American aid to the *mujahidin* in Afghanistan eventually had. One major, inadvertent effect had been to help underwrite anti-Soviet elements in Afghanistan that later became American opponents: AQ and the Taliban. The Obama administration was determined to avoid the possibility of a repeat of the 1980s mistake, and thus conditioned its proposals for assistance to the rebels on certification of groups that would not turn on the United States (a position that brought condemnation from Republicans and hard men who argued this hamstrung efforts to aid the "good" Syrian resistance). The AQI participation was one of the worrisome possibilities, and trying to figure out how to aid the so-called "moderate" Syrian opposition but to avoid aiding the terrorists slowed down the aid process.

This screening process, however, first brought IS, then still known as AQI, onto the American radar screen. As AQI transformed itself into ISIS and began to grow and expand its territorial base in 2014, it burst onto the American consciousness as a problem in itself, especially after it moved into Iraq and began its advance toward Baghdad. American policy makers, and especially those who had been a part of the planning for the Iraq War and thus bore some sense of support for keeping Iraq out of IS hands, were particularly influenced.

IS thus became an American problem. As IS moved apparently inexorably across Iraq, Iraqi forces seemed incapable or uninterested in stopping the advance. The Iraqi armed forces were, after all, mostly Shiites and the parts of Iraq being swallowed by IS were mostly Sunni, attenuating their enthusiasm and leaving only the Kurds to pose any effective opposition. The Americans were unwilling to sacrifice their accumulated interest in Iraq easily, and became a leading part of the air campaign to slow the IS advance. In the process, Boot stated in March 2015 that "U.S. air strikes have killed more than 6,000 IS fighters." Whether this figure is precisely accurate or not, the United States thus has become an IS problem.

The question, still not resolved, is what the United States should do about the IS problem. The answer is not as clear as proponents on either side (but especially those pushing for an active military role) would argue. The options range from doing nothing about IS (effectively leaving it to those in the region to deal with), playing a role limited to helping anti-IS forces by providing military equipment and possibly continued air support), or becoming a major military force seeking to destroy the terrorists (up to and possibly including the insertion of American ground forces into the fray). Not all these options are equally likely or appealing. Deciding which one is requires looking at the conflict from four vantage points: the nature of the conflict, U.S. interests in various outcomes, the viability and nature of threats to those interests, and thus options and likely outcomes attached to each.

What is the nature of the situation? The answer is not clear at all. There are three ways to look at it. One is as an internal war within the Muslim community between the Sunni and Shiite communities. It is not a classic civil war in the sense of being fought within the boundaries of a single state, but instead bridges the confessional boundaries of the faithful in Iraq and Syria, and potentially more widely into some of the other neighboring artificial states. If it has the dynamics of an internal conflict, its purpose is to realign the boundaries of the area along confessional lines, and it is not at all clear that this process is entirely undesirable (the result could be reasonably coherent—along confessional lines—new states) or that there is any particularly positive impact outsiders like the United States could have on the outcome by their active involvement. Moreover, the record of outside states attempting to influence the outcome of internal conflicts between truly dedicated principals on both sides is generally abysmal at best. Is there any reason to believe this would be different?

The second and third possibilities are more worrisome in an international sense. The second is that the current conflict between IS and Iraq is the opening theater of a broader Islamic confessional war between the Sunnis (led by Saudi Arabia) and the Shiites (led by Iran) to establish religious dominance in the region. Such a conflict could become quite bloody and could upset the region in ways not dissimilar to the impact of the Thirty Years' War in Europe. The interruptions that could occur include supplies of petroleum out of the area. The third possibility is that the conflict is essentially an imperial war led by IS to establish religious governance in an expanding caliphate—which is its stated objective. This nature of the conflict could redraw the map of the Middle East, essentially balkanizing the region and leaving both Iraq

and Syria as smaller and less powerful, if potentially more coherent politically, entities and a fairly large but probably poor caliphate in the middle.
Depending on the ambitions and successes of IS, it could intrude on a number
of surrounding states and destabilize the entire region. Since the caliphate's
expansion would be as a *Sunni* state, it could transform IS imperialism into a
religious war along confessional lines.

What threats do these possible outcomes pose to the United States?
It has been stated American policy in the Middle East generally to prefer
as much stability as is possible, because comparative tranquility allows the
United States to balance countervailing influences toward its other interests,
access to petroleum, and its security commitment to Israel. Since those who
have the oil are at least rhetorically opposed to Israel (or Israeli policies like
its settlement of the West Bank), this requires something of a balancing act.
It is, for instance, difficult for any American administration to approach Iran
on anything but a very adversarial basis for fear of alienating Israeli and its
American supporters.

The caliphate poses a threat to these interests, although it is not quite
certain how dire the threat may be. If the conflict is a contained internal
war that does not go beyond (or far beyond) Iraq and Syria, the threat to the
United States is minimal, because the outcome will not likely have much
impact on America's two notable commitments: oil access and Israel. The
reason for saying this is that the result, be it the caliphate or restored boundaries in Iraq and Syria, will likely not upset the regional balance of power
much—Iraqi oil will not fall under its control, and the caliphate will not be
strong enough to threaten Israel.

If the conflict is either a surrogate confessional war where the Saudis and
Iranians become increasingly involved or where an imperialist caliphate
becomes much more powerful, then the threats become more real. The danger
for the United States is that a Sunni-Shiite conflict backed by its major clients
spins out of control by either side or by outsiders. In that case, one side or
the other might conclude that it could gain support in the region by becoming
aggressive toward Israel, or oil supplies could be endangered. The movement toward shale oil and gas shields the United States—but not many of
its allies—from an oil interruption. Were Israel to become an object in the
conflict, the matter could be more serious and a prospect the United States
would find hard to avoid.

What are American interests in these outcomes? Proponents of all sorts
of American involvement state that there are important American interests
involved in the outcome, but they rarely specify what outcome they are
talking about (what the nature of the situation is) or what those interests
are (other than being important enough so that American involvement is
justified). Those interests differ depending on the nature of the conflict and

likely outcomes. It is hard to see how any of them rise to the level of vitality that would unambiguously justify a large American military role.

The interests are clearest and most bounded if the war is essentially an internal communal affair limited to the Sunni and Shiite communities of both Iraq and Syria. The Sunnis, through IS leadership, are clearly the instigating force in this conflict, although it will be interesting to see what happens if the more extreme manifestation of IS rule in liberated Sunni areas turns the other Sunnis against them (which the United States hopes will happen). If that is the essence of the conflict, the result could be a redrawing of territorial lines, with the caliphate as the Sunni state, a Syria deprived of its eastern areas (which are some of its least valuable lands) and probably a Shiite and Kurdish state in Iraq. Such an outcome would not threaten access to Iraqi oil, since almost all the known reserves are in the Shiite and Kurdish regions. Breaking Iraq into three states has long been one of the options for solving the endemic instability of that country. If the United States adopted a neutral posture toward the resulting states—including the caliphate—it is not certain the United States could not live with the outcome, even if it would be displeased by an IS sovereign state. The United States has not been dependent on oil from Iraq, and the caliphate is probably not powerful enough to threaten Israel. The United States would much prefer that IS and the caliphate disappears, but it probably could live with a confined caliphate.

Interests become murkier if the current campaign is the opening salvo of a broader religious war in the region. Whether an all-out confessional war might occur is, of course, conjectural. Countries in the region, notably leaders of Saudi Arabia and Iran, are much more adept at posturing and sponsoring proxies than they are fighting themselves, and this would seem to mitigate the prospects they would allow matters to deteriorate to the point they might actually have to fight themselves. Since there are more than three times as many Iranians as there are Saudis, the odds will be with the Iranians in a large war, and this could be troubling for the United States. As long as the United States retains some dependence on Middle Eastern oil, it wants a viable Saudi government on our side, and it is not clear the Saudis can do this on their own. If Iran prevails, it would take a major rapprochement with Tehran to assure the flow of petroleum. It is not clear what the outcome of a confessional war might be. It is possible to derive apocalyptical outcomes that would leave the regions in flames. It is equally possible that such a war would quickly peter out if the actual major contestants found out they might personally have to fight. Israel would predictably put the worst possible face on these prospects and would be supported by their supporters in the United States.

If the ultimate dynamic of the war is the establishment of an imperialist caliphate, American interests are somewhat different. In this scenario, the major problem is how to frustrate the growth of the caliphate while balancing relations with Sunni and Shiite regimes in the region. The staunchest opponent of IS expansion will be Iran on confessional grounds, and an aggressive American opposition to IS would effectively align it with Tehran. Given that a much milder level of cooperation in Iraq has raised partisan concerns in Washington, it is not clear whether such an alignment would be politically viable. Two other possibilities exist. The success of the caliphate could, as already suggested, prompt a confessional war if Iran acts forcefully to help the affected countries (Iraq and Syria) regain territory lost to the Sunni caliphate. Which side does the United States then align with? The other possibility is that a radical established caliphate could become an international troublemaker, assaulting less fundamentalist regimes in the Middle East and extending its reach outside the region, largely through terrorist activities. The former possibility could affect the flow of oil; the latter the American homeland, at least in a minor way. It might even drag in the Turks, who have been conspicuously absent in active efforts to deal with IS.

One way to ameliorate the more dire prospects is through the defeat and destruction of IS, which would allow a return to the status quo. Allowing or forcing this outcome would be divisive within and between some Sunni states, where some support for the goals of IS resonate with parts of the population. The ideal solution would be for the Sunni states and the Sunni residents of the caliphate to rise and throw IS out. The latter possibility exists because, like the Taliban and other religious fanatics, their puritanism alienates the people it is supposed to save. It is probably unlikely that this will happen, certainly in the short run and without some outside assistance. The question, therefore, is: what are the meaningful options available to the United States in this process.

There are three broad options. They are doing nothing (essentially withdrawing from the competition with IS and letting others deal with it), a full-scale military intervention designed to topple IS, or a limited role of supporting, even providing some political and military leadership, to the effort to overthrow the caliphate but stopping short of introducing American ground forces into the conflict. Of the three, the two extreme options are both the most restrictive in terms of what to do and the least attractive and likely. The middle option is actually a whole series of graded actions between the extremes. The best (or least worst) solution probably resides somewhere within those options.

The extremes are reasonably easy to dismiss. The United States will not back completely out of the competition with IS for several reasons. One is that the United States has already expressed the goal of destroying IS, and abandoning that option altogether would be politically and militarily unacceptable, particularly among the chicken hawks who are such a vocal influence in the American debate. Another is that doing so would appear an abrogation of

American world leadership to many critics, which is also politically untenable. It would also cede any real ability the United States might have to influence a settlement to the crisis. It is not at all clear that any outsider, including the United States, can succeed in brokering anything resembling a negotiated outcome to the imbroglio, but this country cannot seem not to be trying to help broker a settlement either. The American flag must be shown—at least discretely. As well, it appears that regional actors—Saudi Arabia, Turkey, and Iran, most notably—lack the will or ability to act decisively.

The other extreme is equally unacceptable. An all-out intervention almost certainly would not work on the grounds that such interventions almost always fail (for an explanation of why, see my *The Case against Military Intervention*). In light of the outcomes of the missions in Iraq and Afghanistan, the public would be unlikely to support a large American effort, and it is not clear that anyone (especially the Anwar Sunnis) would welcome an American "liberation." Virtually no one has proposed "sending in the Marines" to knock the caliphate over, and it is just as well that they have not.

That leaves the option of some form and intensity of limited involvement as the only alternative. The extreme options are discrete: one stays out altogether or intervenes in a large way where the objective is for the United States to act as the primary actor in overthrowing IS. The middle option, however, actually encompasses a whole range of possibilities along the continuum. I will highlight three of these: "soft" intervention, the Nixon Doctrine, and showing the flag. The options are arrayed in Figure 5.1.

The options are more or less attractive depending on where one stands regarding the efficacy of American military intervention in internal wars generally—and thus the IS conflict in particular. Showing the Flag, for instance, goes a step beyond doing nothing at all, and probably includes condemnations of IS at the United Nations and elsewhere, rallying support for the anti-IS forces in the region, and providing some logistic assistance to anti-IS forces (e.g., satellite recognizance). The Nixon Doctrine response follows the pronouncement by President Nixon after the withdrawal from Vietnam was completed. In the future, he argued the United States would provide material support (weapons, training, etc.) and financial aid to beleaguered friends, but would not commit American forces to the conflict. Soft intervention would consist of the Nixon Doctrine plus limited American military participation

Least Intrusive				Most Intrusive
Do Nothing	Showing the Flag	Nixon Doctrine	Soft Intervention	Full-Scale Intervention

Figure 5.1   IS Intervention Options.

such as providing air resources and possibly some trainers and special forces on the ground, but would stop short of committing American combat forces.

These options, of course, vary in terms of the potential American impact on the situation. If one feels that a maximum effort is necessary, then the options on the right are most appealing. Given political realities in the wake of Iraq and Afghanistan, the all-out intervention option is politically toxic, and most American military activists—the chicken hawks—have instead settled on soft intervention as their compromise. Boot captures this position: "With a slightly larger commitment of American forces, we might be able to galvanize more local opposition to ISIS in Syria and Iraq." Others disagree and believe that any involvement would be inadvisable, if for no other reason that, as Jeffrey argues, "U.S. ground troops almost always generate negative reactions among developing-world populations that are suspicious of neo-colonial intrusions." Such a concern would be especially great in Anbar Province. Most anti-interventionists stop short of the "do-nothing" option, because it leaves them open to criticism as isolationist. For them, the "show the flag" option is a reasonable compromise.

There is another reason to oppose large-scale American intervention in the fight: that the primary proponents are IS itself. The argument is fundamentally compatible with points I have made in *The Case against Military Intervention,* which is that outside interveners inevitably are viewed negatively. As Cronin puts it forcefully, "U.S. ground forces . . . almost always generate negative reactions among developing world populations that are suspicious of neo-colonialist intrusions." Vick, writing in *Time* in March 2015, adds that this is especially true in Iraq, where "sending Americans back into Anbar and Saladin provinces would provide ISIS with pure oxygen and fresh waves of volunteers, while feeding the narrative that the U.S. is in a war against Islam." He concludes, "Now they want to lure us in. The fundamental narrative embraced by ISIS calls for a return of U.S. forces to Iraq, modern legionnaires fulfilling the role of 'Rome' in the end-time narrative the group believes it has set in motion."

Ultimately, what the United States does about the IS problem revolves around two concerns. One is how important the outcome is to this country? The bottom line concern is whether the success of IS would create an intolerable condition wherein American vital interests are compromised. The other is whether an American intervention could be successful in overthrowing IS and creating a better situation in the areas now part of the caliphate. Unless one can conjure sustainable positive answers to both questions, intervention is a dubious proposition. Are American vital interests engaged in the outcome? Can the United State prevail and leave a better place? The answers, when applied to American misadventures recently in the area, are not encouraging. Are things any different now?

MIDDLE EAST SCHISMS: THE U.S. DID NOT CREATE THEM, AND IT CAN'T FIX THEM

As stated at the beginning of the chapter, the Middle East is a mess and one into which the United States has felt itself drawn and toward whose problems it feels a compulsive need to interfere, somehow to make right. The original interests that drew the United States into involvement were the troika of petroleum, support for Israel, and opposition to the expansion of Soviet influence in the region (especially its oil). Since the Soviet Union no longer exists and its Russian successor has only pursued active influence in Syria (for which it reciprocates by vetoing anti-Syrian resolutions in the U.N. Security Council), that leaves oil and Israel as the remaining interests. The need for oil is on the wane, but Israel remains a concern, at least partly because of Israeli actions toward its neighbors (e.g., the West Bank).

It has been a matter of foreign policy conventional wisdom that the bridge between the conflicting interests of Israel and oil is greater regional stability and thus tranquility. The idea is that a Middle East that has stabilized itself will continue to pump the oil the West needs and will become less hostile to Israel, thereby overcoming the oil possessors' historic animosity toward Israel. This position is a hypothesis, not a scientific law, and the evidence of its validity is open to question. Nonetheless, peace and stability remain the preferred American outcome in the Muslim Middle East.

The problem is twofold. First, the Middle East is arguably the least peaceful, most unstable area of the world, and thus it is the most difficult place on the globe successfully to pursue a policy of promoting characteristics in short supply and of questionable desirability to the peoples of the region. Second, the reasons for this instability are deep seated, profound, and of long-standing historical origins. They are problems that long precede either the existence of the United States or its entrance into the Middle East as a geopolitical player. The United States, in other words, did not create any of the internal conflicts that divide the states of the Middle East. Moreover, these differences are internal to the region and its peoples, and it is impossible to understand why anyone believes the United States could solve them. Not only did the United States not create the basic divisions, it also cannot resolve them.

There are two basic divides that overlap and form the divisions. The first and most historically developed is ethnic. Whether the division is between Arabs and non-Arabs or between tribes and clans within different ethnic groups, the divisions that plague the area have, in many cases, roots that go back to Biblical times. The oral historians who composed the Old Testament might have to sort out name changes and some geographic dislocations, but they would not be surprised at the pattern of violence and hatreds today. These divisions have been going on for millennia, and the participants have not been able to resolve them. There is a certain irony involved: the Middle East is one of the birthplaces of world civilization and the locale that has produced three of the world's great monotheistic religions. For all this apparently civilizing influence, it remains among the most violent, primitive, and in some important respects, uncivilized places on the earth. What makes Americans think they can do what the parties themselves have not been able to accomplish?

The second and currently more explosive source of division is religious, between the Sunni and Shiite sects of Islam. This division "only" dates back to the seventh century, but it has created a divide and source of hatred between adherents to the two sects that are enduring and has become even more explosive in recent years. The possibility that the struggle with IS represents the opening theater of a religious war is the current "highlight" of this division. Once again, the United States can hardly be blamed for creating a religious schism within Islam that was a by-product of the succession crisis after the death of the Prophet, and it is impossible to imagine how the United States can do anything to resolve this difference.

Layered onto these difficulties is the nature and tenor of Middle Eastern politics. These politics always operate at multiple and apparently contradictory levels that the principals actively seek to hide from outsiders and which create a climate of uncertainty and confusion that is bewildering, a sleight of hand where nothing is exactly as it appears. Turkey's role in the IS crisis is exemplary. Turkey is generally considered the most secularized of regional Islamic state and is a member of the North Atlantic Treaty Organization (NATO). Both of these factors make it appear that the Turks should find IS an anathema they would oppose, and rhetorically they do oppose them. Operationally, however, they have done little about a threat literally on their borders (IS-controlled parts of Syria adjoin Turkish territory). Their lack of response has frustrated Americans. Why have the Turks acted so apparently strangely? The byzantine answer is that there are countervailing influences on the Turks. Defeating IS would strengthen the Assad regime in Syria, whom they also oppose. Similarly, IS failure could encourage the Iraqi Kurds to declare an independent Kurdistan on their border, which they also oppose. Moreover, fundamentalist Sunnis have become a force in Turkish politics that the government dare not alienate. So the Turks basically sit the crisis out—to the bewilderment and frustration of Westerners.

Ignorance has certainly not deterred the United States from becoming heavily involved in the region. There is little evidence that many decision makers have a sophisticated, detailed understanding of either of these underlying forces in Middle East geopolitics, and yet this country continues to involve, or threaten to involve, itself as if it did. As Bacevich pointed out in October 2014, the United States has employed armed force in fourteen

Middle Eastern states since 1980. If one listens to elected officials discussing the region, it sounds like the Middle East and its problems are like those of anyplace else in the world and that the United States, acting like it always does, can overcome regional problems by applying tried-and-true American techniques like the application of American force. All 14 states in which the United States has intervened would not agree.

Until these underlying causes of conflict are resolved, efforts at peace and reconciliation will be cosmetic at best. The United States has stuck its nose into the violence of the area with its armed forces twice, and the results have not even touched on basic divisions. In Iraq, Sunnis, Shiites, and Kurds have long histories of animosity and hatred, and the eight years of American presence did essentially nothing to bring these groups together. In Afghanistan, ethnic groups and their clans and tribes distrust one another and oppose a strong central government that might bring one of their opponents to power, and they always have. The United States believes the country should have a significant central government; the natives do not. Afghan history suggests the Afghans will prevail, not the Americans.

The bottom line in all this is that there are very finite limits to what the United States can expect to accomplish when it inserts itself into the seemingly perpetual fracases that mark the Middle East. This is particularly true in the case of the intervention of American armed forces into these conflicts. Saying this is not an indictment of American forces; rather, it simply recognizes that there are some things armed force can do, and some things it cannot. Among the things it cannot do is resolve millennia-long differences in ethnicity and religion. Maybe it should stop trying to do what it cannot do and try to figure out what it can do. The United States indeed did not create these problems, and it cannot solve them. Then why do we keep talking and acting as if we can?

BIBLIOGRAPHY

Anderson, Scott. *Lawrence in Arabia: War, Deceit, Imperial Folly, and the Making of the Modern Middle East.* New York: Anchor Books, 2013.

Ajami, Fouad. *The Syrian Rebellion.* Palo Alto, CA: Hoover Institution Press, 2013.

Bacevich, Andrew J. "Even if We Defeat the Islamic State, We'll Still Lose the Bigger War." *Washington Post* (online), October 3, 2014.

Betts, Richard K. "Pick Your Battle: Ending America's Era of Permanent War." *Foreign Affairs* 93, 6 (November/December 2014), 15–24.

Boot, Max. "Should the U.S. Send Ground Troops to Fight ISIS? Yes. Uproot the Enemy." *Time* 195, 8 (March 9, 2015), 32.

Brisard, Jean-Jacques. *Zarqawi: The New Face of Al-Qaeda.* New York: The Other Press, 2005.

Clausewitz, Carl von. *On War.* Princeton, NJ: Princeton University Press, 1984.

Cronin, Audrey Kurth. "ISIS Is Not a Terrorist Group: Why Counterterrorism Won't Stop the Latest Jihadi Group." *Foreign Affairs* 94, 2 (March/April 2015), 87–98.

Feaver, Peter. "The Just War Tradition and the Paradox of Policy Failure in Syria." *Foreign Policy* (online), August 22, 2013.

Hashemi, Nader, and Danny Postel (eds.). *The Syrian Dilemma.* Cambridge, MA: MIT Press (Boston Review Books), 2013.

Jeffrey, James F. "Why Counterinsurgency Doesn't Work: The Problem Is the Strategy, Not the Execution." *Foreign Affairs* 94, 2 (March/April 2015), 178–190.

Lesch, David W. *Syria: The Rise and Fall of the House of Assad.* New Haven, CT: Yale University Press, 2013.

Serwer, Daniel. "Iraq Struggles to Govern Itself." *Current History* 109, 731 (December 2010), 390–394.

Simon, Steven N. *After the Surge: The Case for U.S. Military Disengagement from Iraq.* New York: CFR 23, Council on Foreign Relations, 2007.

Snow, Donald M. *The Case against Military Intervention.* New York: Routledge, 2016.

———. *What after Iraq?* New York: Longman, 2008.

Stern, Jessica, and M. Berger. *ISIS: The State of Terror.* New York: ECCO Books, 2015.

Tabler, Andrew J. "Syria's Collapse and How Washington Cam Stop It." *Foreign Affairs* 92, 4 (July/August 2013), 90–100.

Vick, Karl. "Should the U.S. Send Ground Forces to Fight ISIS? No. Don't Take the Bait." *Time* 185, 8 (March 9, 2015), 33.

Von Drehle, David. "The War on ISIS." *Time* 185, 8 (March 9, 2015), 24–31.

Wood, Graeme. "What ISIS Really Wants." *The Atlantic* 321, 2 (March 2015), 78–90.

Zakaria, Fareed. "Obama Needs to Dial Back His Syrian Strategy." *Washington Post* (online). October 17, 2014.

———. "Opinion: Intervention Is Not the Answer." *Washington Post* (online), January 15, 2015.

Chapter 6

The U.S. Posture in the Middle East

The previous chapter showed what a tough and diverse neighborhood the Middle East is, and thus why it is so difficult for any outsider to pursue a coherent and successful foreign policy there. As has been argued consistently, the problems of the region are enormous. They are based on multiple sources of difference among the people of various countries and of the residents within many of those countries. The permutations of cleavage along ethnic and religious lines is so great that almost nothing one might say about the politics and problems of any single country is also true in the same way about any other. Differences among peoples in any part of the world are not unusual, and in many places those differences can have explosive, unsettling influences. In the Middle East, despite millennia as a center in the development of world civilization, those differences are particularly great, and their consequences are particularly combustible. IS represents the most recent evidence of the convoluted nature of regional politics. It is neither the first nor likely the last example of Middle East difficulty.

The United States has been drawn into the maelstrom of Middle East instabilities for a variety of reasons. American involvement is mostly a post–World War II phenomenon, and it was originally centered on two contradictory axes. One was support for the establishment of the Jewish state of Israel, a position that largely arose from the collective guilt the West felt for not having prevented the Holocaust. Once the Israeli state came into being in 1947, that interest was expanded to assuring the security of Israel from those which would do it harm or destroy it. That interest remains central to the American position on the region.

The second axis of American interest was, of course, gaining and maintaining secure, affordable access to the vast stores of petroleum that lay beneath the surface of many Middle Eastern states, and especially those that washed

on the shores of the Persian (or Arabian, depending on one's political preferences). Originally, this interest was largely the result of reinforcement of the
policy of assisting in European recovery by supporting the continent's conversion to petroleum as the primary fuel for its energy needs and to support
the American oil companies that were part of the seven sisters. The interest
became geopolitical when keeping communist powers, first the Soviet Union
and later China, from challenging the Western stranglehold on the oil, was
added to the equation. These two interests were, of course, contradictory,
since a number of the oil-producing states were also among the most vocal
opponents of the Israeli state.

During the Cold War, these interests were difficult to reconcile but were
manageable for a United States much more concerned with the competition for global supremacy with the Soviets and their allies. During the Cold
War period up to 1979, the dynamics were basically untroublesome for a
United States that lacked a detailed knowledge of most of the Middle East
dynamics because of most of the internal cleavages that have become so
prominent were not evident then. Almost all the Middle Eastern states were
ruled by strong dictatorships that managed to keep internal sources of instability suppressed, and these states managed to align themselves with a United
States that was willing to overlook a little tyranny for access to oil. At the
same time, the various Islamic states could use hatred for Israel as a convenient displacement object to obscure the very real differences between them.
The Sunnis of Saudi Arabia and the Shiites of Iran did not like one another,
but they managed to coexist. Losing a war to Israel now and again let off
steam and allowed the area's differences to remain obscured to outsiders like
the United States, which did not truly understand the very real animosities
that lay barely beneath the surface.

Events in and since 1979 have lifted the veil of Middle Eastern instability.
The fall of the Shah was the first such event and, as argued earlier, it forced
the United States to become much more personally and intimately involved
in the region than it had been before. The United States was unprepared conceptually for this immersion into the byzantine life of the Middle East, and it
has shown ever since. Since the United States did not have much of an experiential or academic knowledge base about the region, it treated the unique,
convoluted politics of the area like it had the power politics of Europe. In the
process, the United States made error after error that drew it more deeply into
the regional morass and, eventually, drew a bull's eye on its back in terms of
becoming the object of Middle East terrorism.

The bizarre history of American relations with Iraq's Saddam Hussein is
exemplary. An army general, Hussein came to power in Iraq in 1979 in the
traditional Iraqi manner, as part of a Baathist military coup that overthrew
and killed the previous ruler, King Faisal II, in 1978. The United States made

little note publicly of these acts, at least partially because the two countries had very limited relations and American oil companies were excluded from contracts on Iraqi oil, a practice Hussein continued until his overthrow by the United States in 2003.

Hussein was a prototypical Middle East tyrant. His background was from a Sunni tribe that lived in Tikrit and which formed the basis of his power. The Baath Party, made up almost entirely of Sunnis, ruled the country as a distinct minority (about a third of the population compared to about twice as many Shiites). His rule was dictatorial but mildly reformist, at least to the extent of not being an unofficial theocracy like Saudi Arabia. The major victims of his rule were the members of the Shiite majority, who most benefited from his overthrow. Shiite retaliation against the Sunni minority concentrated in Anbar Province (where Tikrit is located) helps explain why many Iraqi Sunnis welcomed fellow Sunni IS forces and why a number of IS military commanders are former Baathist officers.

Hussein did not appear on the American geopolitical radar until the wake of the overthrow of the Shah. The radical Shiite religious government in Tehran frightened many in Sunni capitals, and Saddam Hussein saw in this reaction an opportunity to assert himself as the new leader of pan-Arabism (an unofficial title formerly held by Egyptian president Gamal Abdul Nasser). To establish this position, Hussein provoked war with the fledgling Iranian regime over the issue of disputed control of the Shatt al-Arab, the river created by the confluence of the Tigris and Euphrates Rivers that forms the international boundary between the two countries and alongside which a good deal of the oil-refining industries of both countries are located.

The ensuing Iran-Iraq War lasted from 1980 to 1988, marking the first major post–World War II clash between Sunni and Shiite states. Iraq is majority Shiite, of course, but it is also Arab, while Iran is Persian, and one interesting question during the war was whether the Arab Shiites of Iraq would prove to be more Arab (in which case they would support the Hussein regime) or more Shiite (in which case they might side with Iran). Arab ethnicity prevailed.

One of the curious aspects of the war was that no one in the outside world wanted either side to win decisively. A triumphant Iran would probably control the Iraqi oil fields in the south of the country, possibly elevating it to a competitive position with the Saudis as a petroleum source. Given the radical nature of the religious government in Tehran, no one outside Iran wanted that to occur. At the same time, hardly anyone wanted to burnish Hussein's claim to Arab leadership, which would have been greatly enhanced had Iraq prevailed. Both countries depended on weaponry from outside the region to fight, and by tacit agreement, shipments to both sides was modulated so that the recipient had enough power to avoid defeat but not enough to prevail.

The United States got involved in this process. It was predisposed to oppose the Iranians because of the events of 1979. It had no love lost for the Iraqis or Hussein, but in geopolitical terms, Iraq was the clear underdog, with a population only about a third of Iran's. As a result, by the mid-1980s, the United States had become a supplier of arms to Iraq and the Iraqis became de facto partners of the United States in the region, despite accusations that the Hussein used chemical weapons against both the Iranians and some Kurds in his own country.

The courtship of Iraq by the United States was short-lived. Iraq worked up a huge financial debt supplying itself in the war with Iran, and after it was over, it pleaded with creditors, most of which were Sunni states like Saudi Arabia, to cancel the debt and to provide Iraq with needed financial assistance as a show of gratitude for its actions against the hated Iranians. When Hussein's former suppliers refused his requests, he turned his eyes south on Kuwait, a tiny kingdom that sits on an oil dome between southern Iraq and Saudi Arabia long the Persian Gulf. In 1990, Iraqi troops poured into Kuwait, quickly conquering it, and the Kuwaiti monarchy fled into Saudi exile. Iraqi forces quickly moved to the Kuwait-Saudi border, a short drive to the Saudi oil fields with no force between them and their occupation.

This threat to world oil supplies galvanized world opinion to stop this blatant aggression—the first time a member of the United Nation had conquered and occupied another U.N. member (a unique act until the United States did the same thing to Iraq in 2003). The United States took the lead in an international effort that included a number of Middle Eastern states to stop the Iraqi invasion and to force Hussein to leave and restore Kuwaiti sovereignty. The coalition, powered mostly by American air and ground forces, counterattacked in January 1991. It quickly routed the Iraqis in a conventional campaign where the Iraqis tried to fight on Western terms and clearly stood no chance. No other developing world state has made that mistake again; the age of Western-style warfare had its swan song for now in the Kuwaiti desert.

There were two other artifacts of Operation Desert Storm. The first was the Saudi role. Saudi Arabia did not play a major direct military role in the fighting to stop the Iraqis or to send them back to Iraq. Instead, the Saudis provided some air forces, host conditions, and financing but no real ground forces *for the defense of their own homeland.* In 2015, the Saudis sent token forces into Yemen and threatened a larger role, but Desert Storm made it clear that the Saudis themselves were not going to engage in standard ground combat if they can avoid it. When discussing a possible religious war in the region featuring Saudi Arabia as the leader of the Sunnis, it is probably safe to assume they will arrive carrying checkbooks, not rifles.

The other artifact was a lingering animosity toward the Iraqis, and especially Saddam Hussein. When the Iraqi army was sent fleeing from Kuwait back into Iraq, there was one line of advocacy that suggested the coalition should pursue the Iraqis back into their country and overthrow the Hussein regime as punishment for his transgression. The leading apostles of this position were a group of very hawkish, pro-Israeli defense analysts known as the neo-conservatives or neo-cons. Their advice was rejected by the George H. W. Bush administration. Bush argued (and his son George W. Bush agreed) that such an action would trigger a long and bitter civil war from which the United States would have trouble extricating itself and that the coalition, which had the U.N. mandate to force Iraq out of Kuwait but not to invade that country, would simply dissolve at the border.

The neo-cons were not deterred. During the Clinton years of the 1990s, they hatched plans for the invasion of Iraq and the deposing of Saddam Hussein. The election of George W. Bush (who somehow forgot his own agreement with his father in the interim) and the 9/11 attacks allowed the neo-cons to realize their dreams. Many became national security advisors in the new Bush administration and revived their calls to overthrow the Iraqi dictator. The post-9/11 "war on terror" provided them the vehicle, as they promoted the accusation of Hussein's cooperation with Al-Qaeda as reason to take him down. These classic chicken hawks prevailed, and the result was the 2003 invasion and occupation of Iraq.

The United States thus ended up spending eight years occupying a country that two decades earlier was a place in which this country had no important interests and less substantive knowledge or understanding. Even after the United States withdrew the last of its combat forces from Iraq in 2011 American involvement has continued, most recently connected to the IS problem.

The primary purpose of this discussion is that it puts some light on the pattern of U.S. policy toward the Middle East in the last third of a century since the fall of the Shah seemed to push America into a more active, prominent role there. Two summary points stand out. The first is the historic lack of interest and knowledge the United States has shown about the region and its problems. Had the United States been at all clear headed, would it have become involved with Iraq, especially to the extent we did? Was there ever any good reason to believe there was any interest the United States had in that country that justified what was done there? Was it worth over 4,000 American lives? Only the most fervent chicken hawks think so.

Second, the United States has been spectacularly unsuccessful in its boldest, most activist incursions into the area. Given the preponderance of very conservative, fundamentalist Shiites in the country, Iran was probably the worst place on earth to try to modernize and Westernize, but when the Shah asked for our help, we joined in the effort. When it failed and the conservatives overthrew the Shah and instituted fundamentalist rule, they blamed the

United States for their situation. How could we have been surprised by this? The neo-cons argued that Iraq relieved of the tyranny of Saddam Hussein could be turned into a beacon of Islamic democracy in the region. Given Iraqi ethnic and religious divisions, it was an absolutely silly assertion, but it was hardly challenged at the time within the Bush White House.

The beat goes on. As the first stirrings of Republican 2016 presidential aspirations were stirring in New Hampshire in mid-April 2015, the most hawkish candidate, Senator Lindsay Graham (R-SC) asserted the standard activist line about IS: if the United States does not send forces to Iraq to destroy IS there, *we will have to confront them here on American soil.* This suggestion is so blatantly outrageous that it should not have to be discussed, unless the senator means that a few terrorists may be dispatched our way. It should, however, never surprise us how far a little ignorance can take us—in the wrong direction.

U.S. NATIONAL SECURITY CALCULATIONS

National security problems can usefully be analyzed with reference to three interconnected variables introduced in my 2016 book, *Thinking about National Security.* The three variables are *interests, threats, and risk.* These factors are familiar to readers who have been introduced to national security, and their meanings are both straightforward and commonsensical.

The framework begins with interests, which are roughly defined as conditions or situations that are valued, or in which the state has an interest. A national border that has no enemies on it is the most basic national security interest, and one can, with a little effort, make a graded hierarchy on interests that any country has. Doing so reveals that, like the barnyard animals in Orwell's *Animal Farm,* not all interests are equal. In terms of national security affairs, there is a critical threshold between those interests whose realization is deemed *vital* and those that are *less-than-vital (LTV).* The distinction describes the consequences to the state if an interest is threatened or obviated. In the case of a vital interest, not realizing the condition is intolerable to the state. A hostile power on the border with Mexico would likely be seen as intolerable and thus its avoidance or reversal vital, for example. An LTV interest is one where the consequences of its non-realization would be troublesome to some degree, but would not be intolerable: the country could live with the situation, even if it did not like it. The existence of a communist country 90 miles off its shore (Cuba) probably falls into this category. This distinction is important because many national security policy makers believe that the boundary between vital and LTV interests is unimportant and that almost any situation can be argued to impinge on vital interests in some way.

The second element is threat, or manmade or natural conditions that interrupt or potentially threaten to interrupt the realization of interests. A threat is essentially a promise to do something harmful to an opponent unless that other party conforms to some condition on which the threatening party insists. Normally in national security affairs, the threats are to important interests that may arguably be vital in nature, and they most dramatically involve the use of some form of organized violence as the means by which harm is inflicted. Threats can also be non-military in nature and can include both political and economic actions. In the present Middle Eastern context, the Arab oil boycotts of the United States in 1973 and 1977 represent the use of economic power to carry out a threat.

Threats are aimed at the sense of security a country has. Security, in turn, can be either physical or psychological. Physical security involves tangible, objective sources of potential harm. Psychological senses of security involve conditions that make one feel safe (or secure), and this dimension of security enters two additional considerations into the mix. First, it means that threats can be subjective: some people will feel more secure in some situations than others, and the psychological basis of their differences means people can disagree about whether a particular situation is threatening or how threatening it may be. Second, this psychological dimension means that the list of situations that are considered threatening can be very long and that it is expandable based on how people feel and how they are led to feel about different conditions.

The third variable is risk. The list of what is considered threatening is always longer than the ability to negate it all, thanks to the subjective nature of threat. The result is that all threats to all interests cannot practically be negated or neutralized, and this means some threats will be at risk of not being realized. The critical element in this determination is the ability (or capability) the state has to neutralize threats, and it will invariably be less than the sum of all the threats to it. In *National Security for a New Era* (fifth edition) I have reduced this relationship to an intuitive, heuristic formula: Risk = Threat−Capability (risk equals threat minus capability). The practical implication of this formulization is that states must decide what is most important to them, take the actions they can to neutralize the threats to those interests they can, and accept that some valued conditions will be at risk.

Clearly, national security policy has as its central goal protecting as many interests as it can, beginning from the really vital and extending downward into LTV interests to the extent it has the resources (capability) to do so. Different people place different priorities on different values and will try to elevate their particular interests high enough in the hierarchy to guarantee that there will be adequate resources to protect it. This in turn leads to a natural tendency to inflate the importance of interests in controversial, debatable ways. In terms of the Middle East, this has meant a tendency to argue that the obviation of almost all untoward situations in the area is "vital" to the United States and thus may justify the use of American force to realize the interests. Whether the professions of vitality are sincere or demagogic is a matter of debate.

U.S.-Middle East relations in the Middle East can be seen in this light. Those interests have changed somewhat with time: there is no longer a communist threat to the region, and terrorism emanating from the region is now a problem but did not used to be. Of the American interests across time, access to petroleum energy has been by far the most important, and given changes discussed in Chapters 3 and 4, it has also become a more variable interest than it once was. Arguably, the presence or absence of oil dependency is the critical variable in the hierarchy of American interests, and that hierarchy changes depending on the nature of the dependency. The other major American interest that has transcended time has been protection of Israel; since the 1990s, terrorism has arguably become the most important interest the United States has in the area.

American Interests with Oil

Had the United States not exhausted easily and cheaply exploitable supplies of domestic petroleum and had the Persian Gulf area not been one large oil dome, would the United States ever have developed any important interests in the Middle East? Or, in the absence of an insatiable need for oil from abroad, would the Middle East and its various locales have remained at a moderate to low level of LTV interest in any American ranking of its most important national security concerns? Had the region remained off the radar of important concerns, would this country ever have become militarily engaged in the Middle East? If we had not, would terrorists have had any reason to single out the United States for their singular wrath?

These are, of course, interesting abstract questions, but they are also counterfactual and thus academic in nature. If the Middle East did not have enormous reserves of readily exploitable petroleum energy, the United States would likely never have been especially interested in the region. Likewise, if American traditionally exploited sources of oil had not essentially dried up, this country would not have had to look abroad for other sources. Both these conditions, however, occurred. Given the growing disparity between U.S. production and consumption, a strategy of going to the biggest "drinking fountain" made more sense than trying to develop alternate sources under and off the shorelines of states elsewhere. Given insatiable global appetites, other sources in Africa, Latin America, and off Asia have also been explored and exploited, but the first and most important source was in the Persian

Gulf littoral. Had this source not been present, the United States (and most of the rest of the world) would have attached little more attention to the Middle East than it does to most of Africa. Oil forms the geopolitical basis for Middle Eastern interests.

The state of Israel forms the other American interest in the region. Supporting both the creation and sustenance of a Jewish state in the Levant area was a largely unavoidable, highly emotional response to the German atrocities of the Holocaust. When the Israeli state came into contact and conflict with its Islamic neighbors over who had the legitimate claim to territories claimed by both sides, the United States became chief protector of Israeli security in a hostile neighborhood. That guarantee has been ironclad and is a commitment that has been proclaimed and honored by every American president since Harry S. Truman. Support for Israel has widespread political backing within the United States, giving Israel a privileged position in American national security policy. Whether current Israeli policies (such as their intransigence on the issue of a Palestinian state) have abused that "special relationship" is a question that is raised in the next chapter.

Other, extended American interests have followed from these two primary concerns, augmented by a concern over preventing the spread of communist influence to the region during the Cold War. In truth, the Soviet appeal in the Islamic world was always quite limited and instrumental. Although some of the social dimensions of theoretical socialism share tenets with Islamic principles, there are hardly two more incompatible basic philosophies than atheistic communism and theocratic Islam. If, as Karl Marx maintained, religion is indeed the "opiate of the masses," that narcotic is particularly strong and controlling in most of the Middle East. Some Islamic states had an instrumental relationship with the Soviets to obtain arms, but there was never any love lost between the Muslims and the communists.

The extension of American interests into parts of the Middle East that do not contain noticeable petroleum resources generally have been extensions either of petroleum addiction or to protect Israel from its numerous regional enemies. Iraq, for instance, was uninteresting to the United States as long as there was no need for Iraqi oil, since Iran, Saudi Arabia, and the Gulf states provided the United States with all the oil it needed and was willing to pay for. When Iran became part of the oil problem rather than its solution in 1979, Iraq suddenly became important to the United States. Prior to Iran's turn to fervent anti-Americanism, the religious rift between Sunni Saudi Arabia and Shiite Iraq was largely unknown and unanalyzed in the United States. A change in the oil equation altered that calculus as well.

The changes and vicissitudes of the region have been bewildering to most Americans and, judging by their words and deeds, a fair amount of the Congress. One hears, for instance, discussions about some countries being "friends" or "allies" of the United States, whereas other states' relations with the United States are depicted in less favorable, charitable terms. Thus, Saudi Arabia is depicted as a reliable American "ally" in the Middle East, and the moderate monarchy of Jordan's King Abdullah is described as a reliable regional friend of this country.

Such depictions can be misleading and, if applied literally, can lead to unfortunate, even confusing, interpretation of situations. The most overused but misused description is the use of the term "ally." If the term means no more than another person or political entity with whom one cooperates most of the time, then the United States has several allies in the region. Israel and Saudi Arabia are the two states about which this depiction is most common, and in the loose sense, it is accurate. The more precise meaning of the term suggests some formal relationship; in security terms, this means some obligation to participate in the mutual self-defense of a particular ally. The United States has such obligations with a number of states, notably those that are part of the North Atlantic Treaty Organization or in terms of bilateral mutual defense treaties with countries like the Philippines.

In a national security dialogue that discussed the possible use of military force, the latter, formal meaning of the term is more appropriate. Under this definition, the United States has *no* formal allies in any Middle Eastern country except Turkey, which is a member of NATO. The United States has very close security relations with a number of states, but it comes in the form of military-to-military relations and the provision of arms, for instance, not in terms of a formal, binding alliance relationship to defend one another.

This depiction is also true of U.S. relations with Israel and Saudi Arabia. The lack of a formal defense treaty does not mean the United States does not have close, morally binding relations with either country. It does, however, mean that there is no formal treaty obligation that requires the United States to come to the military assistance of either country in the event of crisis, or vice versa. The lack of a formal treaty with Israel arises largely because of the extremely negative reaction the Islamic "friends and allies" of the United States would have if such an agreement were forged. The absence of a formal treaty with Saudi Arabia reflects the Saudi reluctance to conclude binding agreements with outsiders.

Understanding this distinction helps clarify some of the misunderstanding and vagaries of the region in U.S. security policy debates. Israel, which is perpetually threatened by the Islamic world, feels the need for constant reassertion that the United States will come to its aid if needed, and much of the behavior of Prime Minister Netanyahu in the United States gains meaning in those terms. The Saudis, on the other hand, do not consider themselves allies of the United States at all. Rather, they have the much more common regional view that they and the Americans have mutual interests some—even much—of the time, and in those areas of policy, they effectively act as partners (or allies in the informal sense). This relationship does not extend to areas of disagreement, wherein the cooperative relationship simply does not apply. When the United States and the Saudis disagree on a particular area and critics wonder aloud how our "ally" could oppose us, it is because they fail to recognize the informal, not formal, nature of the "alliance" between them. The implication is that, like the ground in so much of the region, relationships are built on shifting sands: today's friend may be tomorrow's enemy, and vice versa.

One constant factor in the "friendly" relationship has been the mutual commerce in oil: the Middle East provides "black gold" to hungry consumers, who enrich Saudi and other coffers in return. Occasionally, that oil becomes a weapon, as it did in 1973, and there are periodic threats about production slowdowns and the like. The oil relationship is, however, the solid base on which an American relationship with the region exists. As long as the United States is an oil "junkie" who requires Middle Eastern role, it has a vital interest in the region, at least in ensuring that the supply continues to flow. Oil dependency creates the need for a balancing act with the oil producers about Israel, and it gives this country cause for concern when the "barbarians appear at the gate" intent on upsetting the status quo, as in the case of IS. But what happens if oil is taken out of the equation?

American Interests without Oil

A shale-led deep reduction in American dependence on foreign oil does not obviate the past where that dependence essentially drove U.S. policy, but it potentially does change the way the United States interacts with the region and its member states in the future. Reductions have already begun, and the United States no longer relies as heavily as it used to on Middle Eastern oil as its source of needed energy. If that dependence is even further decreased to the point that North American and other foreign sources (e.g., Nigeria, Latin America) can provide solid, reliable, and adequate source for American energy needs until the world moves away from carbon-based energy sources, the impact could be great. It is not a done deal at this point, however.

There are three variables that cloud projections into the future. The first, discussed in Chapter 4, is the evolution of the shale oil and gas revolution. There is domestic opposition to the practice of hydraulic fracturing, and if experience shows this opposition has legitimate environmental grounds (e.g., earthquakes begin occurring with greater regularity in areas where fracking occurs, as noted), then the movement could be slowed. Second, the projections of resource adequacy from new sources could prove wrong: new supplies may not meet quantitative predictions, demand both locally and globally could grow faster than projected, or both. Third, the objection that the availability of new sources simply prolongs the period of dependence on carbon dioxide injection into the atmosphere could prove catastrophic enough to require change.

Any of these problems could affect the Middle East. If the United States can reduce its need for Persian Gulf oil, the effects are greatest. From the vantage point of the countries of the region itself, the major impact would be to lose revenue on which their economies are based and to reduce the leverage that the threat of product withholding gives them when dealing with currently dependent countries like the United States. For countries like the United States, shale oil and gas acts almost like methadone by producing an alternate way to treat the addiction to foreign petroleum. If the shale revolution turns out to be a lesser source of change than has been advertised, these effects are lessened and things remain more like they have been. From the perspective of narrow Middle Eastern (e.g., Saudi) self-interest, the movement toward a non-carbon burning base of energy is an economic and geopolitical disaster, as the market for their only truly valuable natural resource shrivels. This fate can be ameliorated by investing aggressively in research to find new bases for productivity when oil is no longer burned: taking the lead in research leading to the conversion of their resource to plastics would seem to be one avenue. To this point, the sheikhs have seemed more interested in personal aggrandizement than in future preparation.

Although the end of dependence on Middle Eastern oil may not happen, it also may, and it is worth at least tentatively exploring some of the possibilities. Following the analysis in the last section, the results could be dramatic and transformational for U.S. national security.

The first and most dramatic effect would be on the structure of American interests in the region. Despite generally vague assertions of other interests in specific situations, the key element in American interests in the Islamic countries begins, and sometimes ends, with petroleum. At the most obvious level, the United States has a much greater interest in those countries that are oil producers than those that are not. Other aspects may create some interest: the size and location of Egypt, and the location of Jordan on the Israeli border (at least as long as the West Bank is held by Israel), for instance. It may sound cynical to declare openly, but the lack of decisive American action on Syria may partially be because Syria is not an oil exporter.

If the United States is no longer dependent on the oil producers, could the level of relative indifference that is currently directed at the non-producers not be extended to the producers as well? In April 2015, for instance, Saudi Arabia launched air attacks against Hauthi rebels in Yemen. The raids accomplished very little other than destroying some of the scant infrastructure of the country and killing nearly 1,000 of its citizens, and there is little reason to suggest that the United States has any "dog in the fight" over whether Sunnis or Shiites prevail in the contest. Yet the United States verbally supported the Saudis in their actions, citing vague Hauthi ties to Iran. Where were important American interests other than supporting our major source of Middle Eastern oil engaged? Without the need to be nice to oil producers, what are American interests in who controls Yemen? Could the United States not simply sit out a fight that is, in interest terms, really none of its business?

This same calculation extends to the oil itself. It has been a primary assertion here that the Iranian Revolution and the consequent withdrawal of Iran from its role of guaranteeing the flow of oil is what drove the United States to feel the need for a permanent military presence in the region and toward the orientation that American military forces and efforts were necessary to ensure the flow to market. Would that need disappear if America no longer requires the oil? The most obvious application is the guarantee of free access to and through the Persian Gulf for the oil tankers, since many were headed toward the United States. Does that change if the delivery addresses on those tankers no longer includes American ports? If it is further true that the permanent military presence by the United States has been the irritant that has spawned and nurtures militant anti-Americanism, what impact could a reduction in the American presence have on the region?

Oil may dissolve as a U.S. national security concern, but Israel remains high on the American interest list. This interest has transcended oil in many instances and has had costs. Siding with Israel in 1973 Yom Kippur War, for instance, led directly to the oil embargo of the United States by Arab members of OPEC, after all. Oil and Israel have effectively been delinked in recent years. The only state that is tied to violent anti-Israeli activity, ironically enough, is Iran, which sponsors antiterrorist groups like Hezbollah that at least verbally are committed to destroying the Jewish state. (The irony, of course, is that Iran was closer to Israel than any other Islamic state, and the relationship between the two peoples goes back to Cyrus the Great's sponsorship of the original Jewish state of Israel over a millennium ago.) The only issue on which the Muslim Middle East is united against Israel is over the creation of the Palestinian state, but Muslim support for Palestine has been more rhetorical than physical. An American reorientation of its policies in the region based on petroleum is unlikely to have profound results.

Terrorism has been the other major policy concern since 9/11, and since most of the world's current crop of terrorists have either their roots or their inspiration in the Islamic world, this creates a connection between the United States and regional terrorism. Since terrorists threaten the lives of American citizens, the protection of whom is the highest national interest, there is no question that terrorism containment or erasure is a vital American interest.

The question is what to do about it. This requires three determinations. The first is how great a threat exists. The second is why the threat exists: why has the United States been singled out as the target of terrorist groups? The third is what capabilities the United States has formally to deal with this threat; in terms developed earlier, what is the capability to reduce risk? And is it appropriate or effective?

The magnitude of threat speaks both to the level of American interests that may be engaged in dealing with terrorists and with the severity of risk one may incur in different levels of threat. To the extent that terrorists pose an existential threat to Americans (although not to the United States in the way Soviet ICBMs did a generation ago), they invoke vital interests and thus open the range of possible responses up to and including military force. This depiction underlies most of the more hawkish advocacies about how to deal with IS, for instance, but it is an extrapolation that must be qualified in terms of the extent of threat that particular terrorist threats raise.

This qualification raises the question of acceptable and unacceptable risk. The more "muscular" a response to threats from groups like IS becomes, the more finite resources (capabilities) have to be devoted to it, and the less that are available to nullify other threats. Given the political rhetoric about terrorism, it would be difficult for any political figure to portray the problem in less than dire terms, but what kind and quality of response does the threat require? At one extreme is the position that the threat is so existentially dangerous that extreme responses are justified: sending ground troops into Iraq to try to destroy IS, for instance. If, however, the physical threat is limited to plots involving "lone wolf" (individual) terrorists, then it may be limited enough that the homeland security approach developed since 9/11 acceptably reduces the risk that terrorists pose acceptably.

The second question is why the United States has been singled out for terrorist purposes. As part of his justification for invading Iraq, then President George W. Bush opined that it was because "they hate our freedom." It may be true that the freedom associated with Western-style democracy may not appeal to theocratic terrorists, but is that enough to justify putting the United States at the top of terrorist lists? The United States has, especially since 9/11, been the most vocal of world antiterrorist states in its determination to try to eradicate this evil, and knowing that we are their enemy may partially explain why they have singled us out as theirs. This may particularly be the case with IS, which has become markedly more anti-American since U.S. bombers (manned and unmanned) started killing their members from the sky. One possible implication would be to reduce American presence in the area, thus removing the irritant and making the American target a lower priority for terrorists. Such a possibility does not imply a reduced antiterrorist effort, but instead redirecting it more specifically toward keeping the threat away from the American doorstep.

This leaves the third consideration: what, if anything, will work to reduce the risk of terrorism? This is a complicated question debated hotly among terrorism experts but captured in a 2004 presidential debate between President Bush and his adversary, then-Senator John Kerry. When the candidates were asked what the United States should do about terrorism, their answers reflected the philosophical divide on the subject. Bush argued that we had to "destroy" terrorism, essentially to confront and destroy them "in detail" so they no longer pose a threat. Kerry, on the other hand, depicted terrorism as analogous to gambling or prostitution, as a problem that cannot be made to go away altogether but that should be contained as best one can. Bush's position was vastly more popular with the public; Kerry's was probably more realistic.

It is not clear how to remove the terrorist threat. If there is a single truism about terrorism historically, it is that terrorist groups come and go, but terrorism persists. Just as the Jewish Zealots who died at Masada in 73 AD ceased basically to exist after the mass suicide on that mountain, so have other groups come and gone as their members were killed off or their goals accomplished or overwhelmingly rejected to the point they became irrelevant. Despite the fates of individual terrorist groups, however, terrorism as a means to achieve goals continues to be attractive to new groups that feel it may give them a chance to succeed that they might otherwise not have. Seen in this light, terrorism is akin to asymmetrical warfare, even a strategy for some asymmetrical warriors.

What this suggests is that the pursuit, especially with military force, of terrorists is like playing "whack-em" at an arcade. No one has devised a strategy that effectively nullifies the appeal and success of asymmetrical warfare, and the same is largely true of destroying terrorist-based efforts. It may be that the only effective way to deal with them is, as Kerry suggested, to contain them, reducing their effectiveness by doing things like assassinating their leaders, trying to isolate them physically, and waiting for their appeal to wane among potential converts. This is a frustrating, undramatic, and often frustrating way to proceed, but it may be the best one can do.

Terrorism and oil addiction may go hand in glove for the United States in the Middle East. The need to protect access to oil supplies forced the United States to adopt an increasingly intrusive military presence in the area in the 1980s, a presence that has predictably been opposed by many in the region. Just as the victims of military interventions have schemed and eventually moved to reject and repel the occupiers, this American presence may be one reason the United States is in the crosshairs of Middle Eastern terrorists. If oil addiction is reduced, so is the need for such a large military presence, and it becomes possible at least to consider reducing that presence as a way to see if that is why we are the objects of so much terrorist ire. It may not work and may have to be reversed, but it also may be as promising as advocating a policy of promoting U.S. military solutions to regional problems when such efforts have been less than spectacularly successful in the past.

DEFINING AMERICAN MIDDLE EASTERN OPTIONS

U.S. national security policy has, at the operational if not the declaratory level, elevated the Middle East to the penultimate place in the hierarchy of American security values. It is an orientation that has never been declared as the central tenet of American national security concerns, except indirectly. The Carter Doctrine as implemented created the mandate for a continuous U.S. military presence—with the navy at the center position—in the Persian Gulf region to protect the oil. Since the turn of the millennium, terrorism originating in the region has been interpreted to create a priority to reduce or destroy that threat with paramilitary and military force.

The Middle East is where the United States contemplates and sometimes uses military force as the primary instrument of its foreign policy. The United States maintains military forces elsewhere around the globe (albeit in gradually decreasing numbers in most places); it employs those forces almost exclusively in the Middle East.

There is no real historical, interest-derived basis for this level of attention. In the period after World War II, it was clearly known and articulated that the most important—truly vital—interests were in Western Europe and northeast Asia (mainly, Japan and South Korea, but extended to places like the Philippines). These places were important to this country because they were our allies, shared political and economic values with us, and were thus important partners who needed to be protected from Soviet-led communism. When the Cold War ended, those areas ceased to be under threat and were less of a national security problem. They did not lose importance; they were simply less threatened.

The situation has reversed in the Middle East. This region has always been unstable, but it has not posed a threat to the United States historically except to the extent the actions taken by its governments might endanger the oil flow or pose threats to Israel that sound apocalyptical but are largely devoid of any real ability to be realized. The old Middle East was a mess, but it was a tolerable mess, at least in the pantheon of American values.

That changed in the last quarter of the twentieth century. The militancy from fringe religious and political elements in the region allowed them to gain the ability to upset the political scene in some large measure, thanks to the leftovers from the Soviet invasion of Afghanistan in the forms of Al-Qaeda and the Taliban, both of which were reactions to the old, conventional tyrannies of the region. When Saddam Hussein invaded Kuwait, and Saudi Arabia beseeched the United States to form the coalition to evict him (and in the process move his forces safely away from Saudi oil fields and refineries), the justification for a permanent American military presence on the ground was established. The ingredients for the current regional malaise were thus put in place. It is not the only destabilizing dynamic of the Middle East by any means, but it has proven a combustible mix. The question for American policy is what it can do both to calm the region and in the process reduce the threats to the United States that arise from the combustion there.

Operationally, threats to American interests have effectively been reduced to thwarting terrorism that has its source in the Middle East. The United States has shrinking interests in continued petroleum availability, but that interest is neither so encompassing nor as threatened as it once was. At the same time, many Muslims still hate Israel and wish it poorly, but none are sufficiently suicidal to take on the Israelis militarily—especially since Israeli defense is ultimately based on their unilateral regional possession of nuclear weapons. Neither of these interests is inconsequential, but neither are they sufficiently at risk to justify the devotion of sizable national security assets (capabilities) to ensure their continuing safety.

Terrorism is unquestionably *the* Middle Eastern national security problem for the United States in the contemporary situation. As long as there are terrorist groups in the region and they continue to treat the United States as one of their enemies, the United States retains an unavoidable interest in Middle East–based terrorism. To the extent that these groups directly threaten American lives and soil, this threat rises to the level of vitality: it is intolerable for terrorists to assail the United States and its citizens. The question is what can be done about the threat.

The construction of the problem is crucial here. As stated in the last paragraph, the problem is dual and sequential. There is the problem of the existence of terrorist groups in the Middle East that targets the United States. The problem is sequential because, of course, terrorist groups must exist before they can pose a threat. This does not, however, mean the United States must necessarily destroy all these terrorist groups, most of whom have much more diverse agendas than just attacking America. For the United States, the national security problem is how to get terrorist groups to remove this country (and its allies) from the terrorist list.

One way is to try to destroy the terrorist groups (which has been a favorite political position in the United States), but fortunately it is not the only way. It is "fortunate" because efforts to decimate terrorist groups have historically proven difficult to the point of approaching "fool's work." In fact, the effort to do so may be counterproductive in two ways. One is that efforts like drone attacks may kill enough innocents that it increases rather than decreases terrorist recruitment. Second, outsider violence can become a kind of displacement object that allows terrorists to blame countries like the United States for its own inadequacies. The reported desire of IS to lure the United States into a ground war in Iraq illustrates this point.

If historical experience is any indicator, terrorist groups are very difficult to destroy unless they are small and weak enough not to pose much of a problem, but even the most robust movements eventually wither and disappear. The logic is fairly straightforward. By definition, terrorist groups represent unpopular ideas (if their ideas were broadly acceptable, they would not need to resort to terror to achieve them), and they employ grotesque methods to achieve their goals. IS, for instance, represents a distinctly minority belief set within Islam that most Muslims reject, and their enforcement of extremely primitive forms of sharia law alienates many people in their occupied regions. Eventually, these dual characteristics may convince the target and host populations that the terrorists are intolerable and that they rise to get rid of them. Almost all the Middle East terrorist groups have fellow residents of the region as their primary targets: IS targets Iraqi and Syrian Shiites and what they consider apostate Sunnis as westerners and others. If they can be convinced to concentrate on their more nearby opponents rather than the United States, would that not solve the U.S. problem? This is a cynical suggestion, but it may be necessary to get regional actors to become serious about eliminating IS in their backyards. This is, after all, their "neighborhood."

The question is how to make that happen. One way to approach this strategic question is to employ the options identified in Chapter 5. Doing so may not result in a "yellow brick road" mandate for any one option, but it may help broaden the discussion of what the American options are.

The least aggressive path is a passive approach to the Middle East. This option may make some sense in a kind of detached, academic way: it gets the United States out of making bad decisions in a part of the world it clearly does not understand well enough to take an intelligent leading role, and it greatly reduces overseas commitments of scarce military (including manpower) resources. There is even precedent for this course, which amounts to a new form of isolationism that has never disappeared from the American political repertoire.

It is an option that is today about as popular as reintroducing a military draft. The most recent political figure in the United States to advocate a deep foreign policy retreat is Senator Rand Paul of Kentucky, who quickly found that such an approach only appealed to the libertarian fringe and that devotion to this approach submarined his candidacy for the presidency.

The simple fact is that the United States is invested in the Middle East and that many Americans believe that, in principle, the United States should remain so engaged. More hawkish Americans argue the result of a precipitous American withdrawal would be to throw the area into even more chaos than it is in now. Moreover, an American withdrawal could embolden terrorists in their actions against the United States while reducing the ability of the Americans to counter their efforts. These assertions are debatable (and will be debated in Chapter 8), but they have enough public support to dampen support for withdrawal.

The other extreme, full-scale military activism in the region can similarly be dismissed as impractical. The clearest manifestation of such a policy would be the insertion of regular American combat troops into the fight against IS in Iraq, and conceivably in Syria as well. The premise of interventionist arguments is that American military might represents the only force adequate to crush those committed to regional outcomes unacceptable to the United States such as the establishment of a caliphate that becomes a sovereign terrorist platform. This prospect is frightening enough that Americans are willing to listen to the advocacies of most vocal hawks. If there is a "happy" outcome of the American experiences in Iraq and Afghanistan, however, it is that the American public is currently unwilling to support the commitment of regular American forces into another Middle East imbroglio. If the Vietnam precedent is any indicator, this negative resolve may dissipate over time, but for now, it is a useful barrier to a major American combat presence in the region even without raising questions about the propriety of American forces and the chances of their success if engaged.

If the extremes fail for lack of support, that leaves the middle options as potential bases for American policy, and all three have some support in recent American actions. A "show the flag" option suggests a low level of American commitment and involvement in Middle East regional affairs. Its premise is that a greater level of involvement would simply be futile and might draw the United States into the maelstrom of the byzantine conflicts of the region, where the United States cannot succeed and hence should not try. This position further reflects that the outcomes in most of these cases are not sufficiently vital to the United States to justify American expenditure of blood and treasure.

The American approach to two recent conflicts in the region reflects this position. In Syria, in 2013, the United States could have taken a much prominent role in the opposition to the Assad regime, but decided to limit its involvement to providing limited armaments to Syrian rebels and to leading diplomatic attempts in the United Nations to condemn Assad regime brutality and especially its use of chemical weapons against civilians. As Yemen descended into sectarian chaos in 2015 and the Saudis moved to support fellow Sunnis (some of whom were affiliated with AQ and even IS), the United States also chose a minimalist role limited to sailing naval vessels into the waters off the Yemeni coast, a classic form of flag showing.

Both these limited responses were premised on the inability of the United States to do much constructive in these trying situations and the inability of the United States either to take sides or to determine what outcomes it preferred beyond an end to the violence. In Syria, the problem was finding who the so-called "moderate" rebels were among Assad's many opponents. The danger of simply supplying arms and hoping they got to the "right" people was that the arms would fall into the hands of very radical, pro-AQ elements, an entirely reasonable concern. Yemen had become effectively a failed state well before Sunni versus Shiite violence broke out. How the United States could gain anything by taking sides in a sectarian war in Yemen has never been convincingly argued.

From the intervention side of the ledger, the alternative to a "hard," comprehensive intervention is "soft" intervention, a limited American incursion that offers assistance that includes the employment of specialized American forces in Middle Eastern conflicts. The military role in this case, as explained earlier, probably consists of three elements: American airpower to attack opposition targets, Special Forces to act as spotters for the bombers, and regular American forces acting as trainers and advisors to whichever indigenous forces one is supporting. This position has been associated with many of the hard men in Congress and elsewhere in their advocacy of a more robust American role in confronting and defeating IS in Iraq. Technically, none of these forces would be involved as regular combat forces, but it is impossible to believe that there would not be instances where they would both fight and incur casualties. Critics of this approach suggest it is a backhanded way to move to a more comprehensive, activist form of intervention and that it would not work, as discussed in Chapter 5.

This leaves the most centrist option, the Nixon Doctrine. Although this policy pronouncement has all but been forgotten outside policy circles, its articulation by President Nixon was the capstone of his Vietnam War efforts. The doctrine said, in effect, that in the post-Vietnam future, the United States would come to the aid of beleaguered governments facing communist uprisings, but that American assistance would be limited to the provision of material assistance: funds to help pay for the resistance, the supply of weapons and training on how to use them, and other nonlethal forms of assistance. It specifically stated that the United States would not commit U.S. ground forces into these conflicts and that any aid that even potentially involved American personnel would be extremely limited.

The Nixon Doctrine faded from public discourse when the former president was forced to resign and nobody wanted to embrace anything bearing the name of the disgraced leader. It was further a policy position that was drafted with a specific goal in mind: to define American responses in the event of communist insurgencies in the developing world, a problem that clearly no longer exists. Those infirmities notwithstanding, is there any reason not to consider it as an option in the current environment?

The critics on either side will likely belittle this centrist, compromise approach. There is, for instance, little to suggest that supplying and equipping forces that lack the will or support to succeed will tip the balance in their favor. The Nixon Doctrine, tinged with slight soft intervention attributes was applied to Vietnam and has been the basis for American ongoing support for the Iraqi military, and it has not exactly carried the day in either case. Critics on the right complain that the policy is not "robust" enough and that only a more activist posture can possibly lead the regime to succeed. Critics on the left doubt the sagacity of these entreaties and argue that following this option is little more than a disguised way to promote a more interventionist policy: the Nixon Doctrine as the Trojan horse of the interventionists.

The discussion suggests that there is probably no general policy option that is acceptable to all partisans in the debate and that covers all possible contingencies. As in contemporary American politics generally, compromise solutions are not universally valued, and stolid advocacy of extreme positions is the norm for many. The result is a policy of slogging along in an ad hoc manner that ultimately pleases no one and results in a strategy that, at a minimum, lacks coherence.

THE MILITARY DISENGAGEMENT OPTION

A major theme that has run through this volume has been the general lack of success of American efforts to intrude itself into and improve Middle Eastern situations. One basic reason for these failures have been a lack of understanding of the situations by Americans, and thus a tendency to interject the United States into places and events that its actions are unlikely to improve. Another is the inapplicability of outside force to solve problems that are essentially internal. These conflicts can only be solved by the internal parties themselves if they can be solved at all. Outside military force may tactically change the situation, but it is irrelevant at best and detrimental at worst to any enduring solution. This latter problem is developed at length in *The Case against Military Intervention.*

The clear implication of this observation is that it is generally—arguably almost or always—a bad idea to contemplate intervening in Middle Eastern conflicts with armed force. If this assertion is true, then it suggests that the activist options for American reaction—especially full-scale intervention, but possibly forms of soft intervention as well—are ill suited as American policy alternatives in the region. If that premise flows logically soundly from the initial premise, then American policy considerations should concentrate on the less interventionist options from the Nixon Doctrine to passivity—in other words, on forms of military disengagement.

Even mentioning these possibilities is a red flag in substantial parts of the policy community, and especially among the hard men who have dominated Middle Eastern policy. A sample of their objections might include:

1. Its analysis is wrong: American military force can affect situations positively, and the absence of American force may embolden those who oppose American interests and make it more likely that those U.S. objectives will not be realized.
2. Disengagement sends the wrong message to opponents both in the region and globally: if America's opponents know in advance the United States will not respond to their provocations, they will be more likely to act against U.S. interests than they feel they can now.
3. Disengagement is a sign of American decline and abrogation of its role as leader in the world order: it suggests to the rest of the world that the United States, and the prospects of American force employment, is no longer relevant and that the U.S. reaction in many situations can be ignored. Moreover, some less desirable power—China, for instance—may claim the traditional American role, to American disadvantage.
4. In an anarchical international system (one with no central authority to enforce its norms), military force is the major way in which states ultimately achieve and enforce their interests, and if the United States effectively abrogates the resort to armed force, it denies itself its most important tool to realize its interests.

These are not inconsequential objections, and they are clearly based on the Cold War mindset that energizes the hard men of the traditional policy elite. These critics are well placed in the policy hierarchy, including Congress, and they can be counted upon to denounce any suggestion of a reduced American military role in the Middle East, and especially one that effectively takes the injection of American forces off the table in most Middle Eastern crisis situations. Since crises are in large part the lingua franca of Middle Eastern politics, a general policy of direct military nonengagement represents a considerable alteration of American policy. Whether this line of objection represents a pusillanimous retraction of responsibility or a more responsible assessment of what the United States can and should do is the important question that should be addressed.

American interests in the Middle East have indeed changed. The United States no longer is so dependent on Middle East petroleum; that dependence is declining and, in the best case, could disappear, and if that happened, the structure of American regional interests would radically be altered. It can be argued that the need for large amounts of Persian Gulf petroleum dictated a strong military presence in the Middle East after Iran rejected the role of guarantee of oil flow to the West. That restricting position has changed, and it is now possible to think about alternatives to American military activism in this part of the world. Such an analysis will inevitably be situation specific in many cases, meaning one can only assess disengagement and more engaged policy on a case-by-case basis, as has already been done regarding IS. Chapter 7 begins the process of widening that analysis to other aspects of U.S. Middle Eastern policy.

BIBLIOGRAPHY

Brehony, Noel. *Yemen Divided: The Story of a Failed State in South Arabia.* London: I.B. Tauris (Reprint Edition), 2013.

Day, Stephen W. *Regionalism and Rebellion in Yemen: A Troubled National Union* (Cambridge Middle East Studies). Cambridge, UK: Cambridge University Press, 2012.

Eland, Ivan. *No War for Oil: U.S. Dependency and the Middle East.* Oakland, CA: Independent Institute, 2011.

Held, Colbert C. and John Thomas Cummings. *Middle East Patterns: Places, People, and Politics* (Sixth Edition). Boulder, CO: Westview Press, 2013.

Hoffman, Bruce. *Inside Terrorism* (Second edition). New York: Columbia University Press, 2006.

Khalidi, Rashid. *Brokers of Deceit: How the U.S. Has Undermined Peace in the Middle East.* Boston, MA: Beacon Books, 2014.

Lackner, Helen. *Why Yemen Matters: A Society in Transition* (SOAS Middle East Issues). London: Saqi Books, 2014.

Lesch, David W. and Mark L. Haas. *The Middle East and the United States: History, Politics, and Ideologies* (Updated Fifth Edition). Boulder, CO: Westview Press, 2013.

Luyendijk, Joris. *People Like Us: Misrepresenting the Middle East.* London: Soft Skull Press, 2009.

Mahdi, Ahmed. *Energy and US Foreign Policy: The Quest for Resource Security after the Cold War* (International Library of Security Studies). London: I.B. Tauris, 2012.

Nacos, Brigette. *Terrorism and Counterterrorism: Understanding Threats and Responses in the Post-Cold War World.* New York: Penguin Academics, 2006.

Orwell, George. *Animal Farm: Anniversary Edition.* New York: Signet, 2004

Petras, James. *The Politics of Empire: The US, Israel, and the Middle East.* Atlanta, GA: Clarity Press, *2014.*

Salmoni, Barak A., Bryce Loidolt, and Madeleine Wells. *Regime and Periphery in Northern Yemen: The Huthi Phenomenon.* Santa Monica, CA: RAND Corporation, 2010.

Smith, Dan. *The State of the Middle East: An Atlas of Conflict and Revolution* (Revised and Updated Edition). Berkeley, CA: University of California Press, 2008.

Snow, Donald M. *The Case against Military Intervention: Why We Do It and Why It Fails.* New York: Routledge, 2016.

———. *National Security* (Fifth Edition). New York: Pearson, 2014.

———. *Thinking about National Security: Strategy, Policy, and Issues.* New York: Routledge, 2016.

———. *When America Fights: The Uses of U.S. Military Force.* Washington, DC: CQ Press, 2000.

Stern, Jessica. *Terrorism in the Name of God: Why Religious Militants Kill.* New York: ECCO Books, 2003.

United States Department of State. *Patterns of Global Terrorism.* Washington DC: U.S. Department of State (annual publication).

United States Strategic Studies Institute. *New Realities: Energy Security for the 2010s and Implications for the U.S. Military.* Carlisle Barracks, PA: U.S. Strategic Studies Institute, 2015.

Uzi, Rabi. *Yemen: Civil War and Unification* (Library of Modern Middle Eastern Studies). London: I.B. Tauris, 2015.

Chapter 7

One size doesn't Fit All

Policy toward Very Different Places

The "vexatious" nature of the Middle East was introduced in Chapter 5. The structure and intent of that discussion was to point to particularly difficult structural characteristics of the region and its members—factors like religion and ethnicity that pervade the region in different ways and making dealing with regions and its parts difficult. The problem of IS was used to exemplify those difficulties.

This chapter carries that introduction forward by pointing to the consequences of these characteristics for specific regional difficulties. The chapter begins with a list of shared consequences (or characteristics) of the region that defines its contentiousness and perversity as a place for conducting national security policy. In the bulk of the remainder, these observations are applied to specific situations that affect the area generically known as the Middle East.

The term "Middle East" is, like most large geographical designations, a form of shorthand to describe an area that has many sub-designations and distinguishing characteristics that simply referring to the generic region does not capture. This is true of most geographic regions: Europe, for instance, is made of numerous nationalities and states with different histories, languages, and politics. Saying someone is European does not tell you whether someone speaks any particular language, is likely to be of a particular religious faith, or has any particular political leanings. One has to have more specific information to reach that kind of conclusion, such as whether the person is German, French, or Italian. The Middle East is much the same, even if, to this point, it has largely been treated as a kind of unity.

If all areas are diverse, the Middle East is particularly so. To begin with, the term is geographically misleading, and most people we call "Middle Easterners" live in what they think of as the Near East, a more geographically accurate term. The people and region share some general characteristics such as speaking Arabic, but not everyone does even this. Most Middle Easterners are Muslims, but this does not make them friends. Millennia of close habitation has not bred friendship and comity, but often its opposite. Beyond the most trivial shared characteristics, the Middle East is a very diverse place. The problem is that nearly all of the shared characteristics of different places in the region are both different from one another and are negative. Some of the bases were introduced in Chapter 5; some of the implications are explored here. The differences are so much more overwhelming than the similarities that it almost begs the question to introduce them. Doing so does, however, create some common base against which to assess the situation and policy alternatives toward different places.

Seven negative shared characteristics are easily identifiable, recognizing that different observers might produce a list with a different number and weighting of factors. They are presented in a very rough descending order of consequence for an outsider trying to make policy in general or in particular circumstances. Rather, the major purpose of listing them is to exemplify the claim of negative commonality and to provide a kind of checklist in individual applications. All have been introduced in one way or another before.

The first regional commonality is its *instability*. What this means is that there is no common political consensus in most countries, and particularly no agreement that the use of violence is an inappropriate way to attempt to bring about change. As a result, virtually, all countries are subject to internal violence, and if they have not already experienced it, they could at some time in the future. The result is volatility in politics both in and between states. The apparent exceptions are some of the oil-rich states of the Persian Gulf, who have dispensed enough petro-dollars to the population to keep them at bay and who have hired enough foreign security to keep the lid on. Should oil revenues begin to fall and subsidies shrink, it is not at all clear that stability would survive.

Much of this instability is, strangely enough, religious, the result of cleavages within Islam. The most obvious source is the divide between Sunni and Shiite sects in those countries where there are significant numbers of followers of each strain. But that is not all. Of possibly more fundamental division is the battle within various Islamic states over secularism and sectarianism. The secularists represent a modernizing faction within states, arguing that modernization requires more of a divorce among Muslims between church and state in areas of governance. The sectarians, on the other hand, are largely believers in a politically dominant role for Islam in all aspects of life. They are known collectively as Islamists, and their general orientation is found in both sects of the religion. John Owen IV describes their basic belief: "Islamism . . . holds that the billion-strong global Muslim community would be free and great if only it was pious—that is, if Muslims lived under state-enforced Islamic law, or sharia." IS and its caliphate are the current poster children for Sunni Islamism. Where Islamism and both sects of Islam vie for power, the instability is likely to be particularly intense. Iraq, Syria, and Yemen are current examples of places where this convergence occurs.

The second commonality is that essentially all the states are *undemocratic or antidemocratic*. It is, of course, one of Israel's loudest selling points that it is the only political democracy in the region (thereby asserting its distinction from the Islamic states with the United States). The absence of democracy or any organized movement in that political direction became evident as the Arab Spring unraveled and the gaudy promises of Westernization and democratization faded under new waves of tyranny and anarchy. The region is mostly ruled by hereditary monarchs or dictators or regimes that came to power other than by the ballot box, and authoritarianism is sometimes tinged with a theocratic rationale. Most of the states are politically underdeveloped or are classic failing or failed states. Dealing with a particular regime as if it represents the legitimate aspirations of the people (a favorite American pastime) is essentially an exercise in futility or self-delusion in the region. One reason the United States has not been able to find any prominent pro-democratic faction in Syria to support, for instance, is because such a faction probably does not exist. Any proponents of political democracy are likely to be viewed as enemies of the state and jailed, killed, or run out of the country, where they hatch plots to return and to pay back their suppressors.

The third common characteristic is that all these states have significant *centrifugal* influences that drive elements of the population apart, not together. Nationalism that is coterminous with state boundaries and that centers on the country rather than some more parochial base—ethnic or sectarian, for instance—is the exception, not the rule. As a consequence, some groups are generally happier with whatever the status quo is than others, and there is at least a latent likelihood of some form of conflict that can, given regional proclivities, turn violent. As practical consequence for the United States, if it seeks to interject into conflicts within these states, is that whatever its actions are, they will advantage and be supported by some groups but will also disfavor others, who will resent the actions. Efforts to create centripetal dynamics are likely to be drowned in intergroup rivalry, even hatred.

The fourth characteristic, flowing from the third, is that each of these societies is capable of and does produce terrorists, one of whose common traits is a dislike for the West and particularly the United States. In places like Yemen or Iraq, the terrorists may be imported but are able to recruit locally, given high levels of frustration and discontent. This phenomenon is even present in the affluent oil-producing states, where wealth cannot buy total happiness. Saudi Arabia, after all, produced most of the 9/11 attackers, has citizens fighting in most Sunni-based terrorist groups, and has private citizens who provide aid and succor to terrorist organizations, including those intent on attacking the United States. Islam's strong tradition of fundamentalist revivalism provides an intellectual hook on which many of these groups justify their existence and actions.

Fifth, all of the Islamic states are at least rhetorically opposed to the state of Israel, a sentiment that finds current voice in bewailing the ongoing fate of the Palestinians. This sentiment is universal, but it should be treated with a grain of salt. For one thing, some states are more anti-Israeli than others. The Turks, at least until recently the most secular of Islamic states, has had considerable dealings with the Israelis, as did Iran under the Shah. Anti-Israeli rhetoric of support generally extends no further than support of anti-Israeli terrorist groups like Hezbollah, which is only supported by Shiite states (notably Iran). At the operational level, no regional state seems in the least bit interested in actually *doing* something about the state of Israel, because their past experience suggests they could fail, they fear that success would lead to an Israeli nuclear attack, and their commitment is only rhetorical anyway, a displacement object to hide the fact that they disagree on almost everything.

Sixth, most of the states have some level of relationship with the United States, but those relationships are almost uniformly instrumental (a way to extract some good—usually financial—from the United States, rather than basic or philosophical). Almost all the Islamic states, after all, are led by elites that have no interest in democracy or see democracy as a way to leverage their advantages internally (Iraqi Shiites, for instance). If American military power can keep them in power and protect them (Saudi Arabia and the Gulf states), that provides a limited form of coincidence of interests. The simple fact is that the United States and any of the Middle Eastern Islamic states cooperate when they have mutual interests on specific matters, and they do not cooperate when they do not. As pointed out in Chapter 6, "today's friends may be tomorrow's enemies," and depictions of one country or regime as a "friend" are dangerously simplistic and misleading.

Seventh and finally, despite all their differences, the Islamic states are all interdependent. Operationally, this means that things that happen in one Middle Eastern country inevitably have consequences in others, even if those effects are unrealized at the time. The rising basis of this interdependence is often sectarian in nature: conflicts involving Sunni or Shiite groups in one state have ripple effects in adjoining states or other parts of the region. It is not clear, for instance, what the outcome of ethno-sectarian strife in Yemen may be, especially with the introduction of outside forces, notably Saudi Arabia, but also AQAP and IS. Yemen itself is relatively unimportant even in regional terms, but it can also be a microcosm of broader dynamics that pervade the region, often in unforeseen ways.

This introduction is intended to serve two purposes. One is cautionary toward American security policy. It suggests, for instance, that the various parts of the Middle East are so idiosyncratic that no general policy could be applied to all of them, especially if that policy suggests much of an activist component. This idiosyncratic nature is, however, not always recognized. Almost anything that happens in the region evokes a response from the American political right that unless the United States does something forceful to deal with whatever the crisis of the day is, there will be dire consequences for the United States. The scramble among 2016 Republican contenders for the presidential nomination to be the most (chicken) hawkish on foreign policy exemplifies this tendency and even suggests a "one size fits all" approach to the region that defies analysis.

The other purpose is to provide the setting for the rest of the chapter. The intent is to look at some of the most important component issues within the region (other than IS) that currently roil U.S. security policy in the region and which, not so coincidentally, demonstrate that one policy does not seem applicable in all circumstances. To that end, the narrative looks briefly at five Middle Eastern-U.S. trouble spots: relations with the Gulf states, including the consequences of an American withdrawal of major naval assets from the Persian Gulf; U.S.-Israeli relations, notably over the issue of a Palestinian state; the United States and Iran, focusing on the nuclear weapons problem; and Syria and Iraq in light of the IS threat. The chapter concludes with a thoroughly immodest suggestion that the United States might be best served letting the regional actors settle their own problems without American intercession.

NOT SO SAVORY STATES THAT HAVE OIL

Not all the countries with which the United States deals represent political systems the United States and Americans would generally approve of unless there was some extenuating circumstance that brought them together. During the Cold War, for instance, there were a number of regimes in developing world countries that would meet no American's definition of virtue but with which the United States carried on cordial relations. For an otherwise unsavory regime to win American friendship, the key was to profess staunch anti-communism, the more fervent the better. In numerous cases, the result was American embrace of tyrannical, corrupt, often venal regimes, which would have likely been ignored or opposed by the United States if not for their loud opposition to communism.

There is an analogy in the Middle East that demonstrates the anomaly and even humbling impact of America's oil addiction—the very "conservative" states of the Persian Gulf littoral. Most are monarchies in a world where monarchism (except where it is symbolic) is considered an anachronism. Their forms of government alone would mark them as anomalies that would likely render them largely pariahs if they did not happen to sit on top of huge petroleum reserves. Oil, however, makes them valuable, even indispensable, to Western (including American) well-being, a fact which their governors are acutely aware of and which they exploit, often with a fair amount of arrogance. The result is both anomalous and even humiliating for the United States. The sheikhs and the monarchs hold the world's democracies at bay with the threat to deny access to the fluid that supports Western oil addiction.

A 2015 example illustrates this dynamic. It was, in some ways, a relatively minor flap, but it also showed the unsatisfying nature of American relations with the oil barons of the Middle East. In May 2015, President Obama issued an invitation to the heads of state of the Gulf Cooperation Council (GCC) to attend a summit of sorts at Camp David in Maryland to discuss the nuclear weapons talks the United States has spearheaded with Iran. (Technically, the organization is the Cooperation Council for the Arab States of the Gulf, but it is universally known outside the region by its more compact acronym.) The GCC members (Bahrain, Kuwait, Oman, Qatar, Saudi Arabia, and the United Arab Emirate) are all neighbors of the Iranians and are conservative Sunni countries under some form of authoritarian rule. All are deeply suspicious of the Shiite Iranians and would likely be part of any Sunni-Shiite religious conflict in the region. All are also considerably smaller than Iran (individually and collectively) and probably could not defend themselves from an all-out Iranian attack. Their defenses consist mainly of foreign mercenaries working for them and American physical security guarantees. Although the United States has no formal alliance with any of them that would ensure an American military response to provocation, the fact that over 35,000 American service members (primarily Navy and Air Force personnel) are stationed in their region provides some foundation for their belief in an American military "umbrella" shielding them.

Under these circumstances, one would think that the leaderships would jump at the opportunity to meet with the leadership of the American government on a clear matter of their own security, but that was not the case. All the GCC members oppose the negotiations with the Iranians on nuclear matters with a passion not often seen otherwise outside of Israel, and they have a Netanyahu-like dislike of the agreement reached earlier in the year to regulate Iranian nuclear development short of weapons acquisition. As a result, President Obama was not exactly at the top of any most loved leader list in GCC capitals.

As the mid-May date for the conference approached, it became clear that only two of the heads of state (from Qatar and Kuwait) would attend the meeting. All others would send representatives, of course, but not the leaders to whom the invitations were extended and whose presence was desired.

Saudi Arabia is, of course, the largest and most consequential member of the group, yet King Salman, its newly installed monarch, declined, stating an earlier commitment regarding the ongoing crisis in Yemen. High on the agenda for all those in attendance was to gain military assurances from the American president about protecting them from Iran, but their leaders could not bother themselves enough to do this in person. When they did not get everything that they wanted from a meeting they declined to attend, they opposed the outcome. Saudi Arabia is the most dramatic case in point.

This snub was not widely publicized at the time but demonstrated the world-class arrogance of the oil-rich states. These states are, to put it mildly, highly dependent on outsiders—which operationally means the Americans— to protect them from their numerous, often well-earned, enemies. The 1990 Iraqi invasion of Kuwait demonstrated that dependency, which one might expect to be accompanied by some gratitude, even deference—like showing up for a summit called by their major protector deference—there was no such show of gratitude. Why not? The answer is clear: the GCC members believe they hold the ace card in the relationship because of Western oil dependence, a form of leverage they believe trumps their virtually total vulnerability to attack by a power the size of Iran.

What does this say about the relationship between the United States and the Gulf oil producers? Basically, it says that these states hold the United States in some level of disdain, essentially as mercenaries who will provide military protection for them to ensure their continued access to oil. The mercenary part of the equation comes from the Desert Storm case in 1990–1991. In that situation, American military might was absolutely critical to reestablishing Kuwaiti sovereignty and protecting the Saudi oil fields from potential Iraqi occupation, but the bill for the American action was mostly paid by the Saudis. The idea that the Americans would do GCC dirty work is not entirely far-fetched from the Saudi viewpoint. Why bother traveling all the way to the Catoctin Mountains and sleeping in a knotty-pine decorated cabin rather than the royal digs at home when you don't have to in order to accomplish your own goal of American military assistance.

The relationship between the United States and the GCC members is one that is clearly built on expediency and mutual need and not from any sense of love or mutual interests beyond the need for oil and security. As already argued, the American dependency on GCC oil is decreasing and could virtually disappear altogether in the upcoming years. If it does, then GCC leverage over the United States shrinks concomitantly. From an objective standpoint, the reason for American military presence in the region essentially begins and ends with the protection of the flow of petroleum. If the United States does not get its oil from the Persian Gulf, the reason to commit large numbers of Americans and military assets to protect the Gulf shrinks as well. In that case, the leverage the Gulf states have over the United States is reduced considerably, whereas their dependence on the United States for military protection remains intact. If anything, it could actually increase. Under such circumstances, would the monarchs dismiss a summon to the Maryland mountains so cavalierly, or would they be asking what kinds of clothes are most appropriate for the Catoctins?

Getting the petroleum monkey off American backs seems an intoxicating prospect, but it probably creates new potential problems that should be antici-pated before any precipitous changes are made. The direst change is that an American military drawdown in the region would leave a military vacuum into which some other power which would like to gain a position of influence with the oil sheikhs might seek to exploit. This would be particularly true in the Persian Gulf itself, through which tankers carrying petroleum products must steam to get to market.

Who would likely be a candidate to try to replace the U.S. Navy if it reduces or eliminates its patrol of these waters? There are relatively few possibilities, but one stands out: China. The Chinese need additional, non-coal-based sources of energy to fuel the growth of their economy, and the Persian Gulf offers an opportunity to gain access to currently unavailable supplies, as well as potentially denying those sources to others (like Japan or India, for instance). Moreover, the Chinese have been constructing a true blue-water navy that may not be any direct challenge to the U.S. Navy, but which certainly could pose a formidable presence in the Persian Gulf if the Americans essentially departed.

Does the United States want to run the risk of turning the Persian Gulf into a Chinese rather than an American lake? In the short run, this might not be a problem, at least as long as the United States does not need Middle East petroleum. But what if that changes? What, for instance, happens if the shale revolution turns out to be less than its enthusiasts proclaim, probably on ecological grounds? What if the world's need for petroleum for the plas-tics industry burgeons beyond the capacity of non-Persian Gulf supplies to service? What if Chinese virtual control makes access difficult for American friends and allies who do need Persian Gulf oil? All these geopolitical ques-tions must be answered before any precipitous action is contemplated and are concerns that will be raised in the next chapter.

THE ISRAELI FACTOR: AN INVERTED ASYMMETRICAL RELATIONSHIP

American relations with Israel are closer than those with any of the Arab states. The United States was one of the cosponsors of the UN resolutions that created the state of Israel in 1947, and it has been a staunch supporter and defender of the Jewish state throughout its nearly 70-year existence. Israel and the United States have the largest Jewish populations of anyplace in the world, and Israel is the only state in the region with a democratically elected government and tradition. At the more interpersonal level, many Americans and Israelis travel freely in and interact with one another, many hold dual citizenship, and the two countries are very economically and intellectually related. Israel is America's closest friend in the Middle East, and the United States is Israel's closest friend and ally in a world that is not entirely sympathetic to the Jewish state and some of its policies.

The two states have significant differences, and always have. For Israel, the Middle East outside its boundaries is a very hostile neighborhood containing numerous states and groups that not only do not wish Israel well, but would like to destroy it. The Israelis, as a result, perceive themselves as living in a perpetual state of existential threat that colors their view of the region in which they live. The United States does not face an equivalent Middle Eastern threat: Islamic religious terrorism may menace the United States, but it does not present a meaningful threat to American existence. Access to petroleum located in the Islamic Middle East further influences how the United States views the region and how the United States must act in it.

In recent years, and especially since the coincidence of the presidency of Barack Obama and the prime ministership of Benjamin Netanyahu, the question of leadership in the relationship has also arisen. As the section title suggests, that relationship has become both asymmetrical and inverted. It has always been asymmetrical in the sense that the United States is objectively far more important to Israel than Israel is to the United States. Without U.S. support, Israel's existential dilemma becomes much more complicated, even potentially untenable. There is no equivalent consequence for the United States if it lacks Israeli support.

One would think that this asymmetry would create an Israeli dependence on the United States that would make it deferential to American leadership, and that has historically largely been the case. In the Obama-Netanyahu era, however, that relationship has largely ceased to work on the most important issues. Indeed, it has virtually been inverted, with the Israeli leadership schooling the Americans on mutual policy concerns rather than the other way around. Some of this has been the result of relentless Republican opposition to anything Obama may attempt to do, but some of it also reflects that the Israeli leadership no longer fears the consequences of taking on the Americans and, in effect, telling the United States what its policy toward Israel should be. The image of Netanyahu speaking before a joint session of Congress in early 2015 and actively lobbying Congress to reject the nuclear agreement between Iran and the West exemplifies this change. The Israelis have acted to seize intellectual control in U.S.-Israeli relations, inverting the direction of leadership that asymmetry would suggest. Why has this occurred?

The short answer lies in Israel wrapping itself in the existential threat against it and the potentially apocalyptical consequences of opposition to its policy preferences. The result is a hard-line, intransigent, and militarized policy toward the region that flies in the face of historic American beliefs about what best serves the interests both of Israel and the region. Netanyahu replies that the Obama administration has proposed or adopted policy positions that could weaken Israel's ability to blunt the existential threat. Within the United States, it has enlisted the hard men to promote its positions in the Congress. It is tempting to draw an analogy between Israeli *chutzpah* in defying the American leadership and the Saudi refusal to send the King to Camp David. That is, of course, a suggestion which Israel and its American supporters would dismiss.

No one questions that Israel lives in a difficult, hostile neighborhood or that it faces significant threats to its existence. Where the two countries come into conflict is over how Israel handles that threat. Among those who find themselves at odds with the Israelis, there is the imputation that Israeli intransigence may actually make matters worse than they need to be and that a more conciliatory position might actually increase the Israeli security dilemma. Such initiatives could cause the Israelis to compromise what have become bedrock positions that supporters of Netanyahu argue are necessary to blunt the existential threat to Israel. Implicitly, a new form of asymmetry is entered into the equation that has come to trump the traditional asymmetry of interests and needs. That asymmetry is that the threat to Israeli existence is so much greater than any threat to American existence that Israeli perceptions trump American beliefs. If the Americans are wrong and Israel follows their lead, Israel could cease to exist. The United States faces no equivalent dilemma and cannot fully appreciate the bind in which Israel is trapped. Given this difference, the Americans should defer to the Israelis: asymmetry of consequences trumps asymmetry of interests. This creates a source of conflict in U.S.-Israeli relations that is particularly obvious over two issues: the creation of a sovereign Palestinian state and the Iranian nuclear program.

The creation of a Palestinian state has been an issue between the two countries since the Camp David Accords of 1979. That agreement did three things: it ended the Israeli occupation of the Sinai Peninsula, returning that piece of territory to Egyptian control; it created the pathway leading to Egyptian recognition of Israel; and it created a mandate to deal with Palestinian statelessness, a condition in which the Palestinian Muslims have found themselves since Israeli independence. The first two parts of the agreement were agreed to and implemented; the third remains unsettled (for a discussion, see my *Cases in American Foreign Policy*).

The advocacy of creating a Palestinian state is internationally widespread, and the United States has been a leading proponent of it since Camp David. The premises of advocacy are: the illegality of continued Israeli occupation of the West Bank of the Jordan River, territory seized by Israel in the 1967 Six-Day War that was formerly part of Jordan; and the legitimacy of claims by the Palestinians for their own state. Backing these claims has been a rhetorical device for creating some strand of unity among the fractious Islamic states of the region. Under Netanyahu, Israeli opposition has hardened and become more intransigent.

Although it risks oversimplifying a very complicated reality, the U.S.-Israeli disagreement can be boiled down to two emphases on each side. From the Israeli perspective, the creation of a Palestinian state is an unacceptable security risk, because it could provide a sovereign refuge within which terrorist and other movements dedicated to the destruction of Israel could operate: a staging ground for the existential threat. At the same time and less explicitly admitted, continued occupation and development of the West Bank allow Israel to promote additional Jewish immigration to Israel, a possibility that is very much limited if Israel must retreat to its pre-1967 boundaries (or something like them): there is simply not enough livable space to attract more of the diaspora without the occupied territories. A larger Jewish Israeli population, it is believed, further enhances Israel's ability to protect itself from hostile neighbors.

The U.S. perspectives (more precisely, the position of those who believe Israel must accept a two-state solution with Jewish and Palestinian states sitting side-by-side) also rests on two fundamental premises. The first is that there cannot be true peace between Israel and its Islamic neighbors as long as the Palestinian issue festers. Allowing the creation of a Palestinian state would both reduce the objective basis for Muslim opposition to Israel and improve Israel's esteem in an international community which views continued Israeli presence as evidence of an illegal, repressive occupation. It would also reduce Arab-American disagreement based on U.S. support for Israel.

The more fundamental basis for implementing a two-state solution is that it is in Israel's enlightened self-interest. This argument is based on the demographics of Israel and the occupied territories. The gist of this argument (which is shared by many Israelis, but not a majority) is that the current policy of resistance is shortsighted, and that its continuation will threaten the Israeli state in the long run.

The dilemma is that Israelis want their country to be both Jewish and democratic. This combination can be sustained in Israel proper (Israeli territory conforming to pre-1967 boundaries), where the Israelis outnumber the non-Jewish population by a ratio of better than five-to-one. A Jewish majority is not threatened in this territory for the foreseeable future. The situation is different if the occupied territories are added to what is considered Israel. These territories are overwhelmingly Arab and Muslim, and population growth rates among the Muslims greatly exceed that of Israelis, a dynamic for which Jewish immigration cannot compensate.

These demographic dynamics are undeniable and not subject to meaningful manipulation: they cannot be changed. They have direct consequences for Israel and its self-image as a democratic, Jewish state. Within the traditional boundaries of Israel, the combination is sustainable, because Israel has an essentially permanent Jewish majority. If the West Bank is part of metropolitan Israel, however, the numbers change. If one adds the Jewish population of traditional Israel and the West Bank and does the same calculation for the Palestinian Muslims, the numbers are roughly equal, and given more rapid fertility rates among the Arabs, are quickly (and inevitably) producing a Muslim majority in the combined territories, and this creates the Israeli dilemma. Israel cannot be *both* a Jewish and a democratic state in this combined jurisdiction. If it wants to remain democratic, it will likely become Muslim, since a majority of its citizens are, or shortly will be, Muslim. It can thus only remain Jewish by effectively becoming nondemocratic, adopting an essentially *apartheid* political system in which non-Jews are denied equal political rights, for example, the ability to outvote the Jewish minority. The only way Israel can remain both Jewish and democratic is to retreat to something like its own boundaries. It cannot continue to occupy the West Bank and be both.

This frames the policy problem on which Israel and the United States disagree. The Israeli government understands these demographic realities, but it does not like to discuss them or their implications. Rather, the prevailing implicit opinion is that serious consideration of Palestinian statehood is unacceptable politically. It raises the existential risk to unacceptable levels, and ceding the territories effectively curtails Israeli desires to bring more of world Jewry to Israel. When Netanyahu went to Paris in 2015 in the wake of terrorist attacks against Jews there, he invited anybody who desired to do so to migrate to Israel. The question was where Israel could put them; the answer was on the West Bank. If a Palestinian state had been in existence, the invitation could not have been issued.

The Obama administration, and others before it, have argued that the creation of a Palestinian state is absolutely necessary: there can be no improvement in Israeli relations and thus security with the Muslim world as long as Palestinian statehood is denied, and Israel is risking its own heritage if it must revert to some apartheid alternative to retain its religious purity. The Israelis implicitly counter that they, not the Americans, are taking all the real risks in pursuing this path, and the possible consequences are unacceptable. As long as current attitudes hold, both sides will continue to be at loggerheads.

The other aspect of U.S.-Israeli disagreement is over the Iranian nuclear program. Both countries, as well as most of the world, agree that Iran's program to build nuclear weapons should not be allowed to continue or to reach maturation. Ironically, the position of Israel and the Sunni states of the Persian Gulf are virtually in total accord on this end, and both share the fear that a nuclear Iran might threaten, on in the worst case even use, these weapons against them. As a result, both the Sunni sheikhs and the Israelis are equally adamant in their categorical opposition to the nuclear agreement reached between Iran and the U.S.-led European coalition. They are unalike in two ways: Israel also has nuclear weapons while the Gulf states do not (although Iranian weapons achievement might force them to develop this same capability); and the Gulf states do not talk as threateningly about how to deal with the Iranians as do the Israelis.

The question that divides Israel and the United States on this issue is how to deal with the Iranians. The United States (at least the Obama White House) prefers negotiating with Iran and reaching an enforceable, verifiable agreement that the Iranians will not violate. The Israelis reject this approach, arguing the Iranians will not honor any agreement they sign and will continue clandestine efforts to reach nuclear weapons status. Netanyahu has, predictably, opposed the agreement that was reached between major Western states and Iran as a "bad deal" and publicly sought support for his position when he addressed the U.S. Congress (an unprecedented open case of lobbying by a foreign leader on U.S. soil) and since. The Israelis prominently do not rule out the use of force (air strikes) to take out Iranian facilities, a tactic it has used in the past to dismantle regional nuclear aspirants, notably Syria and Iraq. Iran's nuclear facilities are heavily protected, and it is not clear that air attacks would work. Moreover, the Obama administration fears that an Israeli attack would trigger an Iranian retaliation that could result in a general war in the region that would be difficult to control.

Like the Palestinian question, the Iranian nuclear weapons problem reflects the difference in perspective between the two countries. The Israeli government believes that if Iran obtains nuclear weapons, they would not hesitate to use them against Israel. This belief effectively cancels the deterrent advantage Israel has in the region due to its own nuclear arsenal (Israel is the only Middle Eastern state to possess nuclear capability). Whether a nuclear Iran would be any more likely to turn those weapons on its adversaries than any other state that has reached nuclear weapons status is purely speculative, but the wrong answer clearly has existential implications for the Israelis, particularly since Israeli population concentrations in a few cities mean the country could effectively be destroyed with a few nuclear explosions on its territory.

The current divide is virtually stereotypical of past proliferation debates (see Snow, *National Security for a New Era*, fifth edition). Whenever the danger arises that a current non-weapons state might "go nuclear," the community of current possessors decries and opposes the possibility, generally on the ground that the new possessor would be less responsible with the weapons than others have been. This condescending assertion has never been clearly demonstrated, and the post-1945 record of nuclear wars remains unblemished. The possibility that the next proliferation might prove apocalyptically different remains a potent argument, however.

Both these issues raise the difficulty of interest and perspectival differences even between the closest of friends. The personal consequences of a Palestinian state are not great and are potentially beneficial for the United States, for instance, because if it could be accomplished peacefully, it is a path to a more peaceful, stable Middle East. For Israel, if the process goes wrong (results in a terrorist-sponsoring Palestine), the threat is existential. Likewise, Iranian nuclear weapons would not directly imperil the United States, since Iran would have no current ability to deliver those weapons to American targets; they do have the ability to strike Israel with them. It is all a matter of perspective and the intensity of interests engaged.

CLASH OF THE GREAT SATANS:
THE U.S. AND IRAN FACE OFF

The relationship between the United States and the largest state in the Persian Gulf region could be the subject of a not very sophisticated television comedy were it not taken so seriously by both sides and have such potentially dire consequences for the region. Iran and the United States were once the closest of friends in the region, and they have become the worst of adversaries: each is indeed a "great Satan" to the other. It is probably a needless level of animosity, but that makes it no less real.

Both sides have legitimate grievances against the other. The United States was the tip of the spear of Shah Reza Pahlevi's attempt to reinvigorate Iran to something like the position of the historical Persian Empire. In return, the Shah, armed to the teeth with state-of-the-art American weaponry, enforced the free flow of oil to the West. American efforts to help modernize Iran, however, included extensive secularization of one of the most conservative Shiite populations in the world. The vast majority of Iranian peasants and the religious mullahs who were their spokesmen and advisors did not benefit from modernization and hated the Shah—and by reflection the United States—for the effort. The United States was also instrumental in engineering the overthrow of the only fully democratically elected government in Iranian history in 1953, alienating even broader parts of the population. When the Shah was finally driven from power in 1979, animosity toward the United States accompanied hatred for the Shah: America thus earned its share of the Great Satan designation.

The Iranians, in their revolutionary fervor, quickly acted to become the Great Satan themselves. Iranian "students," as they were officially proclaimed, seized the American embassy in Tehran, made hostages of its personnel and held them for 444 days, until their release was negotiated on the eve of Ronald Reagan's inauguration in January 1981. The hostage crisis led television news coverage throughout the incarceration: nightly news broadcasts regularly began with a backdrop of how many days the hostages had been held. Americans could not ignore the crisis: the government of Iran also became a Great Satan.

Iran and the United States have essentially ignored one another ever since, other than an occasional slur toward one or the other. This situation is anomalous in geopolitical terms. Iran has, by far, the largest population of any Persian Gulf country (around 80 million, with all its neighboring states having populations of 30 million or less), and Iran represents the modern version of the world's second oldest continuous civilization. It has the world's third largest reserves of traditional petroleum (behind Saudi Arabia and Canada), and it considers itself the pivotal regional power in the area, a claim not without validity. The United States, on the other hand, has been the most prominent external power in the region since France and Great Britain forfeited that role in the 1950s. Moreover, Americans and Iranians developed deep and close ties during the period of Shah-based friendship that ended in 1979, and many of those connections remain. Something like normal relations between the two countries otherwise makes sense, but until recently, the two have not dealt directly with one another on any official level. The Iranian nuclear program has changed that.

The Iranian nuclear program is the centerpiece of American-Iranian discussions and is reflected in other areas of contention between them. Iran maintains that its nuclear program is entirely for peaceful purposes, the generation of energy for the country. That assertion may or may not be true, but a "peaceful" nuclear program can be converted clandestinely to one that can produce nuclear weapons, an intent the Iranians deny but others doubt. Among the most vociferous and militant doubters are the Israelis, the Sunni monarchies of the Persian Gulf, and even some Americans who fear a nuclear-armed Iran could menace this country. How warranted these fears may be is debatable; the fact they are sincerely held is not. Since all those who fear the prospect of Iranian nuclear weapons are connected with the United States, it cannot ignore the prospect and feels it must take the lead in foreclosing the possibility of a nuclear-armed Iran.

The vehicle for trying to restrain the Iranians has been the so-called P5+1 group, composed of the five permanent members of the UN Security Council (the United States, Russia, China, France, and the United Kingdom) plus Germany. The European Union is also represented on questions about the nuclear program. The United States has provided much of the leadership and direction to the non-Iranian efforts on the subject, but it is worth noting that all the others have signed off on agreements that have been agreed to by the Iranian government. Abrogating or short-circuiting the negotiation process has international ramifications beyond the region.

The details of the process and substance of these negotiations are ongoing and beyond the scope of this discussion. Their clear intent is to cause the Iranians to renounce any planning or intention they may have or harbor in the future about acquiring nuclear weapons in a way that is reliably verifiable by third parties. Because of the poisonous relationship between Iran and the United States, Iranian assurances need to be accompanied by adequate means of compliance verification by neutral organizations like the International Atomic Energy Agency (IAEA). This latter requirement is crucial because the Iranians have hidden most of their activities in well-protected underground facilities they argue are made necessary by the possibility of Israeli air attacks. The critics, notably the Israelis, argue the secrecy is a cover for prohibited activities.

These negotiations are highly controversial, but they are probably critical to any future of expanded, less confrontational relations between Iran and the United States. Controversy surrounds the assessment by outsiders that Iranian duplicity makes the talks a sham: the Iranians cannot be trusted. This sentiment is strongest among the Israelis, and it is shared by some American politicians who believe anything the Obama administration does is flawed. It is also shared by the Sunni oil monarchies.

Given the animosity between the Americans and the Iranians, these negotiations would be difficult in the best of circumstances, and a constant chorus of very loud criticism from others does not add to the likelihood of its success. The rhetoric surrounding the consequences of Iranian acquisition of nuclear weapons capability is familiar in the long history of nuclear proliferation and attempts to stem new states from gaining weapons status. It is a simple fact that no agreement between sovereign entities can ever be entirely foolproof and that there will always be some possibility of cheating. The purpose of negotiated agreements is to reduce that prospect to the smallest possibility of breach, but what possibility (what level of risk) is acceptable will always vary, depending on the perspective of the observer.

This impasse also reflects a more fundamental geopolitical reality that is part of the general regional malaise. By virtually any metric, Iran is the dominant regional state, and were it possible to strip away the Sunni-Shiite veneer of regional politics, this position would be recognized within the region.

To the Iranians, the nuclear issue dangles over the region to remind others that Iran is, after all, the successor of the Persian Empire and as such deserves deference. Adding both sectarian and nuclear weapon elements to this witches' brew adds to the dispute's emotional and physical volatility. The Iranian nuclear program would be a problem if the geopolitical or sectarian elements alone energized it. Together, they make it truly combustible.

Israel and the Gulf states face the most dangerous and direct consequences of an Iranian nuclear weapon program. Should there be a breakout that went unnoticed until it became a fait accompli, these consequences would be particularly dire for both. Israel has responded forcefully in two ways. First, it has repeatedly threatened military actions to take out Iranian facilities before the program can reach fruition: effectively, to bomb Iran back into the nuclear stone age. The Israelis have tried to interest the United States in this endeavor but have been rebuffed. The Americans are not convinced such attacks would be effective, and they fear there would be a significant anti-American reaction as a result (such as increased terrorist threats). For the Israelis, an Iranian breakout has existential potential, and no option is off the table. If this fails (as it basically has), the second Israeli strategy has been to submarine the negotiation process. Netanyahu has personally led this international effort, designed to prevent an agreement from being reached or, at a minimum trying to ensure it will not be passed as a treaty through the U.S. Senate.

The position of the states of the Gulf is somewhat different. They lack the wherewithal to attack and try to take out the Iranian facilities, and any attempt to do so would inflame Sunni-Shia animosities and possibly fuel a religious war that has been widely predicted but for which they are hardly prepared. They also lack the Israeli influence and ability to lobby in the United States, meaning their leverage is effectively reduced to the "oil card." Given their inability to solve this problem themselves, it is somewhat more surprising that the leaders did not respond more positively to the Camp David assurance summit.

The consequences of various outcomes also vary. At least some limited form of Iranian-American rapprochement makes geopolitical sense. The United States has no vested interest in taking sides in the Sunni-Shia divide, and ignoring the largest and most significant Shiite country implicitly aligns the country with the Sunni states. Moreover, American and Iranian interests in opposing IS and in Afghanistan might be more fruitful in a less poisonous environment that an agreement could facilitate. There is residual animosity on both sides with roots in the last century, but it serves both countries' national interests to overcome the past and to try to see where they might be able to deal positively with one another.

LESSER, RESIDUAL CONUNDRUMS: IRAQ AND SYRIA

American relations with both these countries currently center on the IS crisis, if for different reasons discussed in Chapter 5. Residual relations with Iraq are concentrated on Anbar Province, the hotbed of IS occupation and the heart of Sunni unhappiness both with Baghdad and the United States, which created their misery by deposing Saddam Hussein. The United States would like Bashar al-Assad to go in Syria, but deposing him might strengthen IS in Syria. Deciding which evil is worse is not an easy choice.

What the situations in the two countries both support is the contention that the United States does not truly understand the Middle East and its constituent parts (states), and that this ignorance leads the country to make bad decisions that do not serve the American national interest very well. This is most clearly the case in Iraq, where the United States is effectively stuck trying to make the best of the disastrous decision to invade and occupy that country and where policies being considered could make the overall situation worse, not better. To this point, the United States has avoided blundering head first into the Syrian civil war, but some of the hard men would not mind a heavier involvement there.

The Iraqi problem is captured in what Thomas L. Friedman first called the "Pottery Barn rule," a dictum that has become somewhat more associated with former Secretary of State and Army General Colin S. Powell. In 2002, Powell is said to have argued to President Bush the essence of the rule in cautioning against the invasion of Iraq: "if you break it, you own it." In the Iraqi case, breakage meant dismantling the Iraqi political system. Powell argued that invading and conquering Iraq would effectively shatter the political system there and would require the United States to occupy it for a prolonged period of time. He was, of course, correct; his counsel was also rejected. Iraq was broken, and the United States (and the Iraqis themselves) has not figured out how to put it back together again. The corollary to the rule is "if you break it, you have to fix it." The United States has not been able to help put it together again. IS presence in Anbar, a Kurdish region that acts increasingly like an independent state (which creates its own problems), and simmering Sunni-Shiite animosities are only the most obvious signs of fractures in need of repair.

Iraq is a problem that never seems to go away. The presence of IS in Anbar, a menace that would not be possible or would be far less dangerous if many Sunnis did not support their being there, guarantees that chronic instability and violence remain dominant leitmotifs in that country. The United States "broke" whatever fragile order existed under the Sunni dictatorship in 2003, but had no effective plan to repair the damage it had done. Its effective disenfranchisement of Baathist Sunnis and their replacement with inexperienced, vengeful Shiites did not reconstruct Iraq. The political and military situations were not much improved in 2015 over what they had been in 2002. If anything, the international situation was worse from an American vantage point: there was no IS before the United States "liberated" Iraq, and Iranian presence and influence were considerably less than they are now. It is not clear the United States has any nostrums for creating a happy ending in Iraq. If that is the case, to what extent and for how long does the United States "own" the Iraq problem? More importantly, is there anything positive the United States can do to improve the situation there?

The continuing drama of Iraq took an ironic domestic turn in 2015, as Republican aspirants for the 2016 presidential nomination jousted over whether they believed President George W. Bush was justified in ordering the invasion in the first place. Americans as a whole overwhelmingly reject a positive answer, but Republican aspirants were reluctant to turn their backs on the last members of their party to win the White House. The answer they tended to give was based on whether anyone else would have reached a different, negative decision based on the intelligence that was given to the president regarding alleged Iraqi weapons of mass destruction (WMD) possession and ties to Al-Qaeda. These qualifications, however, begged the central question about the intelligence, which was whether it was credible at the time or whether it was "cherry picked" by neo-con advocates of the invasion to support their cause. Some analysts (including the present author) argued that the intelligence reports were always incredible: Saddam Hussein and Al-Qaeda, for instance, were sworn enemies, a fact known at the time. Whose fault was it if the President accepted intelligence offerings that he should have known were suspect? It was notable that a number of the neo-con champions of the invasion were foreign policy advisors to Republican aspirants.

Syria is different in the senses that the United States had nothing to do with precipitating the crisis leading to the civil war, has not been an active physical partisan in the violence, and has no deep national security interest in how the conflict ends. In Syria, the Pottery Barn rule does not apply to the United States. Syria is clearly a broken piece of pottery, but the United States did not break it and thus does not own it. Any connection the United States has to whatever the outcome there may be is more abstract and thinly geopolitical. The United States would like to see the end of the Assad regime, but it does not want that event to strengthen the hand of IS in Syria, in effect giving the caliphate a carte blanche to extend its sway into western parts of the country where the wealth and infrastructure is. Like Iraq, however, it is not entirely clear who would succeed Bashar al-Assad or, more critically, whether the replacement would be much of an improvement. Iraq, for instance, may be, as some American politicians maintain, a "better place" with Saddam Hussein gone, but it is hard to argue his successors have been much of an improvement. If the American government knows of a worthy Syrian successor, it has not said who that individual or faction is.

The common element that both Iraq and Syria share is the presence of IS and its caliphate carved from parts of both countries. The two countries share the problem that IS, in essence, represents an extreme Islamist thread of Sunnism and that both regimes are ruled by Shiites. Believers in Shia Islam are, of course, considered apostate by IS and are the subject of the most extreme form of sharia "justice." They differ in that Shiites are in the overwhelming majority in Iraq, whereas they are a distinct minority in Syria. The defeat or prevalence of IS thus has a different impact on each country.

In Iraq, the defeat of IS has majority appeal: indigenous support is basically confined to Sunni Anbar and is opposed within Shiite and Kurdish parts of the country. If IS could be defeated and the Shiite regime in Baghdad convinced to incorporate Anbar Sunnis meaningfully into governance (admittedly not a given), the defeat of IS could contribute to some stabilization of the country. The situation in Syria is affected differently by an IS defeat. IS represents the strongest opposition group to the Assad regime's, and so removing IS from the civil war equation could simplify the regime survival problem for Assad. Whether getting rid of IS would cause the fractious Sunni opposition to Assad to reassemble into a coherent force actually capable of toppling the Damascus regime is problematical. Moreover, whether the success of the rebels would result in a greater likelihood of peace or would instead turn into a recriminatory anti-Alawite bloodbath is also uncertain.

These two fragments of the crisis of the Middle East represent, in their own ways, the ambivalence and difficulty of crafting coherent American national security responses that serve the criteria of service to the American national interest, some reasonable prospect of success, and the likelihood that an American effort will contribute to some greater stabilization in the region. The question of how American policy can move situations from being zero-sum (what one side wins, the other loses) to positive sum (both sides can gain) outcomes is not clear. This calculation applies progressively to the more activist, intrusive purposes for which some Americans propose policy actions. One reaction is simply to adopt a more hands-off approach that requires the principals to work out their own problems.

THE CHAIN LINK FENCE ANALOGY

It would be difficult, arguably impossible, to maintain that American policy in the Middle East has been a rousing success over the past quarter-century or more. The United States has certainly been heavily invested in the region's problems, as its record of military intrusion (in fourteen Middle East countries since 1980) attests. This increasingly prevalent American presence has coincided with the rise of anti-American terrorism in the region. It may be that this coincidence is spurious: terrorism has arisen not because of American presence but independently of it. At this point, no one can tell with any reliability whether the relationship exists or its direction. Making the projection goes beyond the data.

The American interest that underlies this activism has been oil. Most regional analysts deny or downplay that importance, and politicians shy away from it. Admitting that the United States is bowing down in front of oil addiction amounts to admitting the country is trading American blood for Middle Eastern oil. That equation may be accurate, but it is politically dicey, at a minimum, to admit it.

If the need for Middle Eastern oil is removed from the list of American geopolitical interests in the region, the calculation changes dramatically. The reason is simple enough: except for petroleum access and the protection of Israel, the United States does not have very important interests—certainly vital interests—in much of what goes on there. The exceptions are places where the country has violated the Pottery Barn rule, broken the status quo in individual states, and thus has some residual responsibility to clean up the mess and to try to make the country whole again. Iraq and Afghanistan are the obvious examples.

Terrorism is the rhetorical tie that binds the United States to the Middle East in the absence of oil as a vital interest. The premise is that unless the United States confronts and disassembles the terrorist threat at its source, the various terrorist organizations will imperil Americans at home, a clear violation of the most vital interest any country has. No one would deny that avoiding this scenario is vitally important business. There are two residual questions that the scenario does not answer. One is why the threat toward the United States exists: is it because the terrorists inherently hate Americans, or is it because what they hate is the American military's intrusive presence and actions in the region; if it is the latter, removing the irritant may be the more appropriate response.

The other question is what actions are most responsive for reducing the threat? As noted, the United States has devoted considerable resources to the counterterrorism enterprise, and it has had some success against individual terrorists and organizations. The most spectacular efforts have been military and paramilitary, but they have not succeeded in causing the significant shrinkage of the overall problem. Efforts to "terrorist proof" American soil have similarly had general success (there has not, after all, been a successful, coordinated foreign terrorist attack again on American soil since 2001), but they also have not succeeded in making the threat go away. The emergence of lone wolf terrorism demonstrates the threat is different than it was in 2001, but it remains potent.

If American efforts have not been overwhelmingly successful in the Middle East, maybe it is time to look at alternative approaches to the relationship between the United States and this part of the world. One possibility is to reduce American presence and activism in Middle East politics and to force those who live there to settle it themselves. The section heading is a rhetorical device to describe that possibility. It is not to be taken literally, but it does suggest a different general approach that outsiders might take to the current throes in which the contemporary Middle East finds itself.

There is no universal agreement about the dynamics that afflict the region. Certainly, a good bit of it is religious, between Sunnis and Shia and extreme elements within each sect of Islam. The basic Sunni-Shia rift has the potential to resemble the confrontation between Catholicism and Protestantism in the 1500s, and could turn quite bloody in the process. Writing in *Time* magazine in April 2015, Massimo Calabresi suggests that "The post-Arab Spring violence has now devolved into a region-wide proxy war, with Saudi Arabia and Iran, two of the biggest powers and fiercest enemies, squaring off in a new, bloody conflict." It may be that the Saudis will not dirty their hands personally fighting this battle but will instead fight the conflict through proxies in places like Syria and Yemen or that they will essentially hire mercenaries to do their fighting for them. They seem to regard the United States as a candidate for this latter role, based on the Desert Storm precedent of 1990–1991 and American promises to protect them at the May 2015 Camp David summit. This is not a role most Americans would relish if the proposition was put directly to them.

The other side of the religious conflict, of course, is between the fundamentalists and the modernizers both within and among Muslim states. The modernizers have actually lost ground since the Arab Spring: they were prominent in the movement—preaching democracy and secular reform—and they lost in the backlash among conservative Muslims. IS and its barely medieval worldview and methods of operation are the current manifestation of this phenomenon. Although it is unclear that the IS-based extremists will carry the day in the region, they have certainly intensified its level of violence and barbarity. The barbarians are not at the gate in the region; they have become the gatekeepers.

Westerners should not be overly smug at this chaos, because these same basic dynamics played themselves out in the period leading to the Thirty Years' War in Europe. As Owen points out, "Parts of the Muslim world today, in fact, bear and uncanny resemblance to northwestern Europe 450 years ago, during the so-called Wars of Religion. . . . The current legitimacy crisis in the Middle East is neither unprecedented in its gravity nor likely to resolve itself in any straightforward manner." The crisis in Europe nearly a half millennium ago was exacerbated by deep political fragmentation among tiny, antagonistic political entities bearing competing religious affiliations and with no overriding political authority that could straighten matters out. The result was bloodletting of unprecedented proportions (nearly one-quarter of the population of modern Germany died in the Thirty Years' War, for instance). Europe had to purge itself in futile bloodletting before it became so exhausted that peace could prevail.

The current situation in the Middle East is similar. Sunni and Shia, tribally based populations, live side-by-side in seething conflicts within the artificial boundaries created by European withdrawal after World War II. Middle East countries are also divided economically: there are very rich and very poor countries, and the rich countries (the ones with oil) do very little to level the economic playing field. In the poor countries, helplessness and purposeless-ness are potent conditions for extremist recruiters who argue that religious fanaticism and self-sacrifice can bring eternal rewards in a world with no earthly benefits.

There is no direct and decisive way that the United States or any other outsider can shepherd the region from this condition to a modernity in which some level of tranquility can emerge. Once again, Owen draws the historical analogy: "Just as the Ottoman Empire, the Muslim superpower at the time of the Wars of Religion, could not resolve the strife among Christians in the sixteenth century, no outside actor can pacify the Middle East today. *Only Muslims themselves can settle their ideological war*" (emphasis added). The United States cannot resolve the differences among Sunni and Shiism or between the Islamists and the modernizers within and among Muslim states. It is masochistic folly even to try, and the one certain outcome of the effort is that it will not be appreciated by those it is designed to "save." Likewise, the mess that is the current map cannot be solved with a magic wand that redraws boundaries along more objectively rational lines. Once again, the effort would not be appreciated by those who would lose in the process.

Suggesting drawing back from the crisis within the Muslim Middle East—in effect erecting a figurative chain link fence around the area—would provide benefits for this country and the region. From an American vantage point, it would be premised on a greater neutrality toward the various cleavages in the area—not siding automatically with one side or the other in the sectarian struggle between Saudi Arabia and Iran, for instance. Doing so would, of course, not endear the United States to the Saudis, whose cause has had the reliable support of the United States in the past. It would, however, open the possibility that the United States could become an honest broker in regional disputes, offering unbiased diplomatic and political, rather than military, assistance beyond the kind suggested in the Nixon Doctrine.

The United States could, in other words, cease to be a crutch propping up some regimes and positions that this country should feel uncomfortable supporting.

A military disengagement would also reduce whatever resentment that American military presence now creates among Middle Eastern population segments. That presence is the most obvious reason for hatred of the United States and hence the designation of Americans and American territory as prime terrorist targets. Additionally, the physical presence of American fighting forces provides a recruiting tool for regional extremists—including terrorists—who accuse the Americans of neo-colonialism. This dynamic has been particularly apparent where the United States becomes engaged and kills either combatants or civilians under the guise of collateral damage. Drawing back could reduce the ability to depict the United States and its intentions in as invidious a fashion as it is now possible.

Military disengagement would also be more economical and realistic. The monetary costs of American operations in Iraq, Afghanistan, and elsewhere in the region are rarely publicly discussed. The reasons are wrapped patriotically in national security and the need for secrecy, but they also reflect the connection between those political figures who vote for and support large military expenditures for these adventures while opposing expenditures for other priorities. At the same time, a reduced operational tempo for American forces would clearly be good for the physical condition of the force, which has been stretched considerably by deployment in the Middle East for over a decade. A reduced presence is, in other words, more affordable than is a more aggressive stance.

A drawback would also be realistic. The problems in the Middle East are, as has been argued here, both internal in nature and based on dynamics like religion and ethnicity. These are not causes that are amenable to settlement by outside military action, which can make the problems worse and rarely makes them any better. A policy that steps back from active military intervention would reduce the American proclivity for allowing itself to be sucked into quixotic quests where it has no reasonable prospect of success and which end up being spectacular, expensive, and frustrating failures.

Erecting a figurative chain link fence would work in both directions. That fence would contain regional conflicts within the region itself and thus force the indigenous peoples to solve their own problems, which is its large purpose. It would also provide a barrier keeping the United States out of regional conflict. It would not sever relations between the United States and the countries of the region; rather, it would signal that those relations would have a significantly smaller military content.

This "modest proposal" will not, of course, be universally embraced within the American national security community. For one thing, it gores several oxen, because it involves moving away from positions that the hard men have supported and promoted for decades. If one believes, as presumably its champions sincerely do, that American military force is a necessary ingredient in dealing with American interests in the Middle East, the chain link fence is anathema. The hard men and the chicken hawks are likely to sneer at the possibility.

Because the chain link fence analogy proposes a sharp reduction of military intrusion as a part of U.S. national security policy in the Middle East, it will be attacked along predictable lines, two of which stand out. The first is that it is a "weak" policy, because it downplays the prevalence of "hard" military power. The failure to consider and to implement military options will be assailed as isolationist, even pusillanimous in the face of opponents—notably terrorists—who allegedly "only understand force." The military instrument of power is the ultimate recourse the country has to realize its most important interests, and abjuring that instrument will likely be viewed as a lack of resolve, even virility, on the part of the United States.

There is a retort to this position, and it is that the military instrument has been mostly ineffective in Middle Eastern settings. Had the long military occupation of Iraq been successful, after all, there would be no Sunni support for IS, and that crisis would not have occurred or would have been much more easily contained or defeated. It is not particularly the fault of the U.S. military that it did not create Iraqi political reconciliation, because that is a task for which military force is singularly inappropriate. As consistently argued here, internal conflicts are just that, and only the indigenous population can solve them. Asking the military to solve political conflicts is unfair to the military. Military force cannot do everything.

This leads to the second objection, which is that the chain link fence is options-limiting for the United States. This is particularly true in the area of terrorism, where military actions must be available at the source to contain and reduce the threat. In extreme, this argument takes the form of "if we don't stop the terrorists where they live, we will have to stop them here." Given the horrors that terrorist attacks conjure, it is a powerful emotional argument. The recent spate of lone wolf, possibly IS-inspired attacks reinforces this emotion.

Where is the evidence that the employment of armed forces actually reduces terrorist threats? It is certainly arguable that some specialized activities—special forces raids, drone air attacks—have been effective in killing some terrorist leaders, but have those efforts reduced the power or strength of terrorists overall? Even the most surgical forms of "kinetic" attacks produce some unintended deaths, and this collateral damage may do more to replenish terrorist ranks than the attacks do to deplete them.

Most defenses of an activist approach to the Middle East center their rationales on the terrorist problem. The IS caliphate is of prime concern to the United States not because of its existence, its lunatic philosophy or its barbarism (although these are matters of some concern), but because it has threatened terrorist attacks against the United States. Why does it threaten these things? One possibility is because the United States is engaged in a systematic campaign to kill its members from the sky and to aid those who want to defeat it. If the United States were to step back from its ongoing campaign, would IS terrorist threats toward the United States be less important to them? They might not be affected and might continue or even increase the threats if they believed the United States was changing policy out of a lack of resolve. They also might not.

At the bottom line, a policy reorientation like that suggested by the chain link fence analogy rises or falls depending on the success or failure of the current policy direction. "If it ain't broke, don't fix it" is one way to assess that policy. But has the current approach worked? More specifically, has the employment of U.S. armed force in the Middle East represented an effective method for achieving American policy goals? If it has done that, it does not need changing. If it has not, it may be time for a change.

BIBLIOGRAPHY

Aarts, Paul, and Carolein Roelants. *Saudi Arabia: A Kingdom in Peril*. London: Hurst Publishers, 2015.

Aslan, Reza. "What We Got Wrong." *Foreign Policy,* July/August 2010, 109–110.

Barfield, Thomas. *Afghanistan: A Cultural and Political History*. Princeton, NJ: Princeton University Press, 2010.

Bellin, Eva. "Democratization and Its Discontents: Should America Push Political Reform in the Middle East?" *Foreign Affairs* 87, 4 (July/August 2008), 112–119.

Calabresi, Massimo. "Caught in the Cross Fire." *Time* 185, 13 (April 13, 2015), 24–27.

Carter, Jimmy. *Peace Not Apartheid*. New York: Simon and Schuster, 2006.

Cooper, Andrew Scott. *The Oil Kings: How the United States, Iran, and Saudi Arabia Changed the Balance of Power in the Middle East*. New York: Simon and Schuster, 2012.

Della Pergola, Sergio. "Israel's Existential Predicament: Population, Territory, and Identity." *Current History* 109, 731 (December 2010), 383–389.

Ewans, Martin. *Afghanistan: A Short History of Its People and Politics*. New York: Harper Perennials, 2002.

Gilbert, Martin. *Israel: A History* (revised and updated edition). New York: Harper-Collins, 2008.

Goldberg, Jeffrey. "How Iran Could Save the Middle East." *The Atlantic* 304, 1 (July/August 2009), 66–68.

Hamid, Shadi. "The Rise of the Islamists: How Islamists Will Change Politics, and Vice Versa." *Foreign Affairs* 90, 3 (May/June 2011), 40–47.

Haylel, Bernard, Thomas Hegghammer, and Stephane Lacroix (eds.). *Saudi Arabia in Transition: Insights on Society, Politics, Economics and Religious Change.* Cambridge, UK: Cambridge University Press, 2015.

House, Karen Elliott. *On Saudi Arabia: Its People, Past, Religion, Fault Lines—and Future.* New York: Vintage Books Reprint edition. 2013.

Jones, Seth G. *In the Graveyard of Empires: America's War in Afghanistan.* New York: W. W. Norton, 2009.

Kaplan, Robert D. "Living with a Nuclear Iran." *The Atlantic* 306, 2 (September 2010), 70–72.

Kinzer, Stephen. *Iran, Turkey, and America's Future.* New York: Times Books, 2010.

Lacey, Robert. *Inside the Kingdom: Kings, Clerics, Modernists, Terrorists and the Struggle for Saudi Arabia.* New York: Penguin Books Reprint edition, 2010.

Muravchik, Joshua. *Making David into Goliath: How the World Turned against Israel.* New York: Encounter Books, 2014.

Owen, John M. "From Calvin to the Caliphate: What Europe's Religious Wars Tell Us about the Modern Middle East." *Foreign Affairs* 94, 3 (May/June 2015), 77–89.

Polk, William R. *Understanding Iran: Everything You Need to Know from Persia to the Islamic Revolution, From Cyrus to Ahmadinejad.* New York: Palgrave Macmillan Trade, 2011.

Rashid, Ahmed. *Taliban, Militant Islam, Oil and Fundamentalism in Central Asia* (second edition). New Haven, CT: Yale University Press, 2010.

Riedel, Bruce. "The Mideast after Iran Gets the Bomb." *Current History* 109, 731 (December 2010), 370–375.

Shavit, Ari. *My Promised Land: The Triumph and Tragedy of Israel.* New York: Spiegel and Grau, 2013.

Snow, Donald M. *Cases in American Foreign Policy.* New York: Pearson, 2013.

———. *National Security for a New Era,* fifth edition. New York: Pearson, 2014.

Takeyh, Roy. "Time for Détente with Iran." *Foreign Affairs* 86, 2 (March/April 2007), 17–32.

Van Creveld, Martin L. *The Land of Blood and Honey: The Rise of Modern Israel.* New York: Thomas Dunne Books, 2010.

Part IV

CONCLUSIONS

Chapter 8

Moving Ahead

Time for a Change

It used to be an article of faith, part of the American military culture and a pillar of American national security policy, for the United States to avoid fighting ground wars on the Asian continent. The reasons were pragmatic and reasoned. The United States had interests in parts of the region, but none that were so compelling that they justified sending an expeditionary force halfway around the world to prosecute. Because Asia was so far away, so large, and so heavily populated, a ground war on that continent probably could not be won in any acceptable manner. At the same time, such an effort would tax American resources that could be better put to other priorities. Asian wars simply did not make sense.

That orientation was essentially maintained until World War II. The United States did participate in limited forays on the continent (helping put down the Boxer Rebellion in China in 1900) or on the peripheries of the continent (putting down the rebellion in the Philippines after the Spanish-American War), but it was not until the United States and Japan collided in World War II that Asia became a major fighting ground for American armed forces. That change in practice has continued since World War II ended. Since 1945, virtually all the fighting the United States has engaged in has been in one part of Asia or the other. During the Cold War, the commitment was to Cold War flashpoints like Korea and Vietnam. Even before the end of the Cold War and certainly since, about the only part of the world where American forces have been committed in anger is in the southwestern part of Asia—the Middle East.

Why did this country turn its back on its historical dictate to avoid employing force where it now does almost all its fighting? The obvious answer, the equivalent of 1930s bank robber Willie Sutton saying he robbed banks because that is where the money is, is that Asia (and especially the

179

Middle East) is where the fighting is, and thus where violent challenges to American interests have taken place. Europe and the Western Hemisphere have become basically tranquil, and African conflict does not challenge other than American humanitarian interests. Asia, and especially the Middle East, is the center of the action.

It may be coincidental—but probably is not—that American movement militarily into Asia and the decline in favorable military outcomes to American excursions have coincided. The only conspicuous success of American arms on Asian soil since Korea, after all, has been in the Kuwaiti desert where Iraq confronted the U.S. military on American terms and had no chance of success. All the other forays have experienced either much more limited success, had ambiguous outcomes, or been arguable failures.

Could it be that the older tenet of policy about engaging in Asian ground wars was correct? That policy had three basic tenets: the importance of the region (the level of interests involved); the likelihood of success (the ability to apply force effectively to attain sought-after goals); and an assessment of the acceptability of the cost of attaining the goal (the affordability of the enterprise). Considering all three questions effectively discouraged the frequent use of American forces in Asian setting before. What has happened to them?

The short answer is that potential American involvements are no longer assessed (at least in public) in these terms. Instead, whenever violence breaks out in the Middle East—which it regularly does throughout the region—the knee-jerk reaction is that whatever upset is occurring challenges American interests, and that only a "muscular" (military) response will "save" an otherwise intolerable situation. The response, in other words, attempts to address the question of interests, but it does so by merely asserting importance and by painting anyone who opposes the assertion as irresolute or worse. It does not even touch upon the question of whether American force is appropriate to settling the situation and shies away from the question of cost.

Abandoning the rejoinder on direct intervention in Asian land wars may have made sense when American interests were compellingly at risk and American resolve was unquestionable. The Japanese challenge in World War II is the obvious example.

The rejoinder rested most obviously in manpower, as raised in Chapter 2. The simple implication regarding Asia was that the continent was too large and populous to subdue with American ground forces and that the effort was only conceivable if the United States was willing to make a maximum effort that might not succeed. This effort had to include the determination that Americans were sufficiently committed to the outcome to agree to be conscripted and potentially to make the ultimate personal sacrifice in its name. Vietnam exploded that presumption; the ongoing political climate has reflected the belief that this consensus has not been restored.

The limitation on accepting conscription places a real constraint on the use of force in Asia, including the Middle East, for the present and future. Without conscription, what the United States can do with armed force in Asia will always be circumscribed; it is as simple as that. This fundamental recognition has not yet been reflected in many advocacies of an activist Middle East policy. The AVF and military activism in Asia are simply incompatible and probably irreconcilable. If these contradictory dynamics cannot be reconciled, then the paradigm needs modifying.

REPLACING THE COLD PARADIGM

The Cold War experience helped drive American national security policy and military employment in two ways. First, some of the most active Cold War surrogate battle grounds were in Asia. Korea, for instance, was the first instance where the communist and noncommunist worlds clashed violently over an attempt by the communists to spread their domain into the noncommunist world. This action represented a breach of the developing containment line philosophy underlying the Cold War: stopping the expansion of communism beyond those places where it existed in 1948 represented a vital national interest and would be resisted with force if necessary. South Korea was not initially included in the drawing of the containment line, but it was quickly added when North Korean troops poured across the 38th Parallel in June 1950. Communist challenges to the status quo were particularly concentrated in Asia during the 1950s, culminating in the American commitment to South Vietnam in the mid-1960s.

This same concern was also present in the Middle East. In 1946, even before the Cold War was "declared," the United States moved naval forces into the Eastern Mediterranean to threaten the Soviet Union with dire consequences if they did not withdraw assistance to communist followers in Iranian Azerbaijan. The ploy worked. As the lines between Israel, closely associated with the United States, and surrounding Arab state hardened, the Soviets attempted to curry support among the Arabs by arming them. The fundamental philosophical incongruity between the *Quran* and *Das Kapital* made this a limited and strained marriage that did not survive the end of the Cold War except in Syria, where Russia maintains a port of naval call. Resisting communist expansion into the region was always third most important in the troika of American interests behind oil and Israel, but it was present nonetheless.

Tying American Cold War interests to Asia presented a military change for the United States that was hardly recognized at the time. It was buried deeply below the conventional military dictates of the "central battle" in

Europe between the conventional behemoths, the United States and the USSR. In East Asia and the Middle East, the United States ran headlong into opposition that did not fight by European rules but instead employed strategies and rules of engagement (ROEs) that are now referred to as asymmetrical but have deeper roots in Eastern practice. In East Asia, this unfamiliar style took the form of Maoist guerrilla warfare (mobile-guerrilla warfare) as developed by the Chinese communist leader and modified by North Vietnamese general and strategist Vo Nguyen Giap. In the Middle East, it took the form of highly mobile desert warfare of the kind Robert D. Kaplan describes as deriving from the Scythians of the seventh to third centuries BC in parts of modern southern Russia and Ukraine. It represents a style that is intended to frustrate the efforts of conventional war by rendering their greater mass and prowess in set-piece warfare irrelevant, and it works. As Kaplan puts it, "Largely because of the Scythians, the United States has only limited ability to determine the outcome of many conflicts, despite being a superpower."

The end of the Cold War exposed the military dynamic and frustration of attempting to counteract an unconventional problem in conventional ways. Ian Bremmer conventionally describes the U.S. status of remaining superpower as being "the only country able to project military power in every region of the world." The definition, and the common assumption of strategists operating from the essential Cold War mind-set, is that the superpower can *effectively* employ military power everywhere, and this assumption is suspect when the opponents fight asymmetrically. The United States can unquestionably deploy force anywhere in the world, but recent experience raises questions about whether that effort is always effective.

If the Cold War paradigm is premised on the assumption that conventional force—the kind that is the United States' specialty—is effective everywhere against any opponent and that premise is false or questionable, then the viability of the strategy it supports is vulnerable as well. The Cold War paradigm and a preference for and reliance upon conventional military force are coincidental, reflecting that the paradigm developed at a time when both sides had traditional, European-style military forces around which to design the military component of their competition. Originally, the military preparations presumed the very real possibility of armed conflict—a conventional World War III—that nuclear weapons invalidated. Nuclear weapons did not, however, supplant traditional force as the principal military aspect of the paradigm, but instead supplemented it as the ultimate battlefield and strategic element in the military clashes between the two sides. Happily, the anomaly of such preparation—the probability that the employment of the weapons would obliterate both sides—eventually sobered militaristic tendencies, elevated deterrence to the penultimate reason for arming against one another, and eventually contributed to the end of the conflict.

The military tradition of the Cold War transcended that change and forms the core implicit assumption underlying so-called "muscular" approaches to managing the post–Cold War world. What is implicit in this formulation is that the post–Cold War challenges are analogous to those of the Cold War: the opponents remain like the Red Army, not like the Scythians. Moreover, the paradigm foresaw a contest between coalitions of sovereign states, who were presumed to be the core, legitimate members of the international system. States retain their centrality in the post–Cold War world, but they are no longer the opponents that are typically encountered in modern conflict, which is internal in its dynamics and thus is a contest between subnational groups, not sovereign states.

Those who fashioned the Cold War system were traditional realists. This term, as it is applied to international relations, is premised on the centrality of the governments of states as the primary, even sole, repositories of sovereign legitimacy and whose rights and prerogatives are the only matters that ultimately count. In classic realist formulation as it developed after the peace of Westphalia, no entity is or can be superior to the state, state interests are supreme, and the possession and occasional recourse to force by national governments is the legitimate ultimate means of conflict resolution in the system. Because the ideas were developed in a European context, the force that developed to protect and advance national interests were increasingly sophisticated, lethal forms of the European tradition of set-piece warfare by large military units confronting one another. The ultimate expression of that tradition was World War II, the deadliest military event in human history. World War III with nuclear weapons would have dwarfed the carnage World War II produced.

During the second half of the twentieth century, Cold War–style realism dominated international relations, simply because the international system's major conflict was between the last two of its predominant practitioners, the United States and the USSR. The developing world contained challengers to the premises that underlay the paradigm, but their objections were largely ignored by the central players. When the Cold War ended, the remaining superpower continued on the premise that the rules had not changed, but they had.

There were two principal changes. The first was philosophical and derived from a rejection of the premise that the only fully legitimate actor in international relations was the state. In military affairs, fighting was between the organized armed forces of other states for traditional ends. The rules of war and the legitimacy of national armed forces clashing inherent in classic realism were the norm. Wars were increasingly traumatic and lethal events, but their dynamics were at least familiar. A paradigm that was an extrapolation of the experience of the past three hundred years since Westphalia seemed appropriate.

The post–Cold War experience has largely negated those conditions and rendered them increasingly irrelevant. Wars are no longer fought between sovereign states or between conventional armed forces representing states. *Inter*state warfare, in other words, has virtually disappeared. In its place, *intra*state warfare between factions within a state vying for control of state territory and power has become the norm. The rules for such warfare are very different from conventional interstate war to the point that the guidelines for conducting one are not very helpful, and can be terribly misleading, if applied in the wrong context. More to the point, intervening on the side of one state in conventional war offers very little useful instruction about the dynamics—including outcomes—of intervening on the side of one party or another in a civil conflict. It is simply not the same thing. The United States should have learned this lesson in Vietnam, Iraq, and Afghanistan. Not every American has.

The second change was in military application, as the symmetrical warfare model of the Cold War confrontation gave way to asymmetrical, more Scythian formulations. When it is said that the United States' claim to being the surviving superpower derives from its ability to project force globally, that claim needs to be qualified. It refers to two aspects of force projection: the provision of conventional armed forces pretty much anywhere, and the provision of specialized but limited kinds of force, such as Special Forces or aerial bombardment by manned aircraft, drones, or cruise missiles across a wide range of contingencies. This is a limiting qualification. It is not clear that conventional forces are decisive in the internal, asymmetrical situations into which they are insinuated. They are extremely potent at what they do, but they only questionably do the things that are decisive in internal wars. The U.S. armed forces were, for instance, quite adept at invading Iraq, sweeping aside its armed forces, and conquering the country. Their skills were neither particularly effective nor relevant to an eight-year opposed occupation. Special and air forces, on the other hand, are relevant to internal war situations, but they are limited in their effect and not really intended to be decisive. The combined result is that the United States may be the remaining superpower, but that claim is partly hollow in the face of the kinds of lethal situations that exist in the system.

The result is that the Cold War paradigm is questionably helpful in either a political or a military sense in today's environment. It might be transferrable to a world where states still clashed in conventional warfare, but it has not been shown that it applies effectively to understanding or dealing with the political dynamics of internal wars fought for a variety of reasons—like religion or ethnicity—that dominate modern violence and instability. Internal wars are rarely fought by conventional, symmetrical military means, which are the means prescribed by the paradigm. The caricature of the attempt to apply conventional means to unconventional opponents was the Army's "search and destroy" strategy in Vietnam—sending heavily armed columns of forces rumbling into the countryside looking for an enemy who melted into the background when it knew the Yankees were coming.

Maintaining allegiance to the assumptions of the Cold War paradigm will have two major undesirable effects. First, it will cause the United States to misapprehend the political situations and dynamics of violent candidates for American force. When the hard men suggest the United States should move in and destroy IS, what they are implicitly suggesting is an application of force like that which brought down the fascists in World War II. Such an approach does not work in internal wars and can lead to efforts destined to fail. Second, the paradigm implicitly endorses the use of conventional forces against the descendants of the Scythians. Should American forces set out to "search and destroy" IS in the Syrian and Iraqi deserts? Would IS stand, fight, and be destroyed? Or would they melt into the background and wait for the Americans to go away? The United States should know the answer to that question and should be looking for a different approach. The Cold War paradigm does not offer that answer.

THE ALTERNATIVES: MILITARY ACTIVISM OR REFINED REALISM

A national security paradigm should provide guidance that helps answer the two most critical questions that must be asked in any situation in which the use of force might be contemplated. The first question concerns *when* the United States should entertain using force to resolve a problem. What reasons are there? And are they sufficient to justify the recourse to American arms? The second addresses *how* the country should think about employing force. If contemplating the use of force is justified by the situation, how can it be applied to meet the policy goal that drives its employment? The two questions are related in both directions. If force is unjustifiable, then how or whether it can be applied effectively is moot. If force cannot achieve goals that may be deemed worthy, then its contemplation is foolhardy and counterproductive.

Traditional realism does not directly address these questions. Rather, it implicitly assumes positive answers to each question based on the fundamental nature of relations among sovereign states in international relations. At that, the questions sometimes enter calculations. Any extremely weak state must decide if resisting the forces of a very strong state is preferable to submitting to that state's military power, and a powerful state may use its force for lesser reasons against an opponent who stands no chance of defeating it than it would against a more potent foe. The calculus behind the questions is

not novel; raising them explicitly may be a way to move to a more sophisticated method for addressing the national security question.

The two basic questions can, in turn, be restated in terms of three criteria
that can govern the determination of whether force is appropriate in different
situations. These three standards are *importance, attainability,* and *affordability.* These three criteria, their basic meaning, and relationship to the two
basic questions can be placed in a tabular form, as is done in Figure 8.1.

The figure requires one point of clarification. The criterion of importance is
clearly associated with the vitality of interests involved and thus whether it is
worthwhile to think of employing force, and affordability is clearly related to
whether that force's use is worth the cost. The criterion of attainability, on the
other hand, is related both to when and how force should be used. Importance
and attainability are sometimes competing standards: can we do what is worth
trying to do? At the same time, attainability may depend on the extent, and
thus the cost, of using different kinds and amounts of force: are means that
might attain goals worth what they will likely cost?

Overlaying this framework on national security issues and how to plan
them could clarify whether and what kinds of national security responses the
country might consider in individual situations. A negative answer to any of
the three criteria should effectively preclude the commitment of American
force, but does not mean that all forms of response, including those detailed
previously, from being considered. The critical heart of national security calculations, of course, is when or if force is justifiable, so the discussion begins
with the framework.

The first and most critical concern is the importance of achieving whatever
interest is at stake. The idea that interests drive national security determinations is at the heart of traditional realism. As that formulation has traditionally
been interpreted in the United States, the interest threshold dividing those
situations in which force is justifiable lies in the notion of vitality: is an unfavorable outcome intolerable to the United States? If it is, then the employment of American force may be appropriate and necessary. If the outcome of
the situation falls below that threshold in the realm of less-than-vital (LTV)

Question	Criterion	Concern
When to Use Force	Importance	Vitality of Interests
	Attainability	Acceptable Success Chances
How to Use Force	Affordability	Costs and Benefits

Figure 8.1   Force, Interest, and Success.

interests where unfavorable outcomes may be undesirable but not intolerable, the traditional notion is that the direct application of U.S. force is not justified. That does not mean the United States should not act to protect its interests in ways other than the commitment of American forces to combat; it just rules out an overt American role. The principles underlying the Nixon Doctrine may be applicable in these circumstances.

The second concern is whether military force will attain the goal being pursued. It has become an implicit assumption in some national security circles that the American military can accomplish any military goal to which it is assigned. This idea, embedded in the military's own "can do" tradition (discussed in the various editions of *National Security for a New Era*), is an extension of America's superpower status. The notion that the United States can project force anywhere is extended to the assertion it can do so *effectively*. Developing world, including Middle Eastern, experience has, however, rendered this assumption questionable in these kinds of situations.

As argued, American military force (or any outside force) is of questionable decisiveness in settling essentially internal conflicts. This is especially true when those who end up opposing American efforts fight asymmetrically, a style at which the United States has proven less than physically or conceptually adept. When limited American force is dedicated to this kind of conflict and fails to deliver promised results, criticism is not directed at whether the goal was attainable but at the alleged paucity of effort devoted to the enterprise. That the effort was inherently quixotic never seems to enter the criticism.

Levels of interest and attainability are intimately related to one another. As already suggested, an LTV interest is more likely to be pursued with armed force if it appears easily attainable than if it is not. The more important consideration, however, is when interests seem very important but are not readily achievable by applying military force. In that case, what is more important: the effort or its success? More particularly in the contemporary debate, is American prestige in the world better served by making honorable but futile gestures or by admitting it cannot accomplish specific goals with its forces? It would, for instance, clearly be in America's general interests to see IS destroyed, but what can the United States plausibly do to bring that about? Declaring, as President Obama did in 2014, that the decimation of the IS menace is a priority goal was one thing; figuring out how to accomplish it has been another.

An added dynamic, discussed at some length in *The Case against Military Intervention,* is the relative importance the two sides attach to different outcomes. It is almost never true that the outcome of an internal developing world conflict is as important to the United States as it is to the indigenous combatants. In general terms, interests that are vital to attain by the internal sides are usually LTV for the outsider, and this affects the likely success of outside action. As Bremmer warns, "No matter how powerful you are, it's hard to defeat an enemy that cares more about the outcome than you do." Kaplan phrases the same conclusion in a slightly different way: "Largely because of these Scythians, the United States has only limited ability to determine the outcome of many conflicts, despite being a superpower."

The third, and least mentioned criterion in the American debate, is afford-ability. It has two faces. One is the cost-benefit of military involvement: is the attainment of the goal worth what it likely will cost? And can you afford the cost of failure? The other consideration is about priorities. The decision to spend public monies on military adventures means there will be less resources available for other things, whether they be decreased public spending such as tax cuts or funding other things. This distinction is often enshrouded in the murky practices of public budgeting, including most prominently the practice of hiding military expenditures "off budget" by paying for them with "supplemental expenditures" that do not show in the formal budget.

Budgetary legerdemain notwithstanding, however, the employment of mil-itary force does cost public resources. This aspect of the decision process is often obscured because many of the most enthusiastic supporters of employ-ing military force also oppose spending public money for much of anything else. Estimates before the fact tend to be much lower than actual costs turn out to be, and rationales are wrapped tightly in the flag of American respon-sibility in the world, an obligation that overrides the monetary expenses it entails. To deny that the use of military force requires the expenditure of scarce and precious human resources is unrealistic, and it is hard to disagree with Bremmer's conclusion: "Beware those who talk of responsibility but never of price tags."

The AVF-based armed forces have allowed the American political system to sidestep these very real concerns. A large part of the costs of activism are human. Putting armed forces into harm's way involves the risk of the ulti-mate cost: human life. When that cost is borne by a tiny minority who has volunteered to accept that risk, the rest of us are absolved of this consider-ation. This dynamic is acceptable for as long—but only as long—as the AVF produces enough forces willing to accept the bargain. It becomes a potentially paralytical problem if the military costs exceed the conditions of the bargain.

Accepting the categories of the framework does not predetermine how all situations will be approached or resolved. The concepts are all, to some degree, subjective, matters on which people can disagree. This is true through-out the framework. The matter of interests is controversial on two levels. One is the boundary between vital and LTV interests, especially as the framework is applied to different instances. The other is that there is some disagreement (generally associated with the neo-conservatives) about whether the criterion of vitality is too restrictive: if applied too dogmatically, it could prevent the United States from doing some useful things. Similarly, there is no infallible crystal ball that tells one if a given effort will succeed or fail. Past experience may suggest strongly the likelihood of attainability, but it is not an exact predictor. Similarly, what an action will cost is virtually impossible to predict accurately in advance. About all one can fairly confidently predict is that most estimates will be less than the eventual costs turn out to be.

Does this framework provide a useful conceptual foundation around which to ground a new national security paradigm? Is it, in other words, a refinement of traditional realism that applies more adequately to the contemporary environment than does the Cold War paradigm? The criterion of interests and importance certainly grounds it in the realist tradition. Realists do not specify what level of interests should trigger American military responses, but a historical American interpretation would seem to argue that force should be limited to the prosecution of vital interests. Current challenges to American security do not meet the unambiguous level of vitality that the Axis powers of World War II or communist expansionism did during the Cold War, and thus questions of attainability and affordability must be added to keep the framework realistic in the world in which they must be applied. Depending on one's predilections and beliefs, there is a very quickly expansible list of situations that threaten American interests to some discernible degree. The United States cannot afford to pursue all these interests with armed force, and it is unclear that U.S. military muscle can deliver positive results in all cases anyway. In a world of nuances, refinement is necessary. It may be particularly useful in assessing American actions in the Middle East.

The framework is amenable to incorporating all five of the intervention options described in Chapter 5. At one end of the continuum, Doing Nothing or Showing the Flag could be chosen options if situations are not deemed very important, achieving a favorable outcome is problematical, or if the effort is not worth the costs involved in more muscular responses. The ongoing kerfuffle in Yemen probably falls in this category. At the other end of the spectrum, Soft or Full-Scale Intervention could result from an assessment that an unfavorable outcome approaches or surpasses tolerability, if the goal seems attainable employing some level of American force, and if costs are tolerable or overridden by the importance of the event. Where these matters are in contention (which they usually will be), providing assistance but not forces (the Nixon Doctrine) may be the compromise solution.

The framework does not, in other words, preclude a "muscular" approach to dealing with world problems, nor does it guarantee that a rational interest- and attainability-driven approach will carry the day in individual cases. The proponents of a more aggressive approach may argue—not without merit— that the framework is tilted toward a more rational than emotional approach to individual situations and that it does not make automatic provision for considerations such as whether American prestige and standing in the world is enhanced or degraded by different conclusions in particular situations. What it can accomplish is a common frame of reference and set of general criteria that can be applied in different circumstances and around which policy debates could occur. Experience might change elements of the framework and the questions asked in its name; but it is a start.

BREAKING THE MIDDLE EAST TETHER

The basic argument developed in these pages is that American interests in the Middle East have generally been overvalued due to American dependence on Middle Eastern oil. Two things have happened to change that calculation. First, protecting access to oil has essentially disappeared from official American explanations of the reasons for its presence, which is now much more likely to be explained in terms of responding to regionally based terrorism directed at the United States. At the same time, American dependence on petroleum from the region has dramatically decreased, and unless something currently unforeseen causes the shale revolution to founder, that dependence will continue to decrease. The need for Middle Eastern oil, and thus the national interest in protecting access to that resource physically has declined and will likely continue to lessen as the underpinning of U.S. national security policy in the region. Likewise, only speculation about what Iran might do if it obtains nuclear weapons presents a direct threat to the other American important interest in the region, the protection of Israel. If anything, continued Israeli intransigence on the Palestine issue is the greatest threat to its security in its neighborhood.

Actual and threatened terrorism now largely drive American policy in the Middle East. The terrorist problem was certainly a major causative factor in the decisions to use armed force in Iraq and Afghanistan, even if those ties were suspect (Iraq) or overextended (Afghanistan after Al-Qaeda fled). It is hard to imagine why the United States would be especially excited about who controls the sparsely populated desert areas of Syria and Iraq under IS control were it not that aspects of IS activities did not include threatened terrorism directed at the United States and Europe.

Preventing terrorist attacks on American soil clearly represents an important, vital American interest, thus satisfying the first criterion of the framework: the use of force can be justified as a matter of interests. The problems begin to accumulate when one moves to the criterion of attainability. The United States has been attempting to apply military solutions to the problem of terrorism in the region ever since 9/11, and that effort has been less than a rousing success. Full-scale intervention was attempted in Iraq and Afghanistan by the George W. Bush administration, and it changed but did not eradicate or arguably even reduce the terrorist problem. Soft intervention bordering on the Nixon Doctrine has been applied in Iraq since the American physical withdrawal in 2011, but it has also not made that country any more terror free or any less a problem. Critics on one side argue that the United States should ratchet up the American effort toward the more intrusive options, while observers on the other argue that this is an internal Sunni-Shiite problem that only the principals can resolve, an implicit call for less intrusion. Neither side has made a compelling case for the likelihood their solution will actually succeed. Meanwhile, the costs continue to add up, shielded from the public because of the likely appall with which their disclosure would be greeted.

The question of attainability stands at the center of any effort to deal with the Middle East. Advocacy of doing more to influence situations to U.S. favor founder on specifying what that "more" actually is and whether any particular actions would actually improve the situation. Attempts to kill terrorists in their lairs have succeeded in removing some leaders from the board, but they have not been especially effective in weakening or destroying particular terrorist groups or terrorism in general originating in the area. Assassinating Osama bin Laden and many of his lieutenants has badly weakened the original Al-Qaeda organization, but successor AQ organizations have popped up elsewhere in Muslim-majority regions in the Middle East and Africa. Destroying individual terrorists is akin to playing "whack-em" ball at the arcade: no matter how many pop-up figures one hits, there always seem to be more replacements. IS, after all, is the modern version of Al-Qaeda in Iraq, returned in a new and more frightening guise that presents a bigger problem than the original AQI ever did.

The current policy probably falls within the category of soft intervention, whereas the invasion of Afghanistan was an instance of hard intervention. Neither policy worked well, and when the hard men suggest ratcheting up the effort—doing more—as a solution, the burden is on them to demonstrate that their suggestions will meet the criterion of attainability at which they failed before. The standard retort, with origins in Vietnam half a century ago, was that efforts have been too timid, too half-hearted, and that, in effect, those combating terrorism have had to fight "with one hand tied behind their backs" (a common charge regarding Vietnam from military circles). Not only is it not clear what doing more means, it is even less clear that increasing the intensity and violence of the effort would make a positive difference.

This kind of analysis extends to Middle Eastern situations in which terrorism is only part of the mix. The battle for Iraq illustrates the problem. The United States remains involved in Iraq for two basic reasons that represent interests of sorts. First, following the Pottery Barn analogy, it is undeniable that the United States "broke" the Iraqi system by forcing the Sunnis out of power and allowing the ascendancy of the Shiites in the aftermath of the 2003 invasion. The Shiites have proven incapable of governing the country, either because they are too inept to forge alliances with the Sunnis and Kurds or because they are insufficiently ruthless to suppress the other groups, as Saddam Hussein did. The result is that Kurdistan is an independent state in all but name, and the Sunni stronghold of Anbar Province is occupied by IS with at least the tacit support of fellow Sunnis. Second, IS forces remain in power in much of Anbar and poses a rhetorical terrorist threat to the United States.

What should the United States do about all this? The answer begins with interests? Are American vital interests involved in who governs Iraq or whether it splinters into several countries? How much of a threat does IS really pose to the United States beyond recruiting young Americans (most of whom are Arab-Americans) to their cause? Are any goals attainable with the application of American force, as the hard men advocate? In other words, can outside interference resolve the underlying issues that torment the Iraqi state? If, as argued here, the problem is, like in most of the region, primarily internal, what are the dynamics of the conflict? Richard Fontaine, president of the Center for a New American Security, summarizes the situation in a quote in a May 2015 *Washington Post* assessment of the situation: "The issue is one of will—will of the Sunnis in the Iraq security forces to fight for a Shia-led military and the will of Shia to fight for Sunni land." How can any quantity or quality of American interference affect these dynamics? Finally, the United States has already spent well over a trillion dollars to little effect in Iraq. How much more will the American people bear?

The point here is that both these problems are internal, and the interference of the United States either will not affect them positively or even could make them worse. American forces would certainly not be welcome in Anbar, where many Sunnis consider them the vehicle of their misery. An American military presence including attacks from the sky have not diminished the terrorist problem, and it is arguable that American actions may actually have made the threat to the United States worse by serving as a recruitment tool among the victims of American aerial bombardment.

Maybe it is time to rethink the policy of aggressive American military presence in the Middle East region. The original rationale for that presence, protecting the flow of oil to the United States, has receded and will likely continue to diminish. Some condominium will probably have to be reached with other countries having an interest in freedom of the high seas in the Persian Gulf (including the Saudis and Iranians), an accord that has not been necessary to reach as long as the United States provided a security blanket over their livelihood. It is unlikely that most of the countries with an interest in the Gulf would view its conversion into a Chinese lake favorably, and doing something about it would be necessitated by an American announcement that it was severely cutting back or ending its protective control over these waters. Would the regional powers and other states which need the oil step up to the plate and supplement or replace the Americans? That question could be avoided as long as vital interests tied the United States to naval defense of the region. With those interests lessened, could the United States, as Kaplan suggests, "return to its roots as a maritime power in Asia and a defender of land in Europe, where there are fewer Scythians, and more ordinary villains"?

This same logic can be applied in a straightforward way to American air and ground presence in the region justified as the major theater of the war on terror. The rationale for keeping Americans on the ground and in the air has been to take the fight to the terrorists, to attack and destroy them on their own territory rather than allowing them to bring the fight to American soil, and thus increasing the safety of Americans.

This argument has a very strong emotional appeal. Terrorism is indeed frightening (which is its purpose), and avoiding the deaths of otherwise innocent Americans at the hands of jihadist terrorists certainly constitutes a major, vital interest of the United States. That said, does this construction stand up under closer scrutiny, as provided by the framework?

One can accept the vitality of an American interest in thwarting terrorism, but it must be put in context. Not all vital interests are equally vital or important. Clearly, the *most* vital interest any state has is its own physical survival, and no realistic assessment can conclude that terrorism has or ever will have the deadly capacity to decimate this country, certainly not in the way Soviet nuclear-armed missiles could have done during the Cold War. The threat of terrorist attacks is certainly ubiquitous in an environment where multiple groups espouse dangerous intentions against the country, but this does not approach the potential cataclysm of nuclear war. At the same time, the nuclear threat was deadly enough that the policy of having enough similar weapons to vaporize an attacker in retaliation effectively deterred that occurrence. It was an expensive, nerve-wracking policy, but it worked.

In one sense, current U.S. policy toward Middle East terrorism has also worked. The interest that policy is supposed to serve is the prevention of terrorist attacks on American soil, and it has succeeded: there have been no successful attacks since 9/11. The strategy of nuclear deterrence made some analysts nervous because its failure would have been catastrophic. The antiterrorist policy also makes many analysts nervous because they believe it is just a matter of time until it does fail. For that reason, they advocate more active ways to suppress the likelihood. High on the list of suggested changes is, in effect, taking the fight to the enemy through military presence and even the actual employment of American force to decimate the terrorists.

This latter alternative raises the question of attainability. The heart of a policy's acceptable chances of success is whether it will actually work, whether it will prove ineffective, or even if it may make matters worse. One cannot argue that the policy has failed, because that suggests there would have been less terrorism had the United States not have engaged in counter-terrorism activities, which is counterfactual. One can, however, argue that the policy of active forward deployment has not solved the problem, since terrorism continues to be plotted and proclaimed and the terrorists remain at large, even proliferating in numbers and guises. Whether the problem would be worse had efforts not been made is similarly counterfactual, since that has also not been tried. Assessing the attainability of a military approach to reducing or destroying the threat is thus treacherous, subjective ground where competing advocacies can be heartfelt and emotional, given the nature of the problem. The affordability of different options is rarely raised. One reason is that avoiding terrorist consequences is so compelling that it seems penurious to raise the question. At the same time, so much of the ongoing effort is enshrouded in "black" (secret) budgets that nobody outside government really knows how much is actually being spent.

Just as American interference in the political affairs of the region has not been an overwhelming and indisputable success, it is equally clear that the current forward presence of Americans in the region with a counterterrorism role has also not been an unfettered success either. The euphoria that accompanied the death of bin Laden—which seemed like a sign of progress at the time—has faded as new variants of Al-Qaeda and other threats with a terrorist element have emerged. Nobody talks about the imminence of demise of the terrorist threat; rather, it is more often described as, in former Secretary of Defense Donald Rumsfeld's words, a "long slog." It is also expected to be expensive.

Reduced to these terms, the current policy and more robust variations do not seem so attractive and even suggest that it is time to consider change of the terrorism aspect of the American national security element in the region. More specifically, it may be appropriate to consider how the terrorism element of policy might be affected by a general reduction of American military presence in the region.

Why would one even contemplate this alternative? The most obvious answer is that the policies that have been attempted have not succeeded very well, meaning that some other policy direction might be more effective. The alternatives can be arrayed across the spectrum. The current policy of equipping and arming various "friendly" regimes and providing air assistance falls somewhere between the Nixon Doctrine and soft intervention, and it has not worked, especially in Iraq. Nixon Doctrine-like aid has not produced an Iraqi Security Force that competes well with IS or that commands much support outside Shiite areas of the country. The force's will to fight has been derided (by Secretary of Defense Ashton Carter in May 2015, most famously), but it is not clear that simple traditional morale problems lie at the base of its failure. Rather, the poor performance of the force may be the deeper result of the schism within Iraq itself. John McLaughlin argues, "People don't fight because they've been trained; they fight because they believe in something. At present, the biggest believers in the region are with the Islamic State." As argued, the United States cannot bridge the sectarian divide in Iraq (or elsewhere), meaning military aid must be selectively inserted into situations where other dynamics will not negate its impact. Similarly, the soft intervention of air attacks is hardly likely to be decisive. Supporters of a more muscular approach thus are forced to suggest upping the ante more closely to full-scale intervention (although they always stop short of that standard). It is not clear success would be attainable through increasing American presence: if anything, recent past experience suggests it would not. Besides, the American people would not support such a suggestion.

If the more robust forms of policy are off the table or open to major question, then why not consider moving toward a *less* intrusive form of American military involvement in the region? It is probably impossible politically for the United States to remove itself altogether from the region, but a reduced Nixon Doctrine approach that moved closer to showing the flag might be possible. Its most visible manifestation would be a sizable reduction of American military presence in the region: a much smaller American naval presence in and around the Persian Gulf and the downsizing or closing of American ground and air facilities in parts of the region, especially around the Persian Gulf. Such reductions would affect the ability of the United States to respond as rapidly as it now can to provocations (which is not necessarily a bad thing), but would not necessarily preclude the ability of the United States to respond to critical situations where its presence might make a difference. It would, however, mean the United States would become a much less visible element in Middle Eastern instability. For those who use American power as a surrogate from defending themselves, this prospect would be clearly upsetting. For those who use the United States as a bogeyman on whom to blame their own shortcomings, it might make lives more complicated, not an undesirable outcome.

THE EFFECTS OF A REDUCED AMERICAN PRESENCE: GEOPOLITICS, TERRORISM, ENERGY, AND MANPOWER

A policy of reduced American military presence rests on three central tenets. The first is that a higher profile, more "muscular" approach to achieving

American interests has, over the 25 years since American arms prevailed in Kuwait, basically failed. The fault for this failure does not lie especially with the military itself, although the persistent inability of the military to figure out how to fight Scythian-style warfare has been a contributory factor. The fault lies with assigning military tasks that a conventionally organized military establishment like the United States is not good at achieving, a distinction it shares with virtually all Western militaries. The military's complicity is that it refuses to accept this reality and, when asked to perform tasks for which it is ill-suited, to respond "can't do." Those who want to increase American presence basically are beseeching the military to do more of what it does not do well. When it yields to calls to combat in the Middle East, the United States is effectively sucker punching itself.

The second tenet is that the situation in Middle East is such a complex mess that there is very little possibility an activist U.S. national security effort can make much positive difference. The conflicts in the area are, as repeatedly argued, mostly internal feuds based on religious or ethnic grounds, and these are problems the U.S. military cannot ameliorate, either through direct intervention or, in many cases, aiding one side or the other. The solution to the IS crisis in Iraq is not better training of Iraqi forces by Americans; it is figuring out how to motivate Iraqi Shiites to fight and die for Iraqi Sunnis who have tormented them for decades. A quick glance behind any of the multiple violent uprisings that periodically break out in the region reveals some underlying dynamic for which American military power is decidedly not the answer.

The general disarray of the region and the intractability of solving that chaos form much of the rationale for the chain link fence analogy. Its premise is that the ills of the region are internal and can only be solved by the participants. The internal process is likely to be long and bloody, but it is a process the United States can do little to help or facilitate. Reducing the American role places the burden more obviously on the regional actors themselves, where it must rest. Kaplan agrees: "While the Middle East implodes through years of low-intensity conflicts among groups of Scythians, let Turkey, Egypt, Israel, Saudi Arabia, and Iran jostle toward an uneasy balance of power, and the United States remains a step removed."

The third tenet is that American military presence in the area has become more of an irritant than a palliative, and that its removal might actually improve the situation. Uncle Sam's presence has meant that the major participants do not have to solve their own problems, because no matter how bad things get, the Americans can always be counted on to keep the lid on situations. Imagine, for instance, what the dynamics of Persian Gulf security might look like if those who benefit from the commerce the most actually had to provide the protection themselves. At the same time, withdrawing the

American presence might also make the Americans less of a target for the venom produced by terrorists in the region. Americans have made extraordinarily good displacement objects for terrorists: U.S. troops occupy and never seem to leave countries that argue they are liberating, and American attacks against terrorist targets give the terrorists an objective reason to hate and want to attack the United States. The collateral damage of those attacks also helps recruit new victims to an anti-American cause. Remove the American presence and the incentives will reduce as well.

These possibilities could not have been seriously raised a decade ago, when American geopolitical interests were more intimately tied to what happens in the Middle East than they are today. Both aspects of American geopolitical interests have moderated. The United States is no longer so dependent on Middle Eastern oil, and the American need for that commodity will almost certainly continue to decline. Israel, the other American geopolitical responsibility, does not face the same level of threat from regional foes that it once did. The exception is a potentially nuclear-armed Iran, but it is not clear how an American physical military presence in the area affects that prospect one way or another. The other source of Israeli estrangement is the continued occupation of Palestine. It is probably a tribute to the degree to which Israel has reinforced its security that the major threat connected to Palestine comes from Hezbollah unguided missiles that mostly miss their targets. The United States would very much like Israel to cede the occupied territories, but American military presence or level of regional activism does not affect those efforts particularly. The geopolitical "neighborhood" has, from an American vantage point, changed considerably since the turn of the millennium.

The apparent counter to the receding geopolitical necessity of American influence is in the area of terrorism. The rise of Middle Eastern–based jihadist Islamic terrorism has become the central geopolitical obsession of the United States since 2001, and if one includes the cost of the Iraq and Afghanistan wars in the accounting, it is probably true that the United States has spent more nonmandated public dollars on the "war on terror" than on any other single governmental activity. No one questions the importance of the effort, but one can raise questions about the attainability of the goal of terrorist abatement through the forward-based counterterrorism efforts both being conducted and proposed to achieve that effort. It is also not clear that the results have been especially cost-effective either.

There are essentially three aspects to the effort to prevent terrorist actions in the United States, only one of which would be negatively affected by a policy of reduced military presence. That area is military and paramilitary actions in the home bases of terrorist activities, most of which are located in the Middle East or, increasingly, in Muslim-dominated areas of Africa adjacent to the

Middle East. From a terrorist vantage point, this campaign is the most vexing, frustrating, and anger producing. As such, these actions provide the most concrete reasons for targeting the United States as a means of retaliation. If they were removed as considerations, would the terrorists reduce their focus on Americans and increase their attention to the areas where they actually have some prospects and have enjoyed success? Put another way, would IS continue to devote scarce resources to anti-American activities if American air strikes were not killing and impeding their members?

Reducing or dismantling the military aspects of forward-based counterterrorism would be controversial. It is the most proactive form of American direct response to terrorist activities against American and other targets. It does kill significant numbers of terrorist leaders and rank-and-file members, although it does not seem to reduce their total numbers. Moreover, reducing the program would permit the terrorists to organize and operate with more impunity than they now can. The cry would be that this was yet another form of tying the hands of those trying to protect the public from a hideous fate.

Whether the objections have adequate merit to carry the day depends on a cost-benefit look at an activist versus a reduced commitment. It is clear, however, that a policy of trying to hunt down and kill terrorist leaders has not successfully "terrorized the terrorists" to the point that they have redirected their verbal efforts away from the United States. Backing away from direct military actions arguably would be viewed as an act of surrender by the terrorists that might embolden them even more. It might also allow the terrorists to redirect their efforts more fully to their real opponents in the region.

Pulling back militarily does not necessarily mean lowering the ability to combat terrorist activities. First, it does not mean or entail the other prongs of policy would be neglected or compromised. The other prongs of policy are foreign intelligence that is aimed at monitoring terrorist activity at its source and antiterrorist activities in the United States, notably monitoring possible terrorist planning and execution. Neither of these aspects of the antiterrorist effort entails any real military component, and both would continue in a demilitarized environment. In fact, the demilitarization of the policy might actually free some funds to strengthen those efforts. Such efforts would, of course, require some arcane manipulation of the convoluted nature of public budgeting within the federal budget.

It is likely those who perform nonmilitary functions would initially react negatively to dialing back military efforts, because whatever effectiveness military attacks achieve reduce the number of terrorists who can penetrate the United States, making their job quantitatively easier. It is also possible that a policy of less military assertiveness would reduce the frequency of attacks if terrorists downgraded their incentives against American targets.

Moreover, the policy would contain the implicit or explicit warning that the attacks could be resumed—possibly with greater vigor—in the absence of their compliance.

The energy situation is an enabler of policy alternatives. The lessened dependency of the United States on Middle East fossil fuels means that the leverage those regimes have over the Americans is decreased. In a number of cases, that leverage has been wielded by regimes with whom the United States would have little comity in the absence of the need for their oil. After the end of the Cold War, simply declaring one's opposition to communism lost much of its currency in terms of currying American favor, and it is possible to think of American relations with some of the more despotic, medieval oil-rich states becoming less close in the future. Notably, a reduction of American military presence might raise the question for some of these leaders about whether the United States would necessarily provide the military muscle for their defense, or whether they might have to assume that burden themselves or come to political accord with those who may threaten them.

The military manpower situation in the United States would be the most obvious beneficiary of a policy of reduced American military presence in the Middle East. The problem of overdeployment of troops that has been one of the negative artifacts of the Iraq and Afghanistan experiences would clearly be improved. Calls for sending thousands of American "trainers" into Iraq to deflect IS would be reduced, and the danger of a limited or full employment of ground forces into the anti-IS conflict would be virtually eliminated. The force could be returned to American soil for replenishment and rest, making it better prepared for future uses in other parts of the world. An American armed force that was not deployed in any war zone for a period of time would represent a unique circumstance in contemporary terms: Americans have been at war continuously since 9/11. In the historical scheme of things, that has been an aberration. Returning to an actual peacetime condition is not entirely undesirable.

A TIME FOR CHANGE

For the past 25 years, the United States has been trying to make sense of the byzantine politics of the Middle East, and it has not succeeded terribly well—an indictment shared by just about everyone who deals with the region. Before 1979, the United States was active there, but the national security obligations entailed in protecting the flow of oil fell on the willing shoulders of Iran. When the Iranian Revolution severed that marriage of convenience, the United States had to insert itself personally into the region. In 1990, the Iraqi invasion of Kuwait cemented the military content of that change in the direction and content of commitment. American military presence and activism in the region have been constant ever since.

The Middle East has become de facto the heart of national security concern. The United States has maintained forces in the region, although local sensibilities often dictate that they be hidden from public view. This is especially true of the Saudis, who sequester Americans in remote desert bases where the average Saudi does not have to be reminded of them on a daily basis. The message is clear: the natives do not particularly want the Americans around, but they are a necessary evil and surrogate for real, personal self-defense.

The major factor in upgrading the salience of the area as a national security concern has, of course, been the emergence of regional terrorist organizations espousing deadly intent against the United States. The major stimulus for this emergence was the jihadi response to the Soviet decade-long occupation of Afghanistan during the 1990s: the mujahidin resistance spawned both the Taliban and Al-Qaeda. Their common thread was their birth as resisters to foreign intrusion, both an Afghan and a regional sentiment. After the Soviets were expelled, many of the Afghanis (foreign mujahidin) went home to their native countries, where they were generally unwelcome as potential troublemakers. The seeds of discontent that became the terrorist movement of the 1990s and beyond were certainly spawned partially from this dynamic. It is still present, and it grew and matured at the same time the U.S. military was becoming an additional piece of the regional mosaic, and one that was about as welcome as the Soviets in some quarters. The terrorist attacks of 9/11 by Al-Qaeda and the military responses of the United States in Iraq and Afghanistan squared the circle: the United States became the opponent of the Taliban (mostly Ghilzai Pashtun Afghan veterans of the Soviet days) and AQ, including AQI which morphed into IS. All of these events were reactive rather than part of any conscious, purposive regional national security strategy.

The United States has never developed a coherent, consistent national security policy to deal with this change of circumstance and orientation. American terrorism suppression programs have, like the efforts of most countries, been largely reactive: antiterrorism efforts to make it more difficult to attack American targets (from screening people entering the country to blocking off streets around public facilities) and counterterrorism initiatives, such as military and paramilitary attacks on terrorist concentrations overseas. Very little of the public effort has gone into trying to identify what specifically motivates Middle Eastern terrorists to want to attack this country and thus to try to devise methods to reduce those incentives.

The United States may be a high priority because it is apostate and the symbol of modernization and secularization that undermines fundamentalist beliefs in the virtue of returning to the values of earlier times. If that is the case, then rallying support in the mainstream Muslim community worldwide against the extremists may be the best approach, combined with physical attrition of the fanatics who hate Americans for being so unlike them. On the other hand, the reasons Americans are special targets may be because of the obtrusive, unwanted American military presence in the region. If that is the case, then a reduction in that presence may be the most productive way to undermine the appeal of a terrorist strategy against the Great Satan the United States represents.

There are two major lines of objection to this suggestion. One is that it is passive and "weak," not the kind of muscular leadership the world expects from its remaining superpower. Withdrawal in this construction can be viewed as an exploitable sign that the United States can be cowed "when the going gets tough," and this will encourage others to challenge American mettle (Russia's Vladimir Putin is a prime candidate). Since no one else possesses the military muscle the United States does, American abrogation of activism—a "muscular" foreign policy—is an invitation to global chaos.

There is a counter to this line of reasoning: military strength does not necessarily imply stupidity. The last quarter-century of American military activity has effectively demonstrated the limits of military activism by inserting American military force into situations where it was inappropriate and could not possibly succeed (intervention in foreign civil wars). Continuing to use American force in these kinds of ways does not demonstrate American resolve or leadership, but instead suggests that the United States is the large, not very bright bully on the international block. The continual insistence from some political quarters in the United States on using American force whenever violence flares becomes an example of Albert Einstein's definition of insanity: doing the same thing in similar situations and expecting different results.

The other objection is that it misses the point and will not work. No one in the U.S. government really knows (or if they do, they are not sharing it) exactly what motivates Islamic terrorists against the United States and Americans. It may be that the reasons are purely visceral, a calculation of the clash of civilizations and their priorities (modernization and secularization against tradition and sectarianism), or even, to recall George W. Bush's cryptic explanation, because they "hate our freedom." If the latter is the case, then a military approach may be appropriate, although an effective strategy to attain victory over the opponents at some acceptable cost has not been articulated. Sending a few thousand military trainers to help the Iraqi army is not such a strategy.

Backing away from the Middle East may not work either, but it is worth a try. Such a strategy cannot work especially more poorly than the ongoing approach, which has not succeeded and shows no particular evidence it is heading in the right direction. If withdrawal either does not work or produces and even more brazen, emboldened opponent, the policy change, like present policy, is not irreversible, and could be replaced by either a return to something like the present effort or by yet a different direction.

A policy of reducing or eliminating a permanent U.S. military presence in the Middle East was not possible 35 years ago as the United States was reacting to revolutionary changes in Iran that thrust it into the lead role in protecting Middle East oil. That situation has changed: the United States does not personally need Persian Gulf oil the way it once did and, in all likelihood, that dependence will not return as American and other Western Hemisphere production increase and as conservationist and environmentalist pressures reduce American and worldwide dependency on "black gold." The Cold War "tradition" of a globally assertive, even aggressive American military posture is almost entirely an artifact of the Cold War. It was the right and only thing to do in that confrontation, but it represented a dramatic change from the American historical role in the world. The Cold War is over, and Russian grumbling notwithstanding, those conditions have disappeared as well. Yet, the American Cold War posture and attitude toward the role of force inherited from that era remain the de facto underpinning of American policy in the Middle East and elsewhere. Maybe the change whose time has come is to return to a more American approach to the world.

BIBLIOGRAPHY

Anderson, Scott. *Lawrence in Arabia: War, Deceit, Imperial Folly, and the Making of the Modern Middle East.* New York: Anchor Books, 2013.

Bacevich, Andrew. "Even If We Defeat the Islamic State. We'll Still Lose the Bigger War." *Washington Post* (online), October 3, 2014.

Betts, Richard K. "Pick Your Battles: Ending America's Permanent State of War." *Foreign Affairs* 93, 6 (November/December 2014), 15–24.

Bremmer, Ian. "What Does America Stand For?" *Time* 185, 20 (June 1, 2015), 26–31.

Carter, Ashton B. "Running the Pentagon Right: How to Get the Troops What They Need." *Foreign Affairs* 93, 1 (January/February 2014), 101–112.

Goldstein, Joshua. *Winning the War on War: The Decline of Armed Conflict Worldwide.* New York: Plume, 2012.

Haass, Richard N. "The Unraveling: How to Respond to a Disordered World." *Foreign Affairs* 93, 6 (November/December 2014), 70–79.

Hashemi, Nader, and Danny Postel (eds.). *The Syrian Dilemma.* Cambridge, MA: MIT Press (Boston Review Books), 2013.

Hoffman, Bruce. *Inside Terrorism* (2nd edition). New York: Columbia University Press, 2006.

Joffe, Greg. "Obama on the Defense Again As Yet Another Defense Secretary Speaks." *Washington Post* (online), May 26, 2015.

Kaplan, Robert D. "The Art of Avoiding War." *The Atlantic* 313, 5 (June 2015), 32–33.

Kinzer, Stephen. *Overthrow: America's Century of Regime Change from Hawaii to Iraq.* New York: Times Books (Macmillan), 2007.

McLaughlin, John. "How the Islamic State Could Win." *Washington Post* (online), May 27, 2015.

Nacos, Brigette I. *Terrorism and Counterterrorism: Understanding Threats and Responses in the Post-9/11 World.* New York: Penguin Academics, 2006.

Obama, Barack. "State of the Union." Text Reprinted in *Washington Post* (online), January 29, 2015.

Pinker, Steven. *The Better Angels of Our Nature: Why Violence Has Declined.* New York: Penguin Books, 2012.

Snow, Donald M. *The Case Against Military Intervention.* New York: Routledge, 2016.

———. *National Security for a New Era* (fifth edition). New York: Pearson, 2014.

Stern, Jessica. *Terrorism in the Name of God: Why Religious Militants Kill.* New York: ECCO Books, 2003.

Stern, Jessica, and M. Berger. *ISIS: The State of Terror.* New York: ECCO Books, 2015.

Index

About the Author

Donald M. Snow is professor emeritus of political science at the University of Alabama, where he served from 1969–2006. At UA, he also served as Director of International Studies, Director of Faculty Development and Services; at the departmental level, he was Director of Graduate Studies and Chair of the Tenure and Promotions Committee. In addition to his service at UA, he held visiting faculty positions at the U.S. Naval, Army, and Air War Colleges and the Air Command and Staff College, as well as adjunct appointments at Auburn University (Montgomery), Dickinson College, and the University of South Carolina (Beaufort). He currently teaches in the Lifelong Learning Program on Hilton Head Island, SC.

Additionally, he has served as chair/president of the Section on Military Studies (now International Security Studies Section) of the International Studies Association (1983–1985) and the International Security and Arms Control Section of the American Political Science Association (1996–1998). He has lectured widely around the country for organizations such the Freedoms Foundation and the U.S. Air Force. He presented an Olin Lecture at the U.S. Air Force Academy in 1994. He has also been a fellow in the Inter-University Seminar on Armed Forces and Society.

Snow is the author of nearly 60 books and monographs on international, foreign policy, and national security topics, and over forty articles and book chapters. His most recent books include *The Case against Military Intervention* and *Thinking about National Security* (both Routledge) and *The Middle East, Oil, and U.S. National Security Policy* (Rowman and Littlefield). He is working on the sixth edition of *National Security* and new editions of *American Foreign Policy* (with Patrick J. Haney) and *Cases in American Foreign Policy*. His book writing career now spans three and a half decades (1980–present) and includes books published by 15 publishing houses.

He holds the BA and MA degrees (1965, 1967) from the University of Colorado and the PhD degree from Indiana University (1969). All degrees are in political science.

Snow and his wife split Donna their time between a primary home on Hilton Head Island and a secondary residence in Black Mountain, North Carolina. He is the father of one son (Eric) and has three grandchildren.